# DATA LINK PROTOCOLS

Uyless Black
Bell Atlantic Education Services

PTR PRENTICE HALL
Englewood Cliffs, New Jersey 07632

*Library of Congress Cataloging-in-Publication Data*

BLACK, UYLESS D.
    Data link protocols / Uyless Black.
        p.    cm.
    Includes index
    ISBN 0-13-204918-X
    1. Computer network protocols.    I. Title
TK5105.5.B564  1993                                    92-21202
004.6'2—dc20                                             CIP


Prentice Hall Computer Communication Series
Wushow Chou, *Advisor*
Editorial/production supervision: *The Wheetley Company*
Buyer: *Mary Elizabeth McCartney*
Acquisitions editor: *Michael Hays*

©1993 by PTR Prentice-Hall, Inc.
A Simon & Schuster Company
Englewood Cliffs, New Jersey 07632

The publisher offers discounts on this book when ordered
in bulk quantities. For more information, contact:

Corporate Sales Department
PTR Prentice Hall
113 Sylvan Avenue
Englewood Cliffs, New Jersey 07632

Phone: 201-592-2863
Fax: 201-592-2249

Printed in the United States of America
10  9  8  7  6  5  4  3  2  1

ISBN 0-13-204918-X

PRENTICE-HALL INTERNATIONAL (UK) LIMITED, *London*
PRENTICE-HALL OF AUSTRALIA PTY. LIMITED, *Sydney*
PRENTICE-HALL CANADA INC., *Toronto*
PRENTICE-HALL HISPANOAMERICANA, S.A., *Mexico*
PRENTICE HALL OF INDIA PRIVATE LIMITED, *New Delhi*
PRENTICE-HALL OF JAPAN, INC., *Tokyo*
SIMON & SCHUSTER ASIA PTS. LTD., *Singapore*
EDITORA PRENTICE-HALL DO BRASIL, LTDA., *Rio de Janeiro*

*This book is dedicated to Pat Webster.*
*A fine builder of fine houses...*
*and thanks for ours.*

# Contents

## 4   ASYNCHRONOUS DATA LINK CONTROLS        73

## 5   BINARY SYNCHRONOUS CONTROL (BSC)        91

# *Preface*

Most of us have attended many business meetings, and this writer is no exception. Several years ago, I attended a meeting that provided the impetus for writing this book. This meeting was held to determine if two companies would be able to exchange some files with each other through their respective data communications systems. My role in this meeting was to monitor the information exchange, and ensure that the companies were on the right track in their initial data communications endeavors.

One speaker at the meeting stated that the companies' systems were compatible in one aspect—both systems used the high level data link control (HDLC) for their data link protocol.

The technicians in the meeting did not challenge this statement, because they (apparently) were not aware that HDLC has many options and subsets and that most HDLC implementations use selected parts of HDLC. For example, the widely used protocol HDLC is used as the foundation for numerous other protocols, such as link access procedure, balanced (LAPB), link access procedure for the D Channel (LAPD), and link access procedure for modems (LAPM). As it turned out, the link control systems of these two companies were not compatible.

On many occasions since this meeting, I have found that many otherwise competent data communications engineers have substantial knowledge gaps about data link protocols. Consequently, I decided a book was needed to provide guidance to the data communications professional about these important protocols. I hope you will find the book useful in your work.

The emphasis of this book is on synchronous data link protocols. Notwithstanding, I have also included a chapter on asynchronous systems with emphasis on personal computer protocols.

The chapters in the book are relatively self-contained, and the experienced reader should be able to read an individual chapter without reading earlier chapters. However, it is recommended that all readers at least review the first three chapters to ensure basic terms and concepts are understood. The beginner is urged to read these chapters more carefully.

# 1

# *Introduction*

## INTRODUCTION

This chapter introduces the major features of data link controls (DLCs). We examine the purpose of data link controls and their contribution to a data communications system. The Open Systems Interconnection model is reviewed in relation to how data link controls fit into the model. The relationship of data link controls to a data communications network also is explained in this chapter.

## PURPOSE OF DATA LINK CONTROLS

The transfer of data across the communications link between computers, terminals, and workstations must occur in a controlled and orderly manner. Since communications links experience distortions (such as noise), a method must be provided to deal with the periodic errors that result in the distortion of the data.

The data communications system must provide each workstation/computer on the link with the capability to send data to another station, and the sending station must be assured that the data arrive error-free at the receiving station. The sending and receiving stations must maintain complete accountability for all traffic. In the event the data are distorted, the receiver site must be able to direct the originator to resend the data.

Services also must be available to manage the traffic that is sent between the machines. Since computers have a finite amount of storage, measures must be taken to prevent one machine from sending too much data to another machine; otherwise, data would be lost due to the receiving machine's inability to receive the data and store them. Additionally, even though storage may be available to receive data, a computer may be busy with other tasks, and/or might not have the computational resources to deal with incoming traffic. Therefore, some means must be available to match the rate of incoming traffic to the ability of the machine to handle the load.

Then there is the important issue to consider concerning keeping data on the link in the proper sequence. For a variety of reasons discussed later in this book, data may arrive at the receiving machine in an order different from that in which it was transmitted. The user application often is expecting data to arrive in a set, predetermined order; missequenced data may create problems at the receiving user application.

A communications system also must distinguish the signals on the link that represent data from extraneous signals such as noise and other nondata elements. The ability to determine when user data begin and when they end is an important aspect of proper communications system operations.

Once the user traffic has arrived safely at the receiving computer, some means must be available to determine the recipient(s) of the data. After all, it does little good to undertake all the aforementioned efforts and have no procedure to pass the traffic to the proper entity (software, data base, a memory buffer, etc.) at the receiving computer.

In summary, data link controls provide important services. They manage the orderly flow of data across the communications path (link) and ensure that this traffic arrives error-free at the receiving machine. In addition, they make certain that data are distinguished from other signals and ensure that data are presented to the receiving machine and a recognized application in their proper order.


## SCOPE OF DLC'S RESPONSIBILITIES

A data link control operation is limited to one individual link. That is, link control is responsible only for the traffic between adjacent machines on a link. For example, consider a network or an internet (multiple networks connected) in which multiple communications links connect routers, networks, and other components. The data are transmitted from one node (such as a router) to the adjacent node. If this node accepts the data, it can send an acknowledgment of this transmission to the originating node. The link control task is then complete for that particular transmission. If the data are relayed to yet another node on another link, the first link's data link control is unaware of this activity. Indeed, the particular type of DLC on each link within this network can be entirely different. This approach could be costly, since the enterprise would have to train its technicians to know different types of DLCs; nonetheless, the data link control protocol is responsible for the integrity of all transmissions on the link. For example, if a communications link has several users accessing it, the DLC is responsible for transporting the data error-free (or as error-free as possible) for all users to a receiving machine on the link.

The DLC generally is unaware that the data on the link belong to multiple users (if, indeed, they do). Most DLCs are designed so they do not know the contents of the user data they are "transporting" to the receiving machine. Their main concern is to deliver the traffic safely from the sending to the receiving machine(s).

This holds true for the user of the DLC, as well. The user is unaware of the activities of the DLC; its operations usually remain transparent to the user and to the other protocols operating in the data communications system.

## IS A DATA LINK CONTROL SERVICE NECESSARY?

Data transmitted correctly from the source computer to the receiving computer may be damaged on the channel enroute, such that the binary ones (1s) and zeros (0s) representing codes and symbols are misinterpreted by the receiver.

To gain an understanding of the magnitude of the problem, consider some performance measurements of a dial-up connection between two user stations on long-distance carriers in the United States. A 1.2 Kbit/s speed transmission experiences a bit error rate (BER) of 1 in $10^5$ (moderate quality) to $1:10^3$ (very poor). In other words, over a period of time we may expect that one bit will be damaged in every 1,000 to 100,000 bits transmitted. While this study does not take into account a transmission over optical fibers, it takes little imagination to recognize that bit errors may be frequent.

Also, bit errors often are random; they cannot be predicted. Even though an error may or may not occur in a "block" of data, studies reveal that a dial-up telephone line experiences an incidence of 0.7 to 142.6 errors in every one thousand blocks sent (each block consisting of 1,000 bits).

Is this a problem? It depends on the needs of the user. The transmission of certain textual data may not require extensive error-detection efforts, since an occasional corrupted character can be ignored as no more serious than a typing error. On the other hand, an error by an electronic funds transfer system can have far-reaching consequences. The distortion of a decimal place or zero could have either disastrous or serendipitous consequences (disastrous for the individual "losing" the decimal place and serendipitous for the individual who gained it).

One solution to the problem is the use of a link that is as error-free as possible. Substantial relief results from the use of conditioned dedicated links and other high-quality media. Moreover, circuits using optical fiber offer superior performance over conventional copper wire media and microwave media. Nonetheless, errors will occur, and some method must be used to deal with them—regardless of how frequent or infrequent they are. After the preventive maintenance efforts of using high-quality links and well-designed hardware and software, the next line of defense is to: (a) check for transmission errors at the receiver, (b) attempt to correct the error at the receiver; and (c) request the sender to retransmit the damaged data.

## IS IT NECESSARY FOR DATA LINK CONTROL TO RECOVER FROM ERRORS?

One certainly can argue with validity that the error-checking and retransmission services provided by a data link control protocol can be provided by other processes that reside in the computer, such as an end-user application program, or even another communications protocol.   In later chapters we examine several data communications systems wherein error checking and retransmission of errors are passed to another component in the computer.   Moreover, with the increasing use of optical fibers (and their very low incidence of errors), some systems do not use a data link control for error checking at all, but assume the end-user (or another protocol) will execute the error-checking and retransmissions services.

Nonetheless, even if the communications channel is of superior quality, and/or if another protocol in the machine is providing error-checking and retransmission operations, the data link layer still must be present because, as introduced previously in this section, it performs other important functions. These will be examined in subsequent chapters.

## CLARIFICATION OF TERMS AND CONCEPTS

Before proceeding to describe the operations of a data link control system, it will be useful to define some terms and concepts.  The user application program resides in the data terminal equipment or DTE (see Figure 1-1).  DTE is a general term used to describe the end-user machine which, as discussed earlier, usually is a computer or terminal.  The DTE could be either a large computer or a smaller machine, such as a terminal or personal computer.  The term *user station* (or *station*) also is used in this book to describe the DTE.

The function of a data communications system is to interconnect the DTEs  so they can share resources, exchange data, and provide backup for each other. The path between the DTEs is called a *line, link, circuit,* or *channel*.  It may consist of wires, radio signals, or light transmissions. Often a telephone company  provides this link between the user devices.

Figure 1-1 shows the data circuit-terminating equipment (DCE), as well.  Its function is to connect the DTEs into the communication line.  The DCEs designed in the 1960s and 1970s strictly were communication devices.  However, in the last few years the machines have incorporated more user functions. Today, some DCEs contain a portion of a user application process; some even contain the data link control operations. Nonetheless, the primary function of the DCE is to provide an interface of the DTE into the communication link.

The DCE may be located inside the DTE or may stand alone as a separate unit. Wherever it is located, it is used primarily to convert the signals representing user data to a form acceptable to the receiving channel.  As a simple example, it might convert an electrical signal from a terminal to a light signal for an optical fiber link.

The DTEs and DCEs communicate with protocols, and one of the protocol types—data link control—is the subject of this book.  Protocols are agreements on the manner in which  the machines "converse" with each other.  They may include the logic and codes that stipulate a required or recommended convention or technique.  Typically, several kinds of protocols are required to support an end-user application and may be implemented both in software and hardware.

The link often is connected by another component, the DSE (data switching equipment) or switch.  As Figure 1-1 shows, the switch allows the DTEs to use different

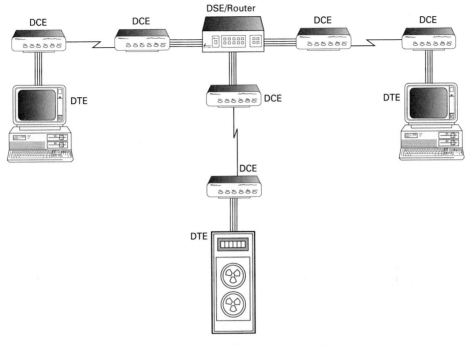

DTE: Data Terminal Equipment (user device)

DCE: Data Circuit - Terminating Equipment

DSE: Data Switching Equipment (switch/router)

⎯⌒: Communications Link (often the telephone line)

**Figure 1-1.** A Typical Data Communications System

channels at different times to communicate with different user stations. This arrangement is known as *networking*. In addition, the DSE provides other important functions such as routing around failed or busy devices and channels. The DSE also may route data to their final destination through other switches.

Many computers and terminals can be interconnected to form networks. The arrangement may or may not use a switch. In Figure 1-1, a switch performs the interconnections to move the data through the network. This type of network is called a *switched network*.

Another approach is the *broadcast network*. All stations share a common channel, and a station transmits its signal to all other stations. The stations "copy" the signal if it is destined for them. Radio systems, such as CB, are examples of broadcast networks. Television and commercial radio are other examples, and most local area networks use some form of broadcast service.

## The Data Link Control Protocol Data Unit (PDU)/Frame

The traffic that is carried across a communications link is described by a number of terms. Some vendors and standards organizations refer to this traffic as a *protocol data unit* (PDU). Since the job of data link control is to "carry" traffic across the communications link, the traffic that is carried on the link also can be called a *data link protocol data unit* (DLPDU). However, a convention more widely used is to identify this traffic with the term frame. Hereafter, in this book the terms *link layer protocol data unit, data unit,* and *frame* will be used interchangeably.

## OPERATIONS OF THE DLC

Data link controls follow well-ordered steps in managing a communications channel.

- *Link establishment.* Once the communicating machines have a physical connection, the DLC "handshakes" with the remote DLC to ensure that both systems are ready to exchange user data.

- *Data transfer.* User data are exchanged across the link between the two machines. The DLC checks the data for possible transmission errors and may send acknowledgments back to the transmitting machine. In the event an error is detected, the receiver may request the transmitter to retransmit the data.

- *Link termination.* The DLC relinquishes control of the link (channel), which means no data can be transferred until the link is reestablished. Typically, a DLC keeps a link active as long as the user community wishes to send data to the other stations.

Figure 1-2 provides a simple example of how data link controls operate. The DCEs are not shown in this example (nor in most examples in this book) because their operations are transparent to data link control.

Before communications can occur  between two machines, the data link control protocol must establish a link *connection.* The term *connection* does not mean connection in the physical sense, because that is a matter for another protocol (at the physical layer). Indeed, the physical connection must be available before any operations can occur with a data link protocol. A link connection means that the two data link control protocols in the DTEs must exchange a number of messages to establish an understanding regarding the manner in which the data link operations will proceed. These initial operations are known as a *handshake.*

The first part of this figure shows the handshake occurring  by DTE A sending a data link control message to DTE B. This message asks DTE B if it wishes to have a link control session with DTE A. In this example, DTE B responds with a positive acknowledgment  (ACK), which is a signal to DTE A that it can begin sending data.

During the link establishment phase, many data link protocols will negotiate various services to be used between the two computers. The services may include the number of data units that can be sent  at  any one time before some type of flow control is established (in order to manage buffers properly). Another negotiation may include an agreement concerning the size of the protocol data unit that flows across the channel.

Once the link establishment and handshakes have occurred successfully, data transfer can begin. The data link control protocol does not initiate data transfer; it receives data from other protocols residing in the machine. The concept of the data link control is to be a service provider to other protocols by conveying the traffic safely across

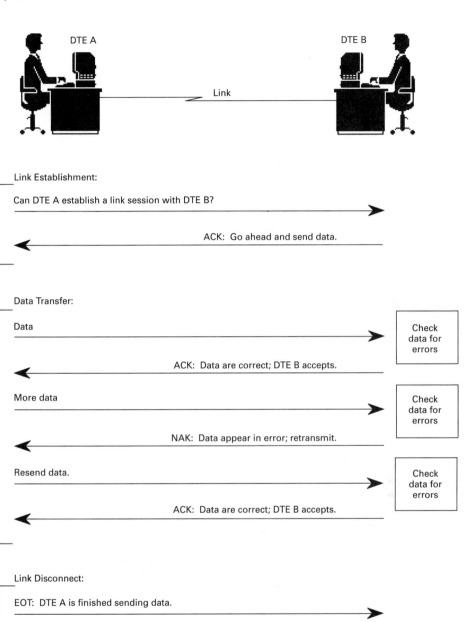

Link Establishment:

Can DTE A establish a link session with DTE B? ⟶

⟵ ACK: Go ahead and send data.

Data Transfer:

Data ⟶ | Check data for errors

⟵ ACK: Data are correct; DTE B accepts.

More data ⟶ | Check data for errors

⟵ NAK: Data appear in error; retransmit.

Resend data. ⟶ | Check data for errors

⟵ ACK: Data are correct; DTE B accepts.

Link Disconnect:

EOT: DTE A is finished sending data. ⟶

⟵ DTE B is finished sending data.

**Figure 1-2.** The Data Link Control Procedures

the link to the other machine. This operation usually is performed by another protocol (with the computer operating system) placing data in a buffer. This buffer is made accessible to the data link control operation by the operating system's communications management software. The data link protocol then places data link control fields around the data and transmits the data to the receiving machine through the physical layer.

This example shows the data transfer operations occurring with Machine A sending data to Machine B. Notice that Machine B checks each data transmission for errors and sends back a positive acknowledgment (ACK) or a negative acknowledgment (NAK). In the event that an ACK is received by DTE A, it assumes that traffic has arrived safely at DTE B and the data link control relinquishes its responsibility for this frame.

However, upon sending any data, data link control keeps a copy of this data in the event that it needs to be retransmitted. Consequently, in our example the receipt of a NAK from DTE B to DTE A requires that DTE A resend the frame that is in error. In this example, this frame arrives safely and is then acknowledged.

After data have been transmitted, a link disconnection operation may occur. The term *disconnect* does not mean that the link physically is disconnected. It means that the two data link control entities disassociate themselves logically. The physical link can still be in operation for later services. However, in most instances data link control does not perform disconnect operations after the transfer of data. The idea of data link control is for it to remain "up" for an indefinite period to provide an ongoing service for user operations and other protocols that reside in the machine. Indeed, in many installations data link control operations remain up 24 hours a day and are taken down only in the event of problems or for preventive maintenance operations.

Not all link control protocols adhere to these handshaking conventions. As we shall see in the next section of this chapter, many link protocols perform no connection setup or disconnect operations, whatsoever.

### Connectionless and Connection-Oriented DLCs

Data link controls can be configured to support either connectionless or connection-oriented operations. With connection-oriented operations (as in Figure 1-2), the data link protocol sets up a logical connection between the machines before the transfer of data. Usually, some type of relationship is maintained between the data units being transferred through the connection in order to ensure that the data have arrived in the proper order and without error.

The connection-oriented service requires an agreement be reached between the two end link control protocols before data are transferred. It allows the communicating parties to negotiate certain options. During the connection establishment, all parties store information about each other, such as addresses, size of the data unit that is to be transferred, etc.

Connectionless operations (also called connectionless-mode) are shown in Figure 1-3. This mode of link layer operations does not set up a logical link connection. Instead, the connectionless type service manages the link layer frames as independent and separate entities. No relationship is maintained between successive data transfers, and few records are kept of the ongoing user-to-user communications process on the link.

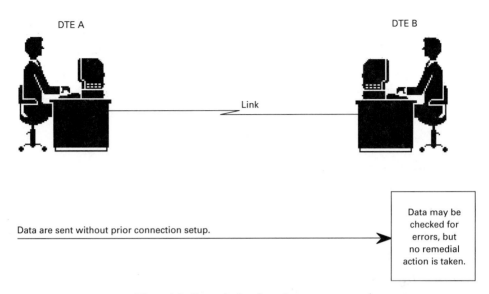

**Figure 1-3.** Connectionless Operations

Moreover, ACKs and NAKs are not provided. Although error checking may be performed on the frame, the receiving data link protocol takes no remedial action. If the frame is in error, it is discarded, and the receiver is not informed about the loss of the traffic.

Generally, the connectionless link layer entities must have a prior agreement on how to communicate, and operation functions, such as the size of the frame, must be prearranged. Alternately (and rarely used), these functions can be identified for each frame that is transmitted. If so, each frame must contain fields that identify the types of service to be performed on the frame.

One might question why connectionless link layer protocols would be employed. After all, if accuracy of data is important, error detection seems to be a prudent action to take. The rationale for the use of connectionless link layer operations is based on two sound notions. First, the nature of the traffic may not warrant the overhead incurred in error checking. For example, the integrity of telemetry data, in which many samples of traffic are being received by a machine, would not suffer if an occasional data unit is received erroneously. Second, protocols other than the data link layer can assume responsibility for error checking. This approach is used in some systems that have been established in the last few years, such as frame relay This is discussed in a subsequent chapter. The trade-offs of error detection and retransmission at the data link layer vis-à-vis performing these operations with other protocols in the machine are discussed throughout this book.

## DATA LINK CONTROL WITHIN THE NETWORK

It might prove useful at this point to examine Figure 1-4 — a view inside the network "cloud." The term *cloud* is used to connote that an end user is not aware of the

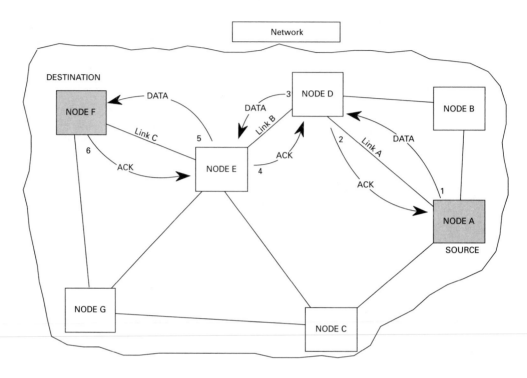

Note: Numbers indicate the sequence in which single frame is sent and ACKed through a network.

**Figure 1-4.** Link Control Inside the Network

operations inside the network. The numbers inside the network show the order of the sending and ACKing of a single frame from Node A to Node F.

If multiple switches are involved in transporting data through the network, the connection-oriented data link layer may be used at each switch to provide link level flow control and error detection. If so, each link between the switching nodes in Figure 1-4 is managed as a separate entity. That is, the link protocols on each link are unaware of each other's operations. Therefore, nothing prevents the network manager from using different link protocols on each link. For example, it is possible to use an IBM link control protocol on Network link A and a Hewlett-Packard link protocol on Network link B. This approach would work because the link layer control fields are stripped off as the data arrive at each switch and then added on for the transmission out of the switch onto another link. This approach is not used frequently, however, because it requires training the communications personnel on multiple protocols.

## POSITION OF THE DLC IN OSI

This book is not intended to be a treatise on the Open Systems Interconnection model (OSI). However, since most data link control protocols are placed in Layer two of the OSI model (and other layered models such as the Internet suite of protocols, DECnet, and SNA), a brief discourse on this model should help in understanding material in subsequent chapters.

## Overview of the OSI Model

The Open Systems Interconnection (OSI) Model was developed by several standards organizations. OSI is intended to diminish the effects of the vendor-specific approach that has resulted in each vendor system operating with unique protocols. This approach "closed" the end users' options of interconnecting and interfacing with other systems, necessitating the purchase of expensive and complex protocol converters to translate the different protocols.

The goal of OSI is to permit different systems to communicate *openly* with each other without changing the logic of the communicating layers (hardware and software). Heretofore "closed" systems that were unable to communicate with each other therefore should be able to communicate with relatively few or no changes to the software and hardware.

As shown in Figure 1-5, the OSI model is organized into seven layers. Each layer includes several to many protocols (entities) which are invoked based on the specific needs of the user. However, each protocol in a layer need not be invoked for every user session; the OSI model provides a means for two users to negotiate the specific protocols that are desired for the session between the users. Data link control protocols reside in layer two, which, logically enough, is called the *data link control layer.*

The lowest layer in the model is the physical layer. This layer is responsible for activating, maintaining, and deactivating a physical circuit between a user device and a

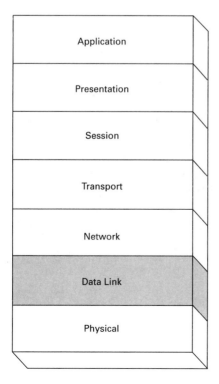

**Figure 1-5.** The OSI model and the Data Link Control Layer

communications device, such as a modem or a data service unit. This layer defines the type of physical signals (electrical, optical, etc.), as well as the type of media (wires, coaxial cable, satellite, etc.). Physical level protocols also are called *physical level interfaces.* Either term is acceptable. The DCE described earlier in this chapter is considered a physical layer device.

The physical layer's most common operations deal with the creation and reception of physical signals. For example, conventions may exist to represent a binary one with a plus voltage and a binary zero with a minus voltage (although some systems are just the opposite).

In addition, the physical connectors are described at this layer. These connectors are published by a number of standards groups. For example, the ISO 2110 connector and the RJ 45 telephone-type connector are used widely in physical level interfaces. Operations at the physical level also describe the speed (typically) in bits per second (bit/s). If analog lines are used, the rules for modulation must be agreed upon, as well.

The physical level also is the layer at which the physical medium is described. For example, the specifications for coaxial cable, twisted pair, optical fiber, and microwave relay are the responsibility of this layer. For proper synchronization between sending and receiving components, clocking functions also must be stipulated—another important responsibility of the physical layer.

The data link layer is the focus of this book. Its functions vary, depending on a connection-oriented or connectionless implementation. As we have learned, the data link layer delimits the flow of bits from the physical layer. Also, it provides for the identity of the bits and usually ensures that the data arrive safely at the receiving machine. Often, it offers flow control to ensure that the machine does not become overburdened with too much data at any one time. One of its most important functions is to detect transmission errors and to provide mechanisms to recover from lost, duplicated, or erroneous data. Traffic is accounted for by the exchange of positive acknowledgments (ACKs) or negative acknowledgments (NAKs).

The physical layer actions are dictated by the control functions of the data link layer. The physical layer provides services to the data link layer and the data link cannot function without the physical layer media-dependent interfaces. This separation allows link control protocols to be transparent to the physical layer, and vice versa.

The network layer specifies (a) the network/user interface; (b) operations of two user computers with each other through a network; and (c) the switching/routing procedures within a network. The network layer allows users to negotiate options with the network and each other. For example, throughput, delay (response time), and acceptable error rates are common negotiations.

Also, the network layer specifies the routing conventions to transfer traffic between networks—a term called *internetworking.* Although it has sequence numbers and flow control capabilities, these operations are used throughout the network and not between the links as in the data link layer.

The transport layer provides the interface between the data communications network and the upper three layers (generally part of the user's system). This layer gives the user options in obtaining certain levels of quality (and cost) from the network itself (i.e., the network layer). It is designed to keep the user isolated from some of the physical and functional aspects of the network.

The transport layer provides for the end-to-end accountability across more than one data link. It is responsible, as well, for end-to-end integrity of users' data in internetworking operations. Therefore, it is a vital layer for users who send traffic to other users on a different network.

The transport layer also has sending and receiving numbers, as well as timers. This feature may seem to be redundant when these timers and sequence numbers also may exist at the network and data link layers. Indeed, they may be redundant. However, in some situations these timers and sequence numbers are quite important. For example, in internetworking situations in which networks are connected, these timers and sequence numbers are used to ensure the integrity of the traffic through *multiple* networks, a service not provided at the lower layers.

Finally, the transport layer provides for flow control between two transport entities through the use of "credit values" issued back and forth between the layers. The credit values provide guidance on how much data the sending transport layer transmits to the receiving transport layer.

In later chapters we explore the interrelationships of the data link, network, and transport layers and examine several configuration options that will reduce some of the potentially redundant operations that exist in these layers.

The upper three layers are not concerned with communications operations. Instead, their task is to support the end user application by offering services such as E-mail, file transfer and management, directories, syntax translation, and so on.

## Logical and Physical Communications at the Data Link and Physical Layers

Figure 1-6 shows the relationship of the layers of the OSI model and specifically, the relationship between the data link layer and the physical layer. The physical signals are

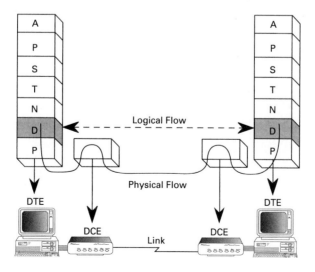

**Figure 1-6.** Relationship of the Physical and Data Link Layers

sent between the sending DTE and the DCE, across the communications link, and then to the receiving DCE and DTE. The physical layer supports the exchange of traffic among all the layers in the OSI model. For this discussion, the logical flow between the data link layers is of interest. The term *logical flow* means that the data link entities in both of these machines are exchanging data with each other. They are not concerned with exchanging data with any of the other layers. The arrow labeled *logical flow* does not mean that traffic is flowing horizontally between the two layers directly (there is no such thing as ether air). Rather, it means that traffic is sent down through the physical channel (link) to be conveyed to the data link layer for execution.

Figure 1-7 shows an example of the manner by which Machine A sends data to Machine B. Data are passed from the upper layers or the user application to the network layer (each layer adds a header to the data as they are passed down to the next layer). The network layer adds a header (labeled NW in the figure) and performs actions based on information in the transaction that accompanied the data from the upper layer.

The network layer then passes the data unit (with all the upper-layer headers) and its header to the data link layer. This layer performs some actions, based on information in the transaction, and adds its header D to the data unit that was passed from the network layer. Notice, in addition, that the data link layer adds a trailer, also labeled D, to the data unit. Thus, all data and headers from the upper layers are *encapsulated* into the data link protocol data unit. This traffic, now called a *frame,* is passed across the communications line (or through a network) to the receiving Machine B.

At B, the process is reversed. The headers and trailers that were created at A are used by the *peer layers* at B to determine what actions are to be taken. As the traffic is

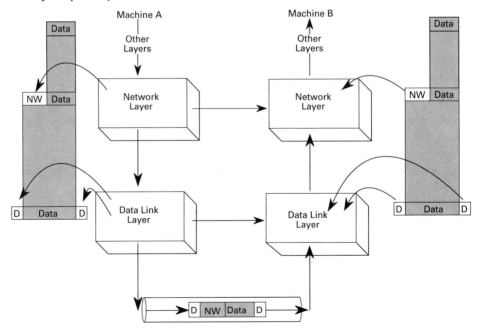

**Figure 1-7.** Link Layer Encapsulation and Decapsulation

sent up the layers, the respective layer removes its header, performs defined actions, and passes the traffic on up to the next layer. This process is called *decapsulation.*

The user application is presented only with user data—which were created by the sending user application. These user applications are unaware (one hopes) of the many operations in each OSI layer that were invoked to support the end-user data transfer.

## Service Definitions

The layers in the OSI model in the same machine communicate with a set of transactions that usually are implemented in program function calls (a software call that allows software modules [layers] to communicate with each other). Figure 1-8 depicts the data link layer providing a service, or a set of services, to the adjacent upper layer—the network layer.

The network communicates with the data link control layer through an address or identifier commonly known as the *service access point* (SAP). Services are provided by the link layer to the network layer through a service access point (SAP). The link SAP (LSAP) identifies the entity in the network layer (for example, a network layer protocol) that is using the service(s) of the data link layer.

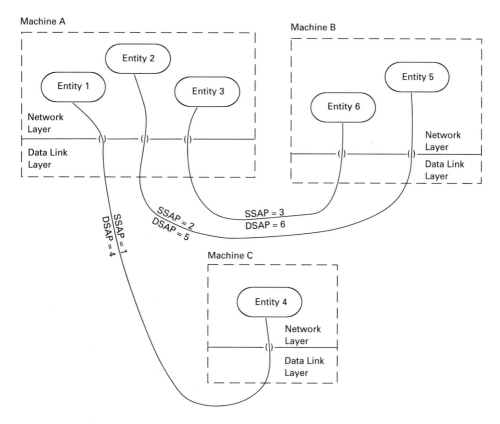

**Figure 1-8.** Service Access Points Between the Data Link and Network Layer

A network entity in one machine can invoke network services in another machine through the use of SAPs. OSI does not define what the SAPs may be. They could be software programs, data bases, files, etc., although the common practice is to use a SAP to identify a software module, such as a specific network protocol. For example, machine A could indicate that it wishes to use the well-known Internet Protocol (IP) at the network layer.

There may be many SAPs in an installation due to the complex operating environment. The well-known services associated with network layer protocols can be associated with a SAP value that is reserved to identify each "well-known" SAP.

Each layer in the OSI model can use SAPs. A common practice is to use SAPs to identify application layer services such as file servers, mail servers, directory services, terminal servers, name servers, and so on.

The idea of a source and destination SAP is relative. For example, in Figure 1-8, at machine A its source SAPs are 1, 2, and 3 and its destination SAPs are 4, 5, and 6. In contrast, machine B considers (when sending data) the SAPs 2 and 3 to be destination SAPs and SAPs 5 and 6 to be source SAPs. Likewise, machine C considers SAP 1 to be a destination SAP and SAP 4 to be a source SAP. This approach simply is a method to keep the endpoint SAPs associated with each other.

## Primitive Operations

As depicted in Figure 1-9, through the use of four types of transactions, called *primitives* (request, indication, response, and confirm), the data link layer communicates with the network layer in order to manage the communications processes on the link between the computers. (Some sessions do not require all primitives.)

- *Request*. Primitive issued by the network layer to invoke services at the data link layer. Data can be passed to the data link layer with the request primitive.

- *Indication*. Primitive issued by the data link layer at the receiving machine to indicate a function has been invoked at a service access point (SAP) and perhaps to deliver any data that were given to the sending data link layer by the request primitive.

- *Response*. Primitive issued by the network layer to complete a function previously invoked by an indication primitive at that SAP. Data may be passed from the network layer to the data link layer with the primitive.

- *Confirm*. Primitive issued by the data link layer to complete a function previously invoked by a request primitive at that SAP, and perhaps to pass data that were given to the remote data link layer with the response primitive.

## Data Link Service Definitions

The International Standards Organization (ISO) has published a data link service definition in the DIS 8886 publication. As we have learned, the services are defined by primitives, and 8886 provides for both connection-oriented and connectionless services.

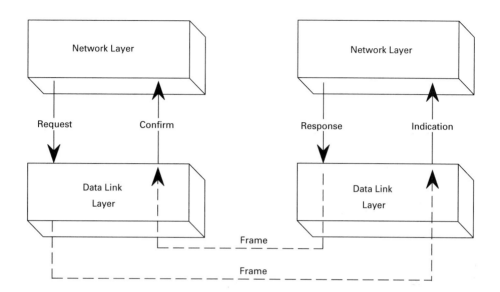

**Figure 1-9.** Primitive Operations Between the Network and Data Link Layers

These primitives are summarized in Table 1-1.

Most of the primitives have associated parameters. These parameters are listed between parentheses with each of the primitive statements. The parameters largely are self-explanatory. For example, called address and calling address are used to identify the receiver and originator of the link layer traffic. Certain link layer protocols support expedited data transfer. If this is the case, the parameter labeled *expedited data selection* can be used to invoke priority operations at the link layer. The quality of service parameters allow a network layer to request certain types of services of the data link layer. In actual implementations, the quality of services (QOS) parameters field either is left blank or contains relatively few values. This lack of QOS is because the data link layer contains a relatively low-function protocol and is not intended to provide very many sophisticated services. Disconnects can be used by data link layers to terminate the data link connections. The originator provides its address in the disconnect and any reason for the disconnect in the reason field. The user data parameter is used to signify that end-user data from the network layer (and upper layers) are carried in the primitive.

Keep in mind that these primitives and the parameters in the primitives are used to create the data link control headers that are appended to the beginning and ending of user data—which results in the creation of the data link frame.

**TABLE 1-1.** DATA LINK CONTROL PRIMITIVES

| Connection-Oriented |
| --- |
| DL-CONNECT.request (Called Address, Calling Address, Expedited Data Selection, Quality of Service Parameters) |
| DL-CONNECT.indication (Called Address, Calling Address, Expedited Data Selection, Quality of Service Parameters) |

DL-CONNECT.response (Responding Address, Expedited Data Selection, Quality of Service Parameters)

DL-CONNECT.confirm (Responding Address, Expedited Data Selection, Quality of Service Parameters)

DL-DISCONNECT.request (Originator, Reason)

DL-DISCONNECT.indication (Originator, Reason)

DL-DATA.request (User-Data)

DL-DATA.indication (User-Data)

DL-EXPEDITED-DATA.request (User-Data)

DL-EXPEDITED-DATA.indication (User-Data)

DL-RESET.request (Originator, Reason)

DL-RESET.indication (Originator, Reason)

DL-RESET.response

DL-RESET.confirm

DL-ERROR-REPORT.indication (Reason)

---

Connectionless

---

DL-UNITDATA.request (Source Address, Destination Address, Quality of Service, User Data)

DL-UNITDATA.indication (Source Address, Destination Address, Quality of Service, User-Data)

## SUMMARY

Data link controls provide for error detection and retransmission on the communications link.  They reside in Layer 2 of a data communications layered model.  While some systems may not need extensive error detection and recovery support, for the foreseeable future data link error checking will remain a vital component of network operations.

# 2

# *Errors and Remedial Measures*

## INTRODUCTION

This chapter examines common transmission impairments that occur on data communication links. Both random and nonrandom errors are explored, as well as problems that occur on telephone type media. After discussion of these errors, the remainder of the chapter is devoted to methods used by data link controls to resolve the transmission impairments. Techniques such as echo, parity checking, and cyclic redundancy checking are examined.

## DIFFICULTY OF DEALING WITH ERRORS

When we consider the differences between the data communications and centralized mainframe environments, it becomes clear that data communications systems are more subject to error because the transmissions take place through a "hostile" environment. A microwave signal is illustrative. During transmission, it may encounter varying temperatures, fog, rain, or snow, as well as other microwave signals that tend to distort the signal. This is one reason, among others, that optical fiber is replacing some of the microwave routes.

A transmission through a communications system travels through several components, and each component introduces an added probability of the occurence of errors. For example, as a signal moves through a network, it must pass through switches, modems, multiplexers, and other instruments. If the interfaces among these components are not established properly, an error can occur. Moreover, the components themselves can introduce errors.

The centralized mainframe operating system (OS) exercises considerable control over its resources. Events usually do not occur without the permission of the OS. In the event an error occurs, the operating system interrupts the work in progress, suspends the problem program, stores its registers and buffers, and executes the requisite analysis to uncover the problem.

A data communications system may not allow for this type of control. First, often it is impractical to suspend and freeze resources because they may be used by other components. Second, their condition may have changed by the time a network control component receives the error indication. Third, networks often are distributed in their control mechanisms and do not always operate under the tight centralized manner found in the centralized mainframe.

Clearly, a distributed data communications system poses formidable challenges to a network manager. However a wide array of remedial measures can be taken to mitigate the effects of these problems, however.

## MAJOR TYPES OF IMPAIRMENTS

Transmission impairments can be defined broadly as random or nonrandom events. The random events cannot be predicted. Nonrandom impairments are predictable and, therefore, are subject to preventive maintenance efforts. These errors may be bothersome only for a voice or video transmission. However, they may be quite serious for a data transmission, since they can result in distortions of the bit streams that represent user data.

The nonrandom movement of electrons creates an electric current on a hardwire that is used for the transmission signal. Along with these signals, all electrical components also experience the vibrations of the random movement of electrons. These vibrations create thermal energy and cause the emission of electromagnetic waves of many frequencies. The phenomenon also is called *white noise* because it contains an average of all the spectral frequencies equally, just as white light does. Other names are *gaussian noise, random noise,* or *background noise.* Excessive noise can undermine the transmission integrity of the link and can prevent the receiving device from detecting the incoming data stream accurately.

Most of us who use the public telephone network have experienced the interference of another party's faint voice on our line. This is crosstalk (or intelligible crosstalk)—the interference of signals from another channel. One source of crosstalk is in physical circuits that run parallel to each other in building ducts and telephone facilities. The electromagnetic radiation of the signals on the circuits creates an inductance and capacitance effect on the nearby circuits. Crosstalk also can occur with the coupling of a transmitter and receiver at the same location, which is called near-end crosstalk, or NEXT. The coupling of a transmitter to an incorrect remote receiver is called far-end crosstalk, or FEXT. Near-end and far-end crosstalk travel in different directions. While crosstalk may be only a minor irritation during a voice call (it might even be interesting), it can lead to data distortions.

In addition, almost everyone using a telephone has experienced echoes during a conversation. The effect sounds like one is in an echo chamber; the talker's voice is actually echoed back to the telephone handset. Echoes are caused by the changes in impedances in communications circuits. (*Impedance* is the combined effect of inductance, resistance, and capacitance of a signal at a particular frequency.) For example, connecting two wires of different gauges could create an impedance mismatch. Echoes also are caused by circuit junctions that allow a portion of the signal erroneously to find its way into the return side of a four-wire circuit. The telephone company must undertake special measures in dealing with echo on data circuits, and if these measures are carried out incorrectly, the link is not adequate for the transmission of data.

The strength of a signal attenuates (decays) as it travels through a transmission path. The amount of attenuation depends on the frequency of the signal, the transmission medium, and the length of the circuit. Unfortunately, signal attenuation is not the same for all frequencies. The nonuniform loss across the bandwidth can create *amplitude distortion* (also referred to as *attenuation distortion*) on a voice channel.

To combat the loss on the line, inductive loading is utilized. The use of inductive loading provides a means of reducing the natural loss in the cable. By placing loading coils at regular intervals in the subscriber loop, the electrical loss throughout a specific range of frequencies can better be managed. Since the natural loss of a cable increases rapidly with frequency and distance, the loading systems can be used to create a consistent performance across the bandwidth in the channel.

However, loaded cable acts like a low-pass filter and severely attenuates frequencies above 3000 Hz. Loaded cable reduces the signal propagation by as much as a factor of three, which increases transmission delay, as well. Loading also introduces significant delay distortion (which requires equalization on longer lines). In addition, VF repeaters are required to obtain additional range, due to the attenuation. These operations must be crafted carefully for data transmissions, since data transmission is more sensitive to attenuation than is voice transmission.

A signal consists of many frequencies. Because these frequencies do not travel at the same speed, they arrive at the receiver at different times. Excessive delays create errors known as *delay distortion* or *envelope delay*. The problem is not serious for voice transmissions, because a human ear is not very sensitive to phase. However, delay distortion creates problems for data transmissions.

Marking and spacing distortion occurs when the receiving component samples the incoming signal at the wrong interval or threshold, and/or the signal takes too long to build up and decay on the channel. This problem can occur in interfaces such as EIA-232-D (and CCITT's V.28) if the standard is not followed. EIA specifies that the capacitance of the cable and the terminator shall be less than 2500 picofarads (a measure of capacitance). If this specification is violated, the transition from a one (mark) to a zero (space), and vice versa, may exceed the EIA-232-D standard stated as "time required to pass through the -3 V to +3 V or +3 V to -3 V transition region shall not exceed 1 millisecond or 4% of a bit time, whichever is smaller."

The net effect of this impairment is that the signal takes too long to complete the transitions from (or to) marks and spaces. Spacing distortion results when the receiver produces space bits longer than the mark bits. Marking distortion occurs when the mark bits are elongated. These problems may cause data errors, especially if the sampling clock is inaccurate and noise exists on the line. The spreading of a pulse signal can affect timing and lead to accumulated timing jitter.

## BIT AND BLOCK ERROR RATES

Since one of data link control's primary functions is to recover from errors that are encountered on the link, the quality of the link from the standpoint of errors encountered determines how much "work" the data link protocol must do. Retransmissions can lead to reduced throughput and increased delay on the communications link. Therefore, the network manager is quite interested in knowing about the quality of the links in the network.

Channel or link quality often is measured by the number of erroneous bits received during a given period. This bit error rate (BER) is derived by dividing the number of bits received in error by the number of bits transmitted. A typical error rate on a high-quality leased telephone line (copper wire) is as low as $1:10^6$. In most cases, the errors occur in bursts and cannot be predicted precisely. The BER is a useful measure for determining the quality of the channel, calibrating it, and pinpointing its problems.

BER should be measured over a finite time interval, and the time measurement should be included in the description of the error rate. The following equation calculates BER:

$$BER = B_e/RT_m$$

Where: $R$ = channel speed in bits per second; $B_e$ = number of bits in error; $T_m$ = measurement period in seconds.

The actual bit sequences are important to BER. Pseudorandom bit sequences have all the appearance of random digital data. These sequences, generated in repeating lengths of $2^n - 1$ bits, will generate all but one possible word combination of bit length n. The most common sequences (defined by CCITT) are 511 and 2047 bits long, representing $n = 9$ and $n = 11$, respectively.

The block error rate (BLER) is a ratio of the number of blocks (we use the term *frame* for *block*) received that contain at least one erroneous bit to the total blocks received. BLER is thus calculated by dividing the number of blocks received in error by the number of blocks transmitted. The BLER is an effective calculation for determining overall throughput on the channel and often is used by network designers to perform line loading and network topology configuration.

The error rate on the link is an important component in determining the size of a data link frame. This topic is revisited later in this chapter, after some other subjects have been introduced.

Another useful calculation is to determine the percentage of seconds during a stated period in which no errors occur. Error-free seconds (EFS) are calculated by:

$$\% EFS = [S - S_e/S] \times 100\%$$

Where: $S$ = measurement period in seconds; $S_e$ = number of 1 second intervals during which one bit error occurred.

The parameter $S$ is important, since, like $T_m$ in BER, it is necessary to specify a measuring interval. The period tested may be hours or even days.

EFS is a valuable measure of performance for channels on which data are transmitted in blocks. BER is not a very good measure of performance of throughput, but it is used widely to evaluate the performance of modems and other DCEs.

## ERROR DETECTION

Since errors are inevitable in a data communications system, some method of detecting the errors is required. While the methods vary, they all have one goal: detecting the corrupted bits.

### Parity Checking

Parity checking is one of the older forms of error detection. Like most data communication error techniques, parity checking requires the insertion of redundant bits that are used to model the content of the bits in the frame. Although the techniques vary on how parity detection is implemented, generally it consists of inserting one bit to a character or a number of bits to a number of characters at the transmitter and checking these bits at the receiver to determine whether distortion has altered any of the bits in the data stream.

**Single Parity.**  *Single parity* (also called *vertical redundancy checking* [VRC]) is a simple parity technique. It consists of adding a single bit (a parity bit) to each string of bits that comprise a character. The bit is set to 1 or 0 to give the character bits an odd or even number of bits that are (a) 1s for a 1-parity protocol or (b) 0s for a 0-parity protocol. This parity bit is inserted at the transmitting station, sent with each character in the message, and checked at the receiver to determine whether each character is the correct parity. If a transmission impairment caused a "bit flip" of 1 to 0 or 0 to 1, the parity check would so indicate. Figure 2-1 shows the single parity check logic. The second bit of the third character is distorted due to noise, etc. Since the VRC bit was set to a 1 to give the third character an odd number of 1 bits (in this case, five 1 bits), the detection of an even

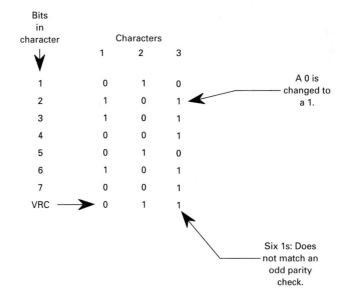

**Figure 2-1.** Single Parity Checking

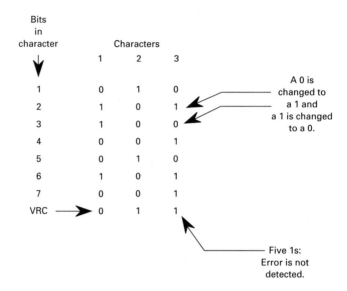

**Figure 2-2.** An Undetected Error

number of 1 bits serves as an indicator of error. The protocol may then ask for a retransmission or may ignore the error, if it is of no consequence.

The single parity check works well enough for a single-bit error, but errors occur in "clusters," as well. Figure 2-2 shows that this type of error will not be detected. At a transmission rate of 1200 bit/s, the probability of more than one errored bit occurring within seven bits is almost 50 percent. Fortunately, the multiple bit errors may not occur within one character in the data stream, but may fall between two successive characters. Nonetheless, the problem is serious enough to apply to other methods. A common solution to the single parity check problem is the use of additional parity checks.

**Multiple or Block Parity.**  *Multiple* or *block parity* (also called *longitudinal redundancy check* [LRC]) is a refinement of the character parity approach. In addition to a parity bit on each character, LRC places a parity (odd or even) on a block of characters.

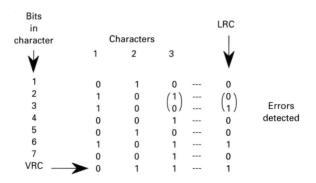

**Figure 2-3.** Multiple Parity Checking

The block check (of a double parity) provides a better method to detect for errors across characters. LRC usually is implemented with VRC and is then called a two-dimensional parity check code (see Figure 2-3). The VRC-LRC combination provides a substantial improvement over a single method. A typical telephone line with an error rate of $1:10^5$ can be improved to a perceived range of $1:10^7$ to $1:10^9$ with the two-dimensional check.

The parity check is expressed mathematically by the use of the EXCLUSIVE OR operation. The EXCLUSIVE OR of two binary digits is 1 if the digits differ; if they are the same (both 0s or both 1s), the EXCLUSIVE OR result is 0.

The following equation demonstrates the use of parity:

$$P_j = b_{1j} \qquad b_{2j} \ldots b_{nj}$$

Where: $P_j$ = parity bit of jth character; $b_{ij}$ = ith bit in the jth character; n = number of bits in the character.

## Checksum

The realization that checking groups of bit streams rather than individual characters would yield better results led to another error-checking technique. Although this technique is known by various names in the field, the process usually is called the checksum. The field used by the checksum frequently is called a *block check character* (BCC). Recall, however, that the term BCC also may be used to describe the double parity check covered in the previous section.

The checksum is a simple sum of the binary, numerical values of the characters in the block of data. At the transmitter, these characters are summed to produce the block check character. At the receiver, an identical checksum is performed and compared with the BCC field that was transmitted with the frame. If the two sums are not equal, it is assumed that an error has occurred during the transmission. Remedial action is then taken.

Checksums are used widely in the industry because of their simplicity and the fact that they can be implemented with a few lines of software code. They are not perfect, however, as they will not detect certain types of error sequences in the bit stream.

## Echoplex

This rather primitive technique is used in many asynchronous devices, notably personal computers. Each character is transmitted to the receiver, where it is sent back or echoed to the original station. The echoed character is compared with a copy of the transmitted character. If they are the same, a high probability exists that the transmission is correct.

Echoplex requires the use of full duplex facilities. In the event a full duplex configuration is not available, a device usually is switched to local echo, which sends the echo through the local modem back to the user device. Local echo permits the system to operate as if it were echoplex, but be aware that local echo does not check for errors across the link.

## Error-Checking Codes

Any discussion of error control must include two widely used error-checking codes: block codes and convolutional codes. The purpose of these codes is to detect errors that have corrupted the signals. (With some codes, the errors also are corrected.)

**Block Codes.**  A block code consists of an information sequence referred to as a *block* or *blocks*. Each block contains k information bits. The block also is called a *message*. For binary-based codes, a total of $2^k$ possible messages exist. An encoder transforms the bits in the message into a code, and $2^k$ code words are possible from the output of the encoder. The term *block code* (or [n,k] block codes) is associated with the set of $2^k$ code words of length n.

Another term important to this discussion is the *code rate* (R), defined as R = k/n. It is the ratio of the number of information bits per transmitted symbol.

For a different code word to be assigned to each symbol, k < n or R < 1. Redundant bits can be added to a message to form a code word if k < n. The number of redundant bits can be n – k. It is these redundant bits that enable a communications system to deal with transmission impairments.

The encoder"outputs" the code based only on the input value of the k-bit message. Therefore, the encoder is said to be "memoryless," and can be implemented with combinational logic.

A block code contains an important attribute called the *minimum distance*. It determines its error-detecting and error-correcting capabilities and is described as the *Hamming weight* or *Hamming distance.* As an example, the Hamming distance between the binary n – tuples of x = (11010001) and y = (01000101), written as d(x,y), is 3. Reading left to right, they differ in the first, fourth, and sixth positions.

It is possible to compute the Hamming distance between any two code words. The minimum distance is defined as:

$$d_{min} = min \{d(x,y) : x, y \ C, x = W\}$$

Where: C = a block code; x and y = code vectors.

When a code v=Vector v is transmitted over a channel, a number of L errors will result in the received Vector r, which is different from Vector v in L places. Hamming theory states that, for Code C, no error of $d_{min}$ –1 (or fewer) can change one code into another. It follows that any code word received with an error pattern of $d_{min}$ –1 or fewer errors will be detected as an error. In other words, the received code word is not a code word of C.

The Hamming code detects all of $d_{min}$–1 or fewer errors and also can detect a large number of errors with $d_{min}$ or more errors. It is preferable to develop a block code with the Hamming distance to be as large as possible. A large minimum distance increases the likelihood of detecting errors.

**Convolutional Codes.**  The convolutional encoder has a memory. It, too, accepts blocks of k-bit information and produces an encoded value of n-symbol blocks. However, in contrast to block coding, the code word value depends on the current k bit message and on m previous message blocks. The encoded value is called a (n,k,m) convolutional code and is implemented with sequential logic.

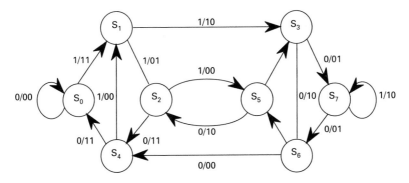

**Figure 2-4.** Convolutional Codes [LIN83]

The sequential aspect of convolutional codes allows us to describe its operation with a state diagram (see Figure 2-4). Each branch on the state diagram is labeled with the k inputs causing the transition and its corresponding n inputs. Starting at $S_0$ the path is followed through the state diagram according to the k bits input [u(1) . . . .u(k)]. The output label is the resulting code symbol [v(1) . . . v(n)]. After the last nonzero bit, the path is followed back to $S_0$, with all-zeros appended to the code.

For example, a bit stream of 11101 produces the code word: 11, 10, 01, 01, 11, 10, 11, 11. The path through the state diagram is:

$$S_0 \ S_1 \ S_3 \ S_7 \ S_6 \ S_5 \ S_2 \ S_4 \ S_0.$$

Convolutional codes also are evaluated in relation to their distance properties. This is achieved by several analyses, but the simplest is the minimum free distance $d_{free}$:

$$\begin{array}{l} D \\ d_{free} = \ \min \ \{d \ (v^1, v^{11}) : u^1 = u^{11}\} \end{array}$$

Where: $v^1$ and $v^{11}$ = code words corresponding to information $u^1$ and $u^{11}$, respectively.

This discussion on block and convolutional codes only touches the surface of error-control coding. However, it provides us with enough background to understand the cyclic codes using block coding concepts.

## Cyclic Redundancy Check (CRC)

Many error detection codes for data transmission use logic based on the cyclic redundancy check (CRC). It is so named because the bits in a message $v = (v_0, v_1 . . . v_{n-1})$ are cyclically shifted through a register one place at a time: $v$ (one place) = $(v_{n-1}, v_0 . . . v_{n-2})$. The CRC method is derived from the concepts of block coding. Thus, the CRC technique is "memoryless" and can be implemented with combinational logic. Moreover, cyclic codes possess algebraic properties that lend themselves to relatively simple error-detection implementations.

With this technique, the transmitter generates a bit pattern called a *frame check sequence* (FCS) based on the contents of the frame. The combined contents of the FCS and the frame (F) are exactly divisible by some predetermined number (with no remainder), or, as an alternative, are divisible by the number with a known remainder. If the contents of the frame are damaged during transmission, the receiver's division will yield a nonzero or a value other than a known remainder— an indication of an error.

CRC detects all of the following errors:

- All single-bit errors
- All double-bit errors, if the divisor is at least three terms
- Any odd number of errors, if the divisor contains a factor $(x + 1)$
- Any error in which the length of the error (an error burst) is less than the length of the FCS
- Most errors with larger bursts

An algebraic notation is used to describe the FCS generation and checking process. The modulo 2 divisor is called a *generator polynomial* (a *polynomial* is an algebraic expression consisting of two or more terms). The divisor actually is one bit longer than the FCS. Both high-order and low-order bits of the divisor must be 1s. For example, a bit sequence of 11001001 is represented by the polynomial:

$$f(x) = x^7 + x^6 + x^3 + 1$$

The leading bits on the left-hand side correspond to the higher-order coefficients of the polynomial.

In general terms, the following rules apply to the CRC operations, although later examples show these rules implemented with EXCLUSIVE OR cyclic shift registers.

- The frame contents are appended by a set of zeros equal in number to the length of the FCS.
- This value is divided modulo 2 by the generator polynomial (which contains one more digit than the FCS and must have high- and low-order bits of 1s). The divisor "can be divided" into the dividend, if the dividend has as many significant bits as the divisor.
- Each division is carried out in the conventional manner, except the next step (subtraction) is done modulo 2. Subtraction and addition are identical to EXCLUSIVE OR (no borrows or carries):

|  |  | 1 | 1 | 0 | 0 |
|---|---|---|---|---|---|
|  |  | - 1 | - 0 | - 1 | - 0 |
|  |  | 0 | 1 | 1 | 0 |

| and |  | 1 | 1 | 0 | 0 |
|---|---|---|---|---|---|
|  |  | + 1 | + 0 | + 1 | + 0 |
|  |  | 0 | 1 | 1 | 0 |

- The answer provides a quotient, which is discarded, and a remainder, which becomes the FCS field.
- The FCS is placed at the back of the frame contents and sent to the receiver.
- The receiver performs the same division on the frame contents *and* the FCS field. The FCS replaces the appended zeros used at the transmitter.
- If the result equals the expected number (a zero or the predetermined number) the transmission is considered error-free.

To illustrate CRC, let us assume the following:

| | | |
|---|---|---|
| Frame contents: | 111011 | |
| Polynomial: | 11101 | $(x^4+x^3+x^2+1)$ |
| Frame contents and appended zeros: | 1110110000 | |

The transmitter performs the following calculation:

$$\overline{100001} \quad \text{(quotient ignored)}$$

```
       _____
11101  1110110000
       11101
          10000
          11101
           1101 (remainder becomes FCS)
```

At the receiver, the frame contents and the FCS are divided by the same polynomial. As this example shows, if the remainder equals zero, the transmission is accepted as having no errors:

$$100001$$

```
       _____
11101  1110111101      (FCS)
       11101
          11101
          11101
          00000     (remainder: no errors)
```

The division operation is equivalent to performing an EXCLUSIVE OR operation. The CRC calculations actually are performed in a cyclic shift register that uses EXCLUSIVE OR gates. EXCLUSIVE OR logic outputs 0 for inputs of 1 or 0; it outputs 1 if the inputs differ. The setup of the register depends on the type of generator polynomial.

Figure 2-5 shows the registers for CRC-CCITT ($X^{16} + X^{12} + X^5 + 1$) and CRC-16 ($X^{16} + X^{15} + X^2 + 1$). The former detects errors of bursts up to 16 bits in length. It detects more than 99% of error bursts greater than 12 bits. The CRC-16 detects more than 99% of error bursts greater than 16 bits.

It is evident from a study of Figures 2-5(a) and 2-5(b) that the feedback logic

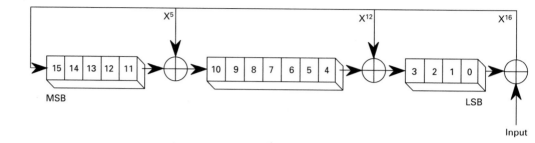

(a) CRC-CCITT ($X^{16} + X^{12} + X^5 + 1$)

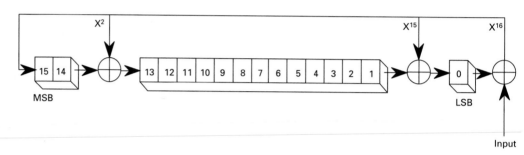

(b) CRC-16 ($X^{16} + X^{15} + X^2 + 1$)

**Figure 2-5.** CRC-CCITT and CRC-16 Polynomials

means that the register contents at a given instant are dependent upon the past transmission of bits. Consequently, the chances of a multiple bit burst creating an undetected error (a zero remainder) is very unlikely.

For the reader who wishes more detail on the frame check sequence, Box 2-1 explains the technique used for HDLC, as published by the European Computer Manufacturers Association (ECMA).

---

**BOX 2-1.** ECMA FCS GENERATION AND CHECKING

FCS GENERATION

1. The FCS is calculated as the sum (modulo 2) of:
   a. The remainder of the division (modulo 2) of
      $I(x) = x^K (x^{15} + x^{14} + \ldots x + 1)$ by $G(x)$.
   b. The remainder of the division (modulo 2) of:
      $x^{16} P_{k-1}(x)$ by $G(x)$
   c. $x^{15} + x^{14} \ldots x + 1$
2. The FCS is transmitted with higher-order coefficient first:
   $M(x) = x^{16} P_{k-1}(x) + FCS(x)$

3. If errors occur, the received polynomial will be:

$M'(x) = M(x) + E(x)$
Where: E(x) represents the error polynomial.

### FCS CHECKING

Received frame checked as the sum, (modulo 2) of the following terms:

4. The remainder of the division (modulo 2) of:
   $x^{16} I(x) = K^{k+16} (x^{15} + x^{14} + \ldots x + 1)$ by G(x)
5. The remainder of the division (modulo 2) of:
   $x^{16} m'(x)$ by G(x),
6. Shall be in the absence of errors:
   $x^{12} + x^{11} + x^{10} + x^8 + x^3 + x^2 + x + 1$.

## ERROR PROTECTION PERFORMANCE OF CRC

As a practical matter, it makes sense to question how far one should go to detect errors. That is, what is the incremental cost to obtain incremental gains in the error control? The cost must be evaluated in terms of a specific system. The incremental gains can be determined by examining several tables published by the National Institute of Standards and Technology (NIST). (Please note: all tables assume the bits assume any random pattern.)

Table 2-1 shows the probability of a pattern of errors that will not be detected by a 16-bit frame check sequence (FCS). For a typical frame of 1122 bits (128 octets * 8 bits of user data + 3 octets * 8 bits of packet header + 5 octets * 8 bits of internal network header + 4 octets * 8 bits of frame header and trailer = 1122 bits, rounded to 1000), the probabilities of an undetected error are approximately $5 * 10^{-10}$ for a link operating in a relatively poor $10^{-4}$ bit error rate.

Table 2-2 shows the maximum undetected bit error rate resulting from (1) a flag destruction; (2) the subsequent interpretation of the last 16 bits of the longer frame as a correct FCS. For our frame of 1122 bits, the maximum undetected bit error rate is approximately $1 * 10^{-11}$.

Table 2-3 depicts the maximum undetected bit error rate resulting from (1) data in a frame garbled into a flag pattern; which (2) divides the frame into two shorter frames; in which (3) the last 16 bits of either of the two frames pass the FCS check. The 1122 bit frame shows a $9 * 10^{-8}$ maximum undetected error rate.

Table 2-4 shows yet another possibility for an undetected error to occur. Two situations are covered in this table. First, a transmission error causes the receiver to leave a stuffed bit in a frame. For example, a bit stream of 111110 (where: 0 is a stuffed bit) is corrupted to 101110. Second, a group of bits is corrupted to resemble a stuffed bit. For example, a bit stream of 111101 is corrupted to 111110, (where: 0 appears to be a stuffed bit). In both cases, the last 16 bits are interpreted as a correct FCS pattern. The 1122 frame at a $10^{-4}$ bit error rate exhibits a $3 * 10^{-7}$ maximum undetected error rate.

Finally, Table 2-5 is an estimate of the overall undetected error rate expected on a link. Our example of the 1122 bit frame on the $10^{-4}$ link shows a very resilient $4 * 10^{-7}$ overall undetected error rate.

To place this data into perspective, it should be recognized that the chances of an undetected error certainly exist, even though they do not occur frequently. As better systems using optical fibers and forward error correction (FEC) are placed into operation, these systems will yield even better results.

**TABLE 2-1.**   UNDETECTED BIT ERROR RATE FROM ERRORS WITHIN FRAMES

| Bits in frame | Bit error rate $10^{-3}$ | $10^{-4}$ | $10^{-5}$ | $10^{-6}$ | $10^{-7}$ |
|---|---|---|---|---|---|
| 100 | $1 \times 10^{-8}$ | $1 \times 10^{-9}$ | $1 \times 10^{-10}$ | $1 \times 10^{-11}$ | $1 \times 10^{-12}$ |
| 300 | $9 \times 10^{-8}$ | $9 \times 10^{-9}$ | $9 \times 10^{-10}$ | $9 \times 10^{-11}$ | $9 \times 10^{-12}$ |
| 1000 | $7 \times 10^{-9}$ | $5 \times 10^{-10}$ | $4 \times 10^{-11}$ | $4 \times 10^{-12}$ | $4 \times 10^{-13}$ |
| 3000 | | $2 \times 10^{-11}$ | $1 \times 10^{-12}$ | $1 \times 10^{-13}$ | $1 \times 10^{-13}$ |
| 10000 | | $1 \times 10^{-10}$ | $2 \times 10^{-11}$ | $2 \times 10^{-12}$ | $2 \times 10^{-13}$ |
| 30000 | | $\sim 10^{-5}$ | $\sim 10^{-6}$ | $\sim 10^{-7}$ | $\sim 10^{-8}$ |

**TABLE 2-2.**   UNDETECTED ERROR RATE FROM SCRAMBLED SINGLE FLAG BETWEEN FRAMES

| Bits in frame | Bit error rate $10^{-3}$ | $10^{-4}$ | $10^{-5}$ | $10^{-6}$ | $10^{-7}$ |
|---|---|---|---|---|---|
| 100 | $1 \times 10^{-9}$ | $1 \times 10^{-10}$ | $1 \times 10^{-11}$ | $1 \times 10^{-12}$ | $1 \times 10^{-13}$ |
| 300 | $4 \times 10^{-10}$ | $4 \times 10^{-11}$ | $4 \times 10^{-12}$ | $4 \times 10^{-13}$ | $4 \times 10^{-14}$ |
| 1000 | $1 \times 10^{-10}$ | $1 \times 10^{-11}$ | $1 \times 10^{-12}$ | $1 \times 10^{-13}$ | $1 \times 10^{-14}$ |
| 3000 | $4 \times 10^{-11}$ | $4 \times 10^{-12}$ | $4 \times 10^{-13}$ | $4 \times 10^{-14}$ | $4 \times 10^{-15}$ |
| 10000 | $1 \times 10^{-11}$ | $1 \times 10^{-12}$ | $1 \times 10^{-13}$ | $1 \times 10^{-14}$ | $1 \times 10^{-15}$ |
| 30000 | $4 \times 10^{-12}$ | $4 \times 10^{-13}$ | $4 \times 10^{-14}$ | $4 \times 10^{-15}$ | $4 \times 10^{-16}$ |

**TABLE 2-3.**   UNDETECTED ERROR RATE FROM FICTITIOUS FLAG

| Bits in frame | Bit error rate $10^{-3}$ | $10^{-4}$ | $10^{-5}$ | $10^{-6}$ | $10^{-7}$ |
|---|---|---|---|---|---|
| 100 | $9 \times 10^{-8}$ | $9 \times 10^{-9}$ | $9 \times 10^{-10}$ | $9 \times 10^{-11}$ | $9 \times 10^{-12}$ |
| 300 | $3 \times 10^{-7}$ | $3 \times 10^{-8}$ | $3 \times 10^{-9}$ | $3 \times 10^{-10}$ | $3 \times 10^{-11}$ |
| 1000 | $9 \times 10^{-7}$ | $9 \times 10^{-8}$ | $9 \times 10^{-9}$ | $9 \times 10^{-10}$ | $9 \times 10^{-11}$ |
| 3000 | $3 \times 10^{-6}$ | $3 \times 10^{-7}$ | $3 \times 10^{-8}$ | $3 \times 10^{-9}$ | $3 \times 10^{-10}$ |
| 10000 | $9 \times 10^{-6}$ | $9 \times 10^{-7}$ | $9 \times 10^{-8}$ | $9 \times 10^{-9}$ | $9 \times 10^{-10}$ |
| 30000 | $3 \times 10^{-5}$ | $3 \times 10^{-6}$ | $3 \times 10^{-7}$ | $3 \times 10^{-8}$ | $3 \times 10^{-9}$ |

**TABLE 2-4.**   UNDETECTED ERROR RATE FROM ZERO BITS ERRORS

| Bits in frame | Bit error rate | | | | |
|---|---|---|---|---|---|
| | $10^{-3}$ | $10^{-4}$ | $10^{-5}$ | $10^{-6}$ | $10^{-7}$ |
| 100 | $2 \times 10^{-7}$ | $2 \times 10^{-8}$ | $2 \times 10^{-9}$ | $2 \times 10^{-10}$ | $2 \times 10^{-11}$ |
| 300 | $9 \times 10^{-7}$ | $9 \times 10^{-8}$ | $9 \times 10^{-9}$ | $9 \times 10^{-10}$ | $9 \times 10^{-11}$ |
| 1000 | $3 \times 10^{-6}$ | $3 \times 10^{-7}$ | $3 \times 10^{-8}$ | $3 \times 10^{-9}$ | $3 \times 10^{-10}$ |
| 3000 | $1 \times 10^{-5}$ | $1 \times 10^{-6}$ | $1 \times 10^{-7}$ | $1 \times 10^{-8}$ | $1 \times 10^{-9}$ |
| 10000 | $3 \times 10^{-5}$ | $3 \times 10^{-6}$ | $3 \times 10^{-7}$ | $3 \times 10^{-8}$ | $3 \times 10^{-9}$ |
| 30000 | $1 \times 10^{-4}$ | $1 \times 10^{-5}$ | $1 \times 10^{-6}$ | $1 \times 10^{-7}$ | $1 \times 10^{-8}$ |

**TABLE 2-5.**   APPROXIMATE OVERALL UNDETECTED BIT ERROR RATE

| Bits in frame | Bit error rate | | | | | |
|---|---|---|---|---|---|---|
| | $10^{-3}$ | $10^{-4}$ | $10^{-5}$ | $10^{-6}$ | $10^{-7}$ | |
| 100 | $3 \times 10^{-7}$ | $3 \times 10^{-8}$ | $3 \times 10^{-9}$ | $3 \times 10^{-10}$ | $3 \times 10^{-11}$ | |
| 300 | $1 \times 10^{-6}$ | $1 \times 10^{-7}$ | $1 \times 10^{-8}$ | $1 \times 10^{-9}$ | $1 \times 10^{-10}$ | |
| 1000 | $4 \times 10^{-6}$ | $4 \times 10^{-7}$ | $4 \times 10^{-8}$ | $4 \times 10^{-9}$ | $4 \times 10^{-10}$ | |
| 3000 | | | $1 \times 10^{-6}$ | $1 \times 10^{-7}$ | $1 \times 10^{-8}$ | $1 \times 10^{-9}$ |
| 10000 | | | $4 \times 10^{-6}$ | $4 \times 10^{-7}$ | $4 \times 10^{-8}$ | $4 \times 10^{-9}$ |
| 30000 | | | $\sim 10^{-5}$ | $\sim 10^{-6}$ | $\sim 10^{-7}$ | $\sim 10^{-8}$ |

## SUMMARY

In the past, error-checking codes used single or double parity checking techniques, and they still are quite prevalent today. During the 1970s and 1980s, checksums became widely accepted in the industry and provided for better error checking performance than the parity operations. Increasingly, systems have developed cyclical redundancy check (CRC) techniques, which yield vastly superior results in the older technologies. Some organizations choose to perform multiple error checking, with a CRC check at the data link layer and a checksum at a higher-layer protocol.

# 3

# *Overview of Data Link Controls*

## INTRODUCTION

This chapter introduces the major operations found in data link control protocols and discusses several key concepts and terms associated with data link layer operations. In addition, an analysis is made of primary/secondary protocols and peer-to-peer protocols.

Half-duplex and full-duplex operations, as well as asynchronous and synchronous transmission systems, are explained. The continuous ARQ systems are examined, too, and are compared with stop-and-wait ARQ. A comparison of the major error-detection schemes used by data link controls also is provided.

## CATEGORIES OF DATA LINK CONTROL PROTOCOLS

Even though link protocols vary widely in how they are implemented, the majority of systems can be described by one or a combination of the categories depicted in Figure 3-1.

An approach widely used to manage the communications channel is through a *primary/secondary* (sometimes called *master/slave*) *protocol*. This technique designates one station as the primary site on the link. The primary station controls all the other stations and dictates when and if the devices can communicate. Primary/secondary systems are implemented with several specific technologies depicted in Figure 3-1.

The second major approach to channel management is a *peer-to-peer protocol*. This technique has no primary station and typically provides for equal status to all stations on the link. However, stations may not have completely equal access to the link, since they can have preestablished priority over others. Nevertheless, the absence of a primary site

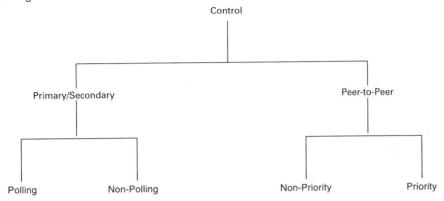

**Figure 3-1.**   Categories of Data Link Control Protocols

usually provides for an equal opportunity to use the communications link and other network resources. Peer/peer systems often are found in local area networks (LANs) with ring, bus, and mesh topologies.

## Primary/Secondary Protocols

**Polling/Selection Systems.**   A prevalent use of primary/secondary systems is polling/selection, usually shortened to *polling*. The configuration in Figure 3-2 shows a host computer at Site A and another machine at Site B. There could be other configurations (for example, a multidrop line or a ring topology). Conceptually, polling/selection works with computers linked to computers. It is possible to have primary/secondary computers, as well as terminals, workstations—any machine that has enough memory and adequate CPU power to execute the operation. Indeed, some machines, such as factory robots and sensory devices, operate with polling/selection protocols.

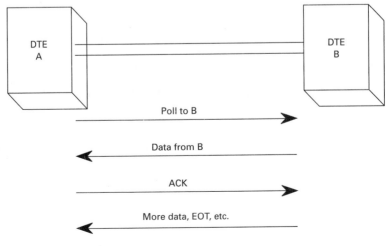

**Figure 3-2.** A Poll Operation

Polling/selection systems revolve around two data link frames, the *poll* and the *select. The* purpose of the poll is to transmit data to the primary site. The purpose of the select is just the opposite: to transmit data from the primary site to the secondary site. Select frames no longer are needed on the newer protocols, because the primary site reserves resources and buffers at the receiver during link establishment; thereafter, data are sent at the discretion of the primary node.

A network often exists as an ordered form of a primary/secondary relationship. Poll and select are the principal frames needed to move data to any site on a channel or in the network. Let us examine how this is accomplished, referring to Figure 3-2. First, a poll command is sent from the primary site to the secondary site. If data are to be transmitted, they are sent back to the polling site. The primary site checks for errors and sends an ACK if the data are acceptable or a NAK if the frame is in error. These two events (data and ACK or NAK) may occur many times until the secondary site has no more data to send. The secondary station must then send an indicator that it has completed its transmission, such as the end-of-transmission code (EOT), or a bit in a control field (called the final bit).

The select command is illustrated in Figure 3-3. Select means the primary station has data for the secondary. The ACK to the select means the station is ready to receive data. The data are transmitted, checked for errors, and acknowledged. (As stated earlier, newer systems reserve resources during the link establishment operations and assume thereafter that the receiver can receive the data. Therefore, no selects are required with this approach.) The process can repeat itself and, eventually, an EOT control indicator is transmitted to complete the operation.

When a poll is issued to the secondary site, it could respond negatively if it has nothing to transmit. The protocol typically uses a NAK to indicate a negative response to a poll.

A disadvantage of a polling/selection system is the potential number of negative responses to polls, which can consume precious resources on the channel. This overhead

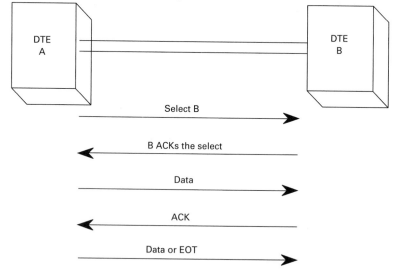

**Figure 3-3.** A Select Operation

especially is evident in systems without multiplexers or terminal cluster controllers that are used to manage the negative responses of the attached devices.

Another approach to decreasing the effect of polling overhead is to use dynamic polling/selection tables. If a machine continues to be polled and does not respond after a certain number of attempts, its priority is moved down in a polling table. Thus, it is serviced less and is polled fewer times. While the nonresponding station is dropped to a lower priority, those devices that have been responding positively to the poll are moved up in the priority table. It is conceivable to design the table to provide multiple entries by the same device. Station A might be polled, then station C, then A again, because A has been busy and responded positively to polls. Dynamic polling/selection eliminates some of the overhead found in the conventional static polling/selection systems.

**Multipoint Polling Systems.**    Figure 3-4 shows the approach used to manage traffic on a multipoint link (most often in wide area networks, and less often in local area networks). Station C is to communicate with Station B. In order for this transmission to take place, the primary station polls C. The data are not sent to B directly, but to the primary station; however, an address header in the frame indicates that the traffic is destined for B, which is shown in the figure as "Data from C to B." The data are checked for errors, an acknowledgment is sent , and, at some point, an EOT terminates the poll operation. When the data arrive at the primary site, this site examines the address header

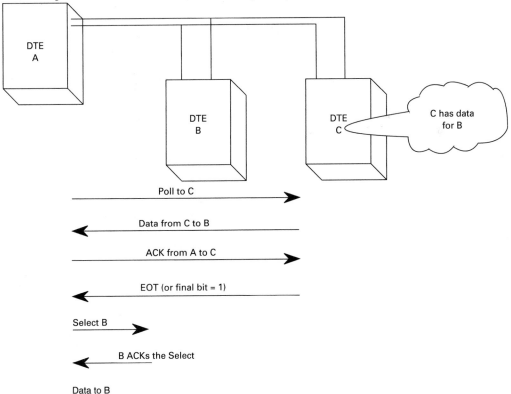

**Figure 3-4.** Polling and Selection Combined

and uses the select to relay the frame (onto the same channel) to B. The figure shows that the select is ACKed, then the frame is sent to B, where it is acknowledged, thus completing the operation.

Multipoint polling introduces delay into the process because of the requirement for switched carrier operations at the secondary stations. (A carrier signal often is used between the DCEs of each station to "carry" the data traffic. The frames are modulated onto the carrier with the transmitting DCE device, called a *modem.*) A multipoint wide area link typically uses two carrier signals (which creates two subchannels on the link). One carrier is sent from the primary station to the secondary stations. The secondary stations take turns using the other carrier signal (the other subchannel on the link) to send traffic to the primary station.

For example, in Figure 3-5 the primary site uses a constant carrier (the modem carrier signal stays on) to the secondary stations. When Station C receives its poll, it turns on its modem carrier signal to Station A. The carrier first is used to synchronize Station C with the primary station. Obviously, this process requires time and introduces delay.

After Station C has completed its transmission, it turns off its carrier signal. Then, the primary station uses its constant carrier subchannel to send the select command to Station B. Station B turns on its carrier to the primary station, the stations synchronize, and frames are exchanged.

The switched carrier operation and its inherent delays have resulted in the use of other link protocols for multipoint operations on local area networks (LANs). Several milliseconds are required to switch the carriers off and on and to synchronize the two machines. This type of delay is unacceptable in local area networks.

**Nonpolling Systems.**    Another approach to primary/secondary systems is the use of nonpolling protocols. One type that is used widely is *time division multiple access* (TDMA). This technique is a sophisticated form of *time division multiplexing* (TDM). Typically, a station is designated as a primary station (often called the *reference station* [REF]). The responsibility of the reference station is to accept requests from the secondary stations, which are an indication that the secondary station wishes to use the channel. The requests are sent as part of the ongoing transmissions in a special control field. Periodically, the reference station transmits a control frame indicating which stations can use the channel during a given period. Upon receiving the permission frame, the secondary stations adjust their timing to transmit within the predesignated slot.

TDMA does not use a polling selection system. Nonetheless, it fits into our classification of primary/secondary networks because the TDMA reference station has the option of assigning or not assigning stations to a slot on the link.

## Peer-to-Peer Protocols

The second major category of link control is the peer-to-peer arrangement. Two examples are provided in this section: (a) nonpriority schemes and (b) priority schemes.

**Nonpriority Systems.**    The carrier sense (collision) protocol is an example of the peer-to-peer nonpriority category of data link control. Several implementations use this technique, notably the Ethernet specification and IEEE 802.3/ISO 8802 standard. It provides a more efficient scheme for multipoint LANs than the aforementioned polling/selection protocol.

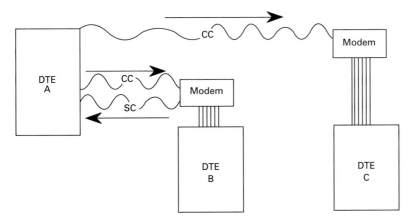

DTE B has switched carrier to DTE A;
DTE A has constant carrier to DTE B and DTE C.

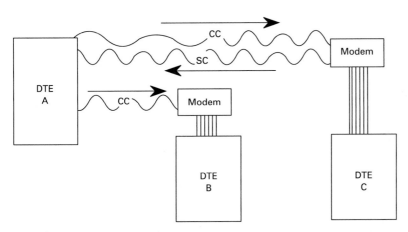

DTE C has switched carrier to DTE A;
DTE A has constant carrier to DTE B and DTE C.

Where:
CC = Constant carrier
SC = Switched carrier

**Figure 3-5.** Switched Carrier Operations

A carrier sense protocol considers all stations equal, so the stations contend for the use of the channel on a peer-to-peer basis. Before transmitting, the stations are required to monitor the channel to determine whether the channel is occupied. If the channel is idle, any station with data to transmit can send its frame onto the channel. If the channel is occupied, the stations must defer to the passing signal.

Figure 3-6 is an illustration of a carrier sense collision protocol. Stations A, B, C, and D are attached to a channel (such as coaxial cable) by *bus interface units* (BIU). If another station currently is using the channel, other stations "listen" and defer to the signal from the sending station. When the channel is idle, all stations can attempt to acquire the channel.

Since a station's transmission requires time to propagate to other stations, they may be unaware that a signal is on the channel. In Figure 3-6, station C could transmit its traffic even though station D supposedly has seized the channel. This problem is called the *collision window*. The collision window is a factor of the propagation delay of the signal and the distance between the two competing stations.

Carrier sense networks usually are implemented on short distance LANs because the collision window lengthens with a longer channel. The long channel provides opportunity for more collisions and can reduce throughput in the network. Generally, a long propagation delay (the delay before a station knows another station is transmitting) coupled with short frames and high data transfer rates gives rise to a greater incidence of collisions. Longer frames can mitigate the effect of long delay, but they reduce the opportunity for competing stations to acquire the channel.

Each station is capable of transmitting and listening to the channel simultaneously. As the two signals collide, they create voltage irregularities on the channel, which are sensed by the colliding stations (in this example, Stations C and D). The stations must turn off their transmission and, after a randomized waiting period, will attempt to seize

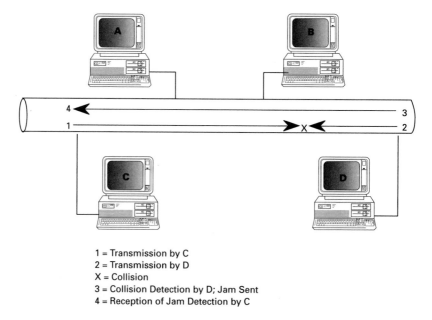

1 = Transmission by C
2 = Transmission by D
X = Collision
3 = Collision Detection by D; Jam Sent
4 = Reception of Jam Detection by C

**Figure 3-6**. Collision Detection Systems

the channel again. The randomized wait decreases the chances of the collision recurring since it is unlikely that the competing stations will generate the same randomized wait time.

**Priority Systems.**    Token passing is a method widely used for implementing both peer-to-peer nonpriority and priority systems. The priority systems are discussed here. The technique is found in many local area networks. Some token-passing systems are implemented with a horizontal bus topology; others are implemented with ring topology.

The ring topology is illustrated in Figure 3-7. The stations are connected to a concentriclogical ring through a *trunk coupling unit* (TCU). Each TCU is responsible for monitoring the data passing through it and regenerating the signal, then sending it to the next station. If the address in the header of the transmission indicates that the data are destined for a station, the interface unit copies the signal and passes the information to the user DTE or DTEs attached to it.

If the ring is idle (that is, no user data are occupying the ring), a "free" token is passed around the ring from node to node. The token is used to control the user of the

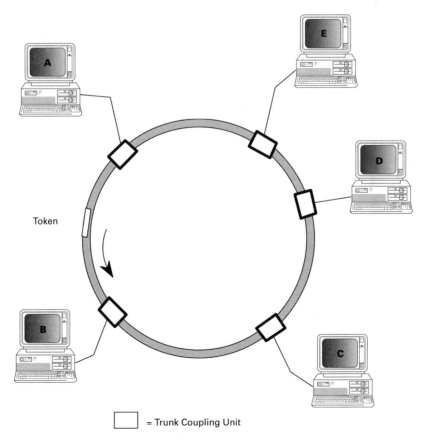

☐ = Trunk Coupling Unit

**Figure 3-7**. Token Ring Operations

ring with a field in the token called the *free/busy bit*. A busy token is an indication that a station has seized the ring and is transmitting data. A free token indicates that no traffic is on the channel; thus any station can acquire (seize) the token, make it busy and send data. The token is passed sequentially from node to node around the ring.

Each station attached to a token network may have a priority assigned to it. Typically, eight priorities are assigned. The object of the token-passing priority scheme is to give each station an opportunity to reserve the ring for the next transmission around the ring. As the token and data circle the ring, each node examines the token, which contains a reservation field. If the individual node's priority is higher than the priority number in the reservation field, it raises the reservation field number to its level, thus reserving the token on the next round. If another node does not make the reservation field higher, then the station is allowed to use the token and channel on the next pass around the ring.

The station seizing the token is required to store the previous reservation value in a temporary storage area at its location. Upon releasing the token when it completes a complete loop around the ring, the station restores the token to its previous lowest priority request. In this manner, once the token is made free for the next round, the station with the highest reservation value is allowed to seize the token. Token-passing priority systems are used widely in local area networks (LANs) and are explained in more detail in later chapters.

## DOES THE END USER HAVE A CHOICE IN THE USE OF A DLC?

One might wonder which category of data link control would best service an end user application. Practically speaking, an end user usually has no choice in which data link protocol is managing the link. The protocols often come as part of the communications product.

The particular DLC often is chosen by the network administrator based on the need to provide compatibility with ongoing systems. In many instances, this approach ties the organization to less than optimum implementations of data link control operations. Even today, some organizations are running with link layer protocols that were developed in the 1960s.

Fortunately, the local area network industry is relatively new to the field of data communications, and the link protocols developed for LANs are developed after some twenty years of experience with older technologies. They are designed to optimize throughput and response time.

Even though the end user usually has no choice in the use of the data link protocol, the operations of the DLC remain transparent to the end user. The user can only hope that the network to which the user is attached is running a reasonably efficient DLC protocol.

## ASYNCHRONOUS AND SYNCHRONOUS TRANSMISSION

Two techniques are used by data link controls to provide timing and proper reception of

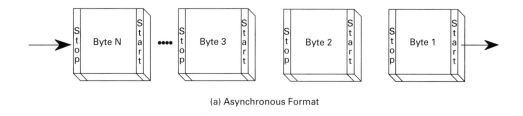

(a) Asynchronous Format

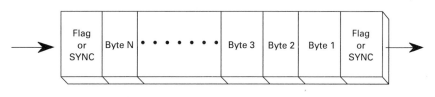

(b) Synchronous Format

**Figure 3-8**. Asynchronous and Synchronous Transmissions

the traffic at the receiver. These two methods are illustrated in Figure 3-8.

The first approach is called asynchronous transmission. With this approach, each data byte/octet (character) has start and stop bits (i.e., synchronizing signals) placed around it. The purposes of these signals are (a) to alert the receiver that data are arriving, and (b) to give the receiver sufficient time to perform certain timing functions before the next character arrives. The start and stop bits really are nothing more than unique and specific signals that are recognized by the receiving device.

Asynchronous transmission is used widely because the interfaces in the computers and communications components, such as modems, are relatively inexpensive. For example, most personal computers use asynchronous interfaces. Since the synchronization occurs between the transmitting and receiving devices on a character-by-character basis, some allowance can be made for inaccuracies, because the inaccuracy can be corrected with the next arriving character. In other words, a "looser" timing tolerance is allowed, which translates to lower component costs.

A more sophisticated process is synchronous transmission. Synchronous formats eliminate the intermittent start/stop signals around each character and provide signals that precede and sometimes follow the user data stream. The preliminary signals usually are called *synchronization (sync) bytes, flags,* or *preambles.* Their principal function is to alert the receiver to an incoming frame and to provide a means to determine when all bits in the frame have been transmitted. This process is called *framing.*

Asynchronous transmission is cost-effective for low-speed and low-volume transmissions such as those from keyboard entry terminals. For larger volumes, synchronous transmission is more efficient. To illustrate, let us assume a 128-byte (8-bit bytes) user block is to be transmitted:

**ASYNCHRONOUS**

2 (start/stop)/8 = .25

**SYNCHRONOUS (HDLC)**

6 (bytes of control overhead) * 8 bits = 48 bits
128 (bytes of data) * 8 bits = 1024 bits
48/1024 = .046

25% Overhead                    4.6% Overhead

As these figures show, asynchronous transmission incurs a 25% overhead with the start/stop bits. A protocol using synchronous formats incurs an overhead of only 4.6%. The decreased overhead of synchronous formats must be weighed against the more expensive circuitry to support it.

## ASYNCHRONOUS LINE PROTOCOLS

As just discussed, asynchronous DLCs place timing bits around each character in the user data stream. The start bit precedes the data character and is used to notify the receiving site that data are on the path (start bit detection). The line is in an idle condition prior to the arrival of the start bit and remains in the idle state until a start bit is transmitted. The start signal initiates mechanisms in the receiving device for sampling, counting, and receiving the bits of the data stream. The data bits are represented as the mark signal (binary 1) and the space signal (binary 0).

The user data bits are placed in a temporary storage area, such as a register or buffer, and later are moved into the terminal or computer memory for further processing.

Stop bits, consisting of one or more mark signals, provide the mechanism to notify the receiver that all bits of the character have arrived. Following the stop bits, the signal returns to idle level, thus guaranteeing that the next character will begin with a 1 to 0 transition. Even if the character is all 0s, the stop bit returns the link to a high or idle level.

## SYNCHRONOUS LINK PROTOCOLS

Synchronous DLCs do not surround each character with start/stop bits, but place a preamble and postamble bit pattern around the user data. These bit patterns usually are called a SYN (synchronization) character, an EOT (end of transmission) character, or simply a flag. They are used to notify the receiver when user data are "arriving" and when the last user data have "arrived."

It should be emphasized that data communications systems require two types of synchronization:

1. At the physical level: to keep the transmitter and receiver clocks synchronized
2. At the link level: to distinguish user data from flags and other control fields

### Character-Oriented Protocols

The character-oriented synchronous data link controls were developed in the 1960s and remain in use today, though in a limited manner. The controls in the binary synchronous control (BISYNC) family are character-oriented systems. These protocols rely on a specific code set (ASCII, EBCDIC) to interpret the control fields; thus, they are code dependent. Both machines must use the same code set in order for the control characters in the frames to be intelligible. Box 3-1 summarizes the functions of the most common character-oriented control codes.

BOX 3-1. TYPICAL CHARACTER-ORIENTED CONTROL CODES
(NOT ALL-INCLUSIVE)

| Character | Function |
|-----------|----------|
| SYN | Synchronous idle (keeps channel active) |
| PAD | Frame pad (time fill between transmissions) |
| DLE | Data link escape (used to achieve code transparency) |
| ENQ | Enquiry (used with polls/selects and bids) |
| SOH | Start of heading |
| STX | Start of text (puts line in text mode) |
| ITB | End of intermediate block |
| ETB | End of transmission block |
| ETX | End of text |
| EOT | End of transmission (puts line in control mode) |
| BCC | Block check count |
| ACK0 | Acknowledges even-numbered blocks |
| ACK1 | Acknowledges odd-numbered blocks |

If machines on a link use different codes (one with ASCII code and one with EBCDIC, for example) the user must contend with two variants of the link protocol. Some type of code conversion is required before the machines can communicate with each other. The problem is shown in Figure 3-9 (a). Let us assume Stations A and B use STX and ETX to represent start of (user) text and end of (user) text, respectively. It is evident that the two devices cannot communicate, since the ASCII and EBCDIC codes use different bit sequences. Consequently, code conversion must be performed by one of the machines.

It also is possible that a code recognized as control could be created by the user application process. For instance, assume in Figure 3-9 (b) that a user program creates a bit sequence that is the same as the ETX (end of text) control code. The receiving station, upon encountering the ETX inside the user data, erroneously would assume the end of the transmission is signified by the user-generated ETX. The protocol would accept the ETX as a protocol control character and would attempt to perform an error check on an incomplete frame, resulting in an error.

Therefore, control codes must be excluded from the user text field. Character protocols address the problem with the DLE control code. This code is placed in front of control codes such as STX, ETX, ETB, ITB, and SOH to identify these characters as valid line control characters (see Figure 3-9[c]). The simplest means to achieve code transparency is the use of DLE.STX or DLE. SOH to signify the beginning of noncontrol data (user data) and DLE.ETX, DLE.ETB, or DLE.ITB to signify the end of user data.

The DLE is not placed in front of user-generated data. Consequently, if bit patterns resembling any of these control characters are created in the user text and encountered by the receiving station, the receiving station assumes they are valid user data, because the

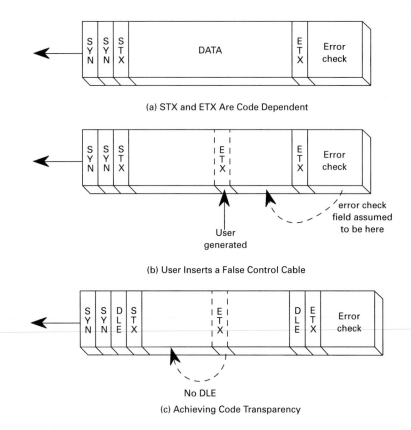

(a) STX and ETX Are Code Dependent

(b) User Inserts a False Control Cable

(c) Achieving Code Transparency

**Figure 3-9**. Character-Oriented Protocols

DLE does not precede the character in question.

The DLE presents a special problem if it is generated by the end-user application process, since it could be recognized as a control code. Character-oriented protocols handle this situation by inserting a DLE next to a data DLE character. The receiver discards the first of two successive DLEs and accepts the second DLE as valid user data.

The character-oriented protocols have dominated the vendors' synchronous line protocol products since the mid-1960s. While still used, they are being replaced by count- and bit-oriented protocols.

## Count-Oriented Protocols

In the 1970s, *count-oriented protocols* (also called *block protocols*) were developed to address the code dependency problem. These systems exhibit one principal advantage over character-oriented protocols in that they have a more effective means of handling user data transparency: they simply insert a count field at the transmitting station. This field specifies the length of the user data field and, as a consequence, the receiver need not examine the user field contents. It need only count the incoming bytes as specified by the count field.

The count-oriented protocols really are a combination of character-oriented protocols and bit-oriented protocols. Figure 3-10 shows that certain control fields are

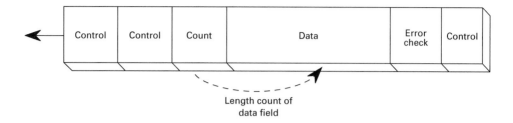

Note: Control codes are code dependent

**Figure 3-10**. Count-Oriented Protocols

code dependent and others are code transparent.

Count-oriented protocols may encounter problems when the signals are transmitted across a digital link. For example, a digital system may delete a digital frame on a link to recover clocks and resynchronize. It also may insert timing/control data into the transmission. A count protocol loses its receive counter in such a situation, and the protocol must recover the lost data with retransmissions.

## Bit-Oriented Protocols

Bit-oriented data link control protocols were developed in the 1970s and now are quite prevalent throughout the industry. They form the basis for most of the new link layer systems in use today.

Bit protocols do not rely on a specific code (ASCII/IA5 or EBCDIC) for line control. Individual bits within an octet are set to effect control functions. An eight-bit flag pattern of 01111110 is the usual flag value for popular bit-oriented protocols. It is generated at the beginning and end of the frame to enable the receiver to identify the beginning and end of a transmission.

There will be occasions when a flaglike sequence, 01111110, is inserted into the user data stream by the application process. To prevent this occurrence, the transmitting site inserts a 0 bit after it encounters five continuous 1s anywhere between the opening and closing flag of the frame. This technique is called *bit stuffing* and is similar in function to the DLE in character protocols and the count field in count protocols. As the frame is stuffed, it is transmitted across the link to the receiver. Figure 3-11 reviews the process.

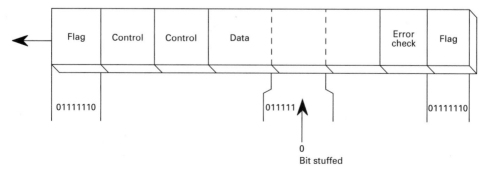

**Figure 3-11**. Bit-Oriented Protocols

The receiver continuously monitors the bit stream. After it receives a zero bit with five continuous one bits following, the receiver inspects the next bit. If it is a zero bit, it pulls this bit out; in other words, it "unstuffs" the bit. In this manner, the system achieves code and data transparency. The protocol is not concerned about any particular bit code inside the data stream. Its function is to keep the flags unique.

Bit-oriented protocols have taken over the market for the newer products and offerings. Consequently, subsequent chapters discuss these systems in considerable detail.

## Comparison of Synchronous Protocols

Box 3-2 provides a comparison of character-oriented, count-oriented, and bit-oriented protocols. It is obvious that no clear distinction exists concerning the attributes of the protocols. The count-oriented protocol actually is a hybrid of the other two protocols.

### Box 3-2. COMPARISONS OF BIT PROTOCOLS

| Attribute | Character-Oriented | Count-Oriented | Bit-Oriented |
|---|---|---|---|
| Start Framing | SYN SYN | SYN SYN | Flag |
| Stop Framing | Characters | Count field | Flag |
| Retransmissions | Stop-and-Wait | Go-Back-N or Selective Repeat | Go-Back-N or Selective Repeat |
| Window Size | 1 | Various (255) | Various (7-127) |
| Frame Formats | Several | Few | 1 |
| Line Mode | HDX | FDX or FDX | HDX or FDX |
| Text Transparency | DLE Code | Count Field | Bit Stuffing |
| Traffic Flow | TTD or WACK | Sliding Window | Sliding Window |
| Line Control | Full Character | Full Character | Bits |

Several terms in Box 3-2 are covered in later sections of this chapter

## MAJOR OPERATIONS OF SYNCHRONOUS LINK PROTOCOLS

This section provides a closer look at data link controls by highlighting the following interrelated topics (these procedures are not used by all link protocols, but are pervasive enough to warrant our attention):

- Flow control of traffic between the machines
- Sequencing and accounting of traffic
- Actions to be taken in the event of error detection

Figure 3-12 illustrates several important points about data link communications. It shows DTE A is to transmit data to DTE B. The transmission goes through an intermediate point, a host computer located at C. This computer might perform routing and switching functions if it also had lines to other stations, and thus fits the definition of data switching equipment (DSE).

The most common approach is to pass the data, like a baton in a relay race, from site to site until they finally reach their destination. One important aspect of the process is in Event 2, in which C sends to A an acknowledgment of the data received. This acknowledgment means station C has checked for possible errors occurring during the transmission of the frame and, as best as it can determine, the data have been received without corruption. It indicates this by transmitting another frame on the return path to signal acceptance.

The data communications industry uses two terms to describe the Event 2 response. We learned in Chapter 1 that the term ACK denotes a positive acknowledgment; the term NAK represents a negative acknowledgment. Usually, a NAK occurs because the signal is distorted due to faulty conditions on the channel (noise, etc.). The frame in Event 2 to A will be either an ACK or a NAK. In the event of an error in the transmission, station A

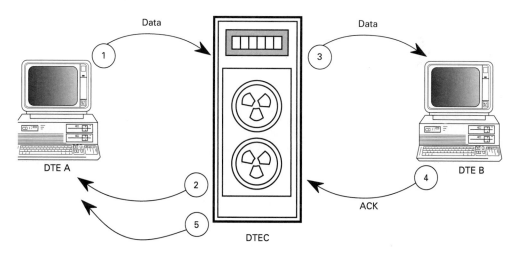

**Figure 3-12**. Link Operations

must receive a negative acknowledgment (NAK) so it can retransmit the data. It also is essential that the processes shown in Events 1 and 2 are completed before Event 3 occurs. If C immediately transmitted the data to B before performing the error check, B possibly could receive erroneous data.

If station A receives an ACK in Event 2, it assumes the data have been received correctly at Station C, and the communications system at Site A can purge these data from its queue. (The application process often saves a copy for accounting, audit, or security reasons.)

Continuing the process in Events 3 and 4, assume that an ACK is returned from B to C. The end user at A may assume through Event 2 that the data arrived at C. A false sense of security could result, because Event 2 indicates only that the data arrived safely at C. If the data are lost between the C and B sites, the A user assumes no problem exists. This scenario provides no provision for an end-to-end acknowledgment. If an end user wishes to have absolute assurance that the data arrived at the remote site, Event 5 is required. Upon receiving Event 4 at C, C sends another acceptance (ACK) to A.

The reader should be aware that the Level 2 data link protocols do not provide end-to-end acknowledgment through multiple links. Some systems provide this service at Layer 3, the network layer. However, the OSI model intends end-to-end accountability to be provided by the transport layer (Layer 4).

## Functions of Timers

Many link protocols use timers in conjunction with logic states to verify that an event occurs within a prescribed time. When a transmitting station sends a frame onto the channel, it starts a timer and enters a wait state. The value of the timer (usually called T1 [no relation to a digital T1 carrier]) is set to expire if the receiving station does not respond to the transmitted frame within the set period. Upon expiration of the timer, one to n retransmissions are attempted, each with the timer T1 reset, until a response is received or until the link protocol's maximum number of retries is met. In this case, recovery or problem resolution is attempted by the link level. If unsuccessful, recovery is performed by a higher-level protocol or by manual intervention and troubleshooting efforts. (The retry parameter usually is designated as parameter N2.)

The T1 timer just described is designated as the acknowledgment timer. Its value depends on (a) round-trip propagation delay of the signal (usually a small value, except for very long circuits); (b) the processing time at the receiver (including queuing time of the frame); (c) the transmission time of the acknowledging frame; and (d) possible queue and processing time at the transmitter when it receives the acknowledgment frame.

The receiving station may use a parameter (T2) in conjunction with T1. Its value is set to ensure an acknowledgment frame is sent to the transmitting station before the T1 at the transmitter expires. This action precludes the transmitter from resending frames unnecessarily.

To illustrate the use of T1 and T2, the following algorithms describe a lower bound on T1 and an upper bound on T2 (T1 is started at the end of the transmission of a frame):

$$T1_T = \geq T2_R + PD + FPT_R + TT_{CUR} + TT_{ACK} + FPT_T$$

$$T2_R = \leq T1_T - PD - FPT_R - TT_{CUR} - TT_{ACK} - FPT_T$$

Where: T is the transmitter; R is the receiver; PD is the round-trip propagation delay;

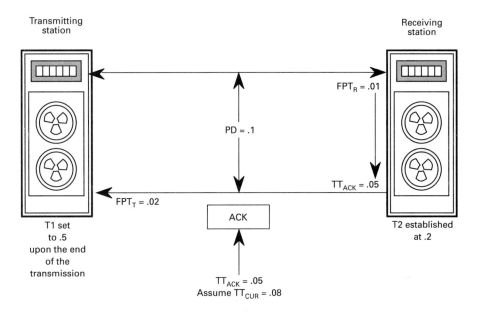

**Figure 3-13.** The T1 Timer and the T2 Parameter

FPT is the frame processing time; $TT_{ACK}$ is the transmission time of the acknowledgment frame; $TT_{CUR}$ is the time to complete the transmission of the ongoing frames that already are in the transmit queue and cannot be pushed down into the queue. ($TT_{CUR}$ also can describe, if relevant to a particular protocol, the queue time at the receiver before the acknowledgment frame is "actioned" and T1 is stopped.)

Figure 3-13 illustrates the use of the T1 timer and the T2 parameter. For the values shown in the figure, the T1 and T2 values are set properly:

$$T1_T \text{ or } .5 = \geq \quad .2 + .1 + .01 + .08 + .05 + .02$$

$$.5 = \geq \quad .46$$

$$T2_R \text{ or } .2 = \leq \quad .5 - .1 - .01 - .08 - .05 - .02$$

$$.2 = \leq \quad .24$$

The number of timers vary, depending upon the type of protocol and the designer's approach to link management. The following are some other commonly used timers:

- *Poll timers* (also called *P-bit timer*): defines the time interval during which a polling station (i.e., a station requesting a frame from another station) shall expect to receive a response.
- *NAK timer* (also called a *reject* or *selective reject timer*): defines the time interval during which a rejecting station shall expect a reply to its reject frame.
- *Link set-up timer*: defines the time interval during which a transmitting station shall expect a reply to its link set-up command frame.

The timing functions may be implemented by a number of individual timers and the protocol designer/implementor is responsible to determining how the timers are set and restarted.

## Asynchronous Systems

Traffic control on an asynchronous link may use the same techniques as a synchronous link. For example, some systems encapsulate an asynchronous data stream into the information field of a synchronous frame and transmit the frame with the synchronous protocol. These methods are examined shortly. For the present, we discuss two simple yet widely used methods for controlling asynchronous traffic: (a) request to send/clear to send, and (b) XON/XOFF.

Request to send/clear to send (RTS/CTS) is considered a rather "low-level" approach to protocols and data communications. Nonetheless, it is widely used because of its relationship and dependence upon the commonly used physical interface, EIA-232.

The use of EIA-232 to effect communications between DTEs is most common in a local environment, because EIA-232 is inherently a short-distance interface, typically constraining the channel to no greater than a few hundred feet. Devices can control the communications between each other by raising and lowering the RTS/CTS signals on the circuits (Pins 4 and 5, respectively). A common implementation of this technique is found in the attachment of a terminal to a simple multiplexer. The terminal requests use of the channel by raising its RTS circuit (Pin 4). The multiplexer responds to the request by raising the CTS circuit (Pin 5). The terminal then sends its data to the multiplexer through the transmit data circuit (Pin 2).

Another widely used technique is XON/XOFF. XON is an ANSI/IA5 transmission character. The XON character usually is implemented by DC1. The XOFF character, also an ANSI/IA5 character, is represented by DC3. Peripheral devices such as printers, graphics terminals, or plotters can use the XON/XOFF approach to control incoming traffic.

The primary station, typically a computer, sends data to the remote peripheral site, which prints or graphs the data onto an output media. Since the plotter or printer may be slow relative to the transmission speed of the channel and the transmission speed of the transmitting computer, its buffer may become full. Consequently, to prevent overflow it transmits back to the computer an XOFF signal, which means "stop transmitting" or "transmit off." The signals can be transmitted across an EIA connection, twisted-pair, or any type of media. As the buffers empty, the peripheral device transmits an XON to resume the data transfer.

## Automatic Request for Repeat (ARQ)

With synchronous systems, when a station transmits a frame, it places a send sequence number in a control field. The receiving station uses this number to determine whether it has received all other preceding frames (with lower numbers). It uses the number also to determine its response. For example, in Figure 3-14, after it receives a frame with send sequence number = 1, it responds with an ACK with a receive sequence number = 2, which signifies it accepts all frames up to and including 1 (for example, 0 and 1) and expects 2 to be the send sequence number of the next frame. The send sequence number is identified as N(S) and the receive sequence number is identified as N(R).

Half-duplex (HDX) protocols need use only two numbers for sequencing, since

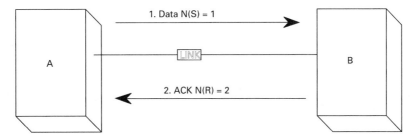

**Figure 3-14.** Link Control Sequence Numbers

they can have only one frame outstanding at a time. Most HDX protocols use the binary numbers 0 and 1 alternately. Full-duplex (FDX) protocols typically use a greater range of sequence numbers because many frames may be outstanding at a time.

The term *ARQ* (automatic request for repeat) describes the process by which a receiving station requests a retransmission. As an example, the reception of a NAK with receive sequence number = 5 indicates that frame 5 is in error and must be retransmitted. The process is automatic, without human intervention (a somewhat antiquated term today). A stop-and-wait ARQ describes a similar half-duplex protocol that waits for an ACK or NAK before sending another frame.

If stop-and-wait is so simple, one might think it is a preferred method for line control. However, it exhibits several deficiencies. First, the delay in waiting translates into idle line time and often it is preferable to keep the line as busy as possible. One possible relief to the idle line is to use a very large frame consisting of many characters. The downside of this approach is that a long frame increases the chances that an error will occur, requiring a retransmission of a large amount of data. Also, it may be impossible physically for a receiving station to store the entire frame in its buffer. As we shall see, although half-duplex may be perfectly acceptable on some links, the approach presents potential response time and throughput problems.

Another technique, continuous ARQ, can utilize full-duplex (two-way simultaneous) transmission, which allows transmission in both directions between the communicating devices. This approach was developed in the 1970s, when better channel utilization became more important (satellite links, fast-response packet networks). Because continuous ARQ has several advantages over a stop-and-wait, half-duplex system, its use has increased in the industry during the past several years.

**Inclusive Acknowledgment**

One advantage of continuous ARQ is called *inclusive acknowledgment.* For example, a receiver might send an ACK of 5, while ACKs of 1, 2, 3, and 4 are not transmitted. The ACK of 5 means the station received and acknowledges everything up to and including 4; the next frame expected should have a 5 in its send sequence field. It is evident from this simple example that Continuous ARQ protocols with inclusive acknowledgment can reduce considerably the overhead involved in the ACKs. In this example, one ACK acknowledges 4 frames–considerably better than the stop-and-wait systems, in which an ACK is required for every transmission.

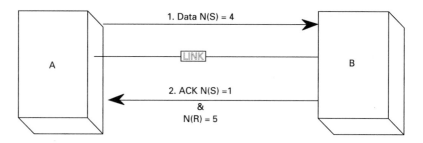

**Figure 3-15.** Inclusive Acknowledgement

## Piggybacking

Most synchronous link protocols permit the inclusion of the N(S) and N(R) fields in the same frame. This technique, called *piggybacking,* allows the protocol to "piggyback" an ACK (the N(R) value) onto an information frame (sequenced by the N(S) value). As shown in Figure 3-15, assume a station sends a frame with N(R) = 5 and N(S) = 1. The N(R) = 5 means all frames up to a number 4 are acknowledged; the N(S) = 1 means Station B is sending a user information in this frame with a sequence of 1.

## Flow Control with Sliding Windows

Continuous ARQ devices use the concept of transmit and receive windows to aid in link management operations. A window is established on each link to provide a reservation of resources at both stations. These resources may be the allocation of specific computer resources or the reservation of buffer space for the transmitting device. In most systems, the window provides both buffer space and sequencing rules. During the initiation of a link session (handshake) between the stations, a window is established. For example, if Stations A and B are to communicate with each other, Station A reserves a receive window for B, and B reserves a receive window for A. The windowing concept is important for full-duplex protocols because they entail a continuous flow of frames into the receiving site without the intermittent stop-and-wait acknowledgments. Consequently, the receiver must have a sufficient allocation of memory to handle the continuous incoming traffic. Clearly, window size is a function of (a) buffer space and (b) the magnitude of the sequence numbers.

    The windows at the transmitting and receiving site are controlled by *state variables* (which is another name for a counter). The transmitting site maintains a send state variable [V(S)]. It is the sequence number of the next frame to be transmitted. The receiving site maintains a receive state variable [V(R)], which contains the number that is expected to be in the sequence number of the next frame. The V(S) is incremented with each frame transmitted and placed in the send sequence field [N(S)] in the frame.

    Upon receiving the frame, the receiving site checks for a transmission error. Also, it compares the send sequence number N(S) with its V(R). If the frame is acceptable, it increments V(R) by one, places it into a receive sequence number field N(R) in an acknowledgment (ACK) frame, and sends it to the original transmitting site to complete the accountability for the transmission.

If an error is detected or if the V(R) does not match the sending sequence number in the frame, a NAK (negative acknowledgment) with the receiving sequence number N(R) containing the value of V(R) is sent to the original transmitting site. This V(R) value informs the transmitting DTE of the next frame that it is expected to send. The transmitter must then reset its V(S) and retransmit the frame whose sequence matches the value of N(R).

A useful feature of the sliding window scheme is the ability of the receiving station to restrict the flow of data from the transmitting station by withholding the acknowledgment frames. This action prevents the transmitter from opening its windows and reusing its send sequence numbers values until the same send sequence numbers have been acknowledged. A station can be completely "throttled" if it receives no ACKs from the receiver.

Many data link controls use the numbers of 0 through 7 for V(S), V(R), and the sequence numbers in the frame. Once the state variables are incremented through 7, the numbers are reused, beginning with 0. Because the numbers are reused, the stations must not be allowed to send a frame with a sequence number that has not yet been acknowledged. For example, the protocol must wait for frame number 6 to be acknowledged before it uses a V(S) of 6 again. The use of 0-7 permits seven frames to be outstanding before the window is "closed". Even though 0-7 gives eight sequence numbers, the V(R) contains the value of the next expected frame, which limits the actual outstanding frames to 7.

We just learned that many systems use sequence numbers and state variables to manage the traffic on a link. As a brief review, please refer to Box 3-3.

---

### Box 3-3. FUNCTIONS OF STATE VARIABLES
### AND SEQUENCE NUMBERS

#### Functions

Flow control of frames (Windows)
Detect lost frames
Detect out-of-sequence frames
Detect errored frames

#### Uses

N(S):  Sequence number of transmitted frame
N(R):  Sequence number of the acknowledged frame(s). Acknowledges all frames up to N(R)–1
V(S):  Variable containing sequence number of next frame to be transmitted
V(R):  Variable containing expected value of the sequence number N(S) in the next frame

**An Example of a Sliding Window Operation.**   This section provides an example of some of the features of sliding window protocols. In Figure 3-16, station A sends frames 1 and 2 to station B. These frames are sequenced as N(S) = 1 and N(S) = 2, respectively.

Station A manages several counters and pointers that are used to direct a "transmit/retransmit" window. The transmit lower window edge (TLWE) identifies the traffic that has been sent and ACKed and the traffic that has been sent and not ACKed. The transmit upper window edge (TUWE) identifies the next sequence number that is to be used for the transmit data unit.

The window limit value points to the value that identifies the last frame that can be sent before the window is opened; that is, when the sequence numbers can be reused to send additional traffic.

The receiving station maintains a set of counters and values to manage its receive window. This receive window mirrors the sending station's transmit/retransmit window; its reflection slightly lags that of station A. The delay depends on the propagation delay of receiving traffic across the LAN and the "speed" in which station B updates its window.

In Figure 3-17, station B responds to station A's transmission by returning a frame with the N(R) value set to 2. This frame states that station B has received and accepted all frames up to and including N(S) = 1 and is expecting the next received frame to be number 2. Of course, by consulting Figure 3-16, one can see that Station A already has sent data unit 2. This overlapping operation is not unusual in full-duplex systems, and station A must be "smart enough" to assume that station B has not yet had an opportunity to check frame 2, or that frame 2 still may be in route across the media. In either case, station B's sending of N(R) =2 is not a NAK. It simply says, "I still am expecting 2." As

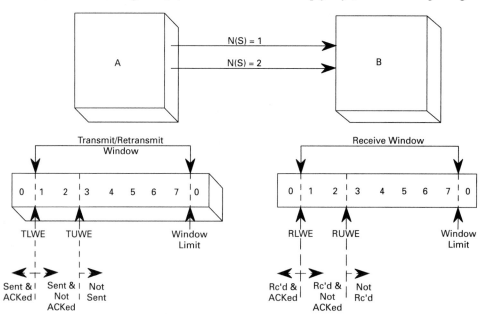

**Figure 3-16.** Sliding Window Variables and Pointers

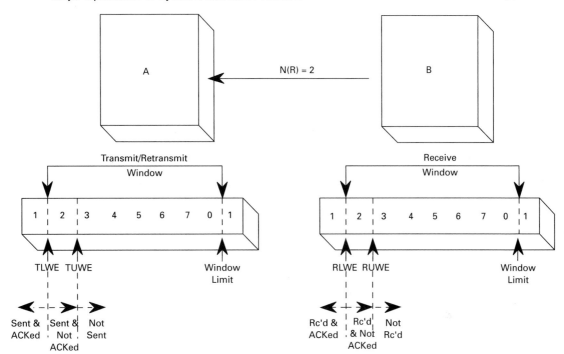

**Figure 3-17.** Station B Acknowledges Frame 1

a common practice, the very next frame that station B sends would have an N(R) value = 3, which means it has indeed received N(S) = 2 and has accepted it.

The effect of these operations can be seen on the transmit/retransmit window on station A and the receive window on station B. The pointers/counters have been updated to reflect the acknowledgment data unit and the window has slid to permit the use of an additional sequence number by Station A [N(S) = 0].

Notice that the windows are implemented with wraparound counters: the numbers 0 through 7 are reused to support the sending and receiving process.

In Figure 3-18, station A sends 4 more frames to station B. In the previous figure, the TUWE value is used to direct station A to begin sequencing the first data unit with N(S) = 3. Thereafter, each sequence number simply is increased by 1.

Notice that the TUWE slides by 1 each time a data unit is sent by station A. After station A has sent data Units 3, 4, 5, and 6, the TUWE = 7, which is the next data unit to be sent. The receive window at station B also is updated to reflect the reception of this traffic.

Station A has only a window of 2 after this transmission. It will be allowed to send data units 7 and 0, after which it has reached its window limit and must stop sending traffic. This means its send window is closed. Likewise, station B understands it is allowed to receive 2 more data units which must be numbered 7 and 0 respectively, after which its receive window is closed. In the event that station A were to violate its send window rule, station B would ignore the traffic, as indicated by its closed receive window.

In Figure 3-19, station B acknowledges all of station A's outstanding traffic by

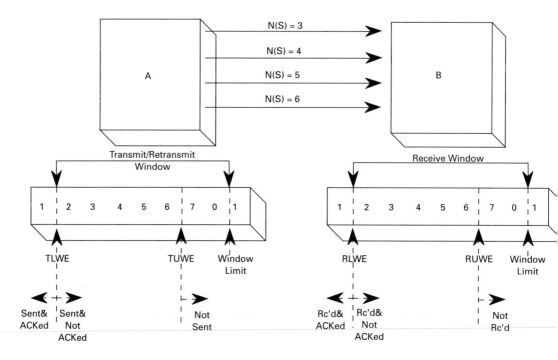

**Figure 3-18.** Sending More Frames

sending back a frame with its N(R) value set to 7. This operation inclusively acknowledges all frames up to and including 6. In this example, this acknowledgment includes frames 2 through 6.

The effect of this operation also is reflected in the transmit/retransmit window at station A and the receive window at station B. The window is open now to its full size, permitting station A to send 7 frames without being concerned about window closure.

This example has illustrated traffic flow in one direction only. Full-duplex operations would allow station B to send its own frames by sequencing them with N(S) values. Additionally, a full-duplex protocol permits both stations to send data units with N(S) values sequencing the traffic and to use the N(R) values to acknowledge previously received traffic.

Why does the protocol place a window limit of 7, when 8 values are available in the sequence space (0-7)? Since the protocol uses the inclusive acknowledgment feature wherein the N(R) value stipulates the next expected data unit, the operation must restrict itself to sequence numbers one less than the total number available. For example, in Figure 3-20, station A has violated its window by 1 by sending 8 successive data units to station B.

This procedure has a potential to create ambiguity, because if station B returns N(R) = 7, station A does not know if it is still expecting N(S) = 7, which is the first data unit sent in this figure, or if it is indeed acknowledging inclusively data units 7, 0, 1, 2, 3, 4, 5, and 6 and is now looking for the next N(S) = 7. This process is known as *modulo 8*, which implies sequence space of one less than the value.

Again, be aware that modulo 8 was employed for this example, but many data link controls employ modulo 128, which uses 7 bits for N(S) and N(R) with $2^7 = 128$.

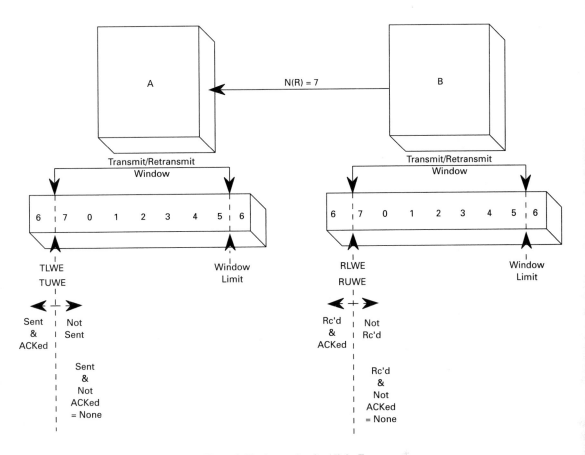

**Figure 3-19.** Accounting for All the Frames

## Other Considerations

A line protocol has three important goals to obtain: (a) high throughput; (b) fast response time; and (c) minimize the logic required at the transmitting/receiving sites to account for traffic (such as ACKs and NAKs). The transmit window is an integral tool in meeting these goals. One of the primary functions of the window is to ensure that by the time all the permissible frames have been transmitted, at least one frame has been acknowledged. In this manner, the window is kept open and the line is continuously active. The T1 and T2 timers discussed earlier are key to effective line utilization and window management.

One could argue that a very large window permits continuous transmissions regardless of the speed of the link and the size of the frames, because the transmitter does not have to wait for acknowledgment from the receiver. While this is true, a larger window size also means that the transmitter must maintain a large queue to store those frames that have not been acknowledged by the receiver.

The goal of the continuous ARQ is to keep the windows open as much as possible for all user sessions on the line. In so doing, the transmitting and receiving stations are more likely to experience fast response time. The continuous ARQ protocols also are

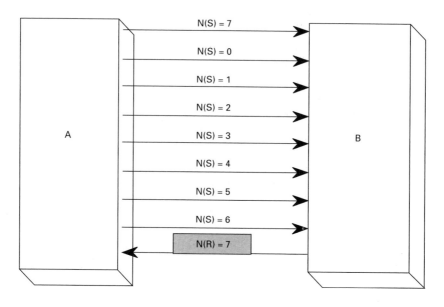

Does this state;
(1) Still expecting N(S) = 7?
or
(2) Acking 7-6 and expecting next N(S) = 7?

**Figure 3-20.**  Window Limits and Sequence Numbers

designed to keep the expensive communications channel as busy as possible.

The concepts of continuous ARQ are relatively simple, yet it should be realized that with a large communications facility, the host computer or front-end processor is tasked with efficient transmission, data flow, and response time between itself and all the secondary sites attached to it. The primary host must maintain a window for every station and manage the traffic to and from each station individually.

## EXAMPLES OF CONTINUOUS ARQ PROTOCOL OPERATIONS

Figure 3-21 provides an example of operations on a data link and allows us to tie together some of the concepts from previous discussions. Station A sends four frames in succession to station B. Station A increments the send state variable V(S) with each transmission and places its value in the N(S) field of each frame. Consequently, the four user data frames would have the N(S) fields set as shown in the figure.

The illustration shows that station A's send state variable is incremented to the next frame to be transmitted and station B's receive state variable V(R) is incremented upon receiving an error-free frame. Thus, the receive state variable always should equal the value of the next expected frame N(S) field. Let us expand this idea further by moving to Event 10 and seeing the effect of the receipt of the N(R) field on station A.

In Event 10, station A receives a frame from station B with N(R) = 4. Notice that station A's V(S) of 4 equals the incoming N(R) = 4. Consequently, station A knows that

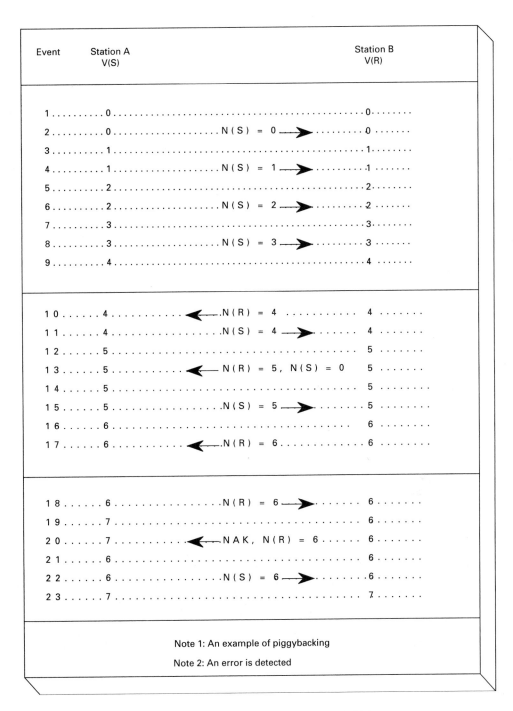

**Figure 3-21.** Sequencing the Frames on the Link

all preceding traffic has been received without problems because its V(S) equals the incoming N(R) value. In other words, the N(R) value is the value of the next expected frame, so it should equal the V(S), which is the value of the next frame to be transmitted.

The process is elegantly simple. Flow control and traffic accountability are maintained by the continuous checking, incrementing, and rechecking of the state variables and sequence numbers.

What happens in the event of an error? As we learned earlier, today's data link controls typically deal with transmission errors through ARQ (automatic request for repeat). User data are transmitted in frames with an error-checking field created by the transmitting site and checked by the receiving site. This field allows the receiver to detect transmission errors and to request the retransmission of errored frames. The transmitter automatically repeats these frames upon request from the data receiver.

In Event 18, station A sends frame 6. However, station B detects an error in the frame. Due to the error, station B does not increment its receive state variable. Rather, it inserts the current value of this variable into the N(R) field and sends it back to station A with a NAK control code or a bit set to indicate a negative acknowledgment (Event 20).

Station A then adjusts its state variables accordingly and retransmits the errored frame. In Event 21, station A resets its send state variable to the received N(R) value of 6, and retransmits frame 6 in Event 22. In Event 23, the channel state variables and sequence numbers once again are synchronized, and the error has been resolved.

With this background information, we now examine several methods for dealing with errors.


## EXAMPLES OF NEGATIVE ACKNOWLEDGMENTS AND RETRANSMISSIONS

To return to the scenario in Figure 3-21, Event 20 can be implemented in a number of ways:

- Implicit reject
- Selective reject (SREJ)
- Rejects (REJ) (or Go-Back-N)
- Selective reject/reject (SREJ/REJ)

*Implicit reject* uses the N(R) value to acknowledge all preceding frames and to request the retransmission of the frame whose N(S) value equals the value in N(R). This technique works well enough on half-duplex links, but should not be used on full-duplex systems. Since a full-duplex protocol permits simultaneous two-way transmission, an N(R) value could be interpreted erroneously either as an ACK or a NAK. For example, if station A receives a frame with N(R) = 4 from station B and the station just sent a frame with N(S) = 4, station A does not know if B is NAKing or ACKing frame 4. On a half-duplex, stop-and-wait link, the N(R) = 4 clearly would mean that frame 4 is expected next. Explicit NAKs really are preferable; they include selective reject, reject, and selective reject/reject.

*Selective reject* (SREJ) requires only that the erroneous transmission be

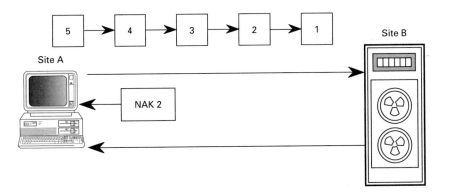

(a) Frames 1 Through 5 Transmitted with an Error in Frame 2

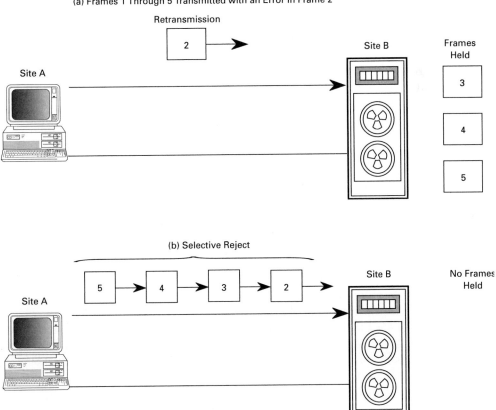

(b) Selective Reject

(c) Reject

**Figure 3-22.** Retransmitting Erroneous Data

retransmitted. *Reject* (REJ) requires not only that the erroneous transmission be repeated, but that all succeeding frames be retransmitted (i.e., all frames "behind" the erroneous frame). Selective reject and reject are illustrated in Figure 3-22.

Both techniques have advantages and disadvantages. Selective reject provides better line utilization, since the erroneous frame is the only retransmission. However, as shown in Figure 3-22(b), Site B must hold frames 3, 4, and 5 to await the retransmission of frame 2. Upon its arrival, frame 2 must be inserted into the proper sequence before the data are passed to the end-user application. The holding of frames can consume precious buffer space, especially if the user device has limited memory available and several active links.

Reject (also called *Go-Back-N*) is a simpler technique. As depicted in Figure 3-22(c), once an erroneous frame is detected, the receiving station discards all subsequent frames in the session until it receives the correct retransmission. Reject requires no frame queuing and frame resequencing at the receiver. However, its throughput is not as high as selective reject, since it requires retransmission of frames that may not be in error. The reject ARQ approach is ineffective on systems with long round-trip delays and high data rates.

One principal disadvantage of selective reject is the requirement that only one selective reject frame can be outstanding at a time. For example, assume Site A has transmitted frames 0,1,2,3,4, and 5, and Site B responds with SREJ with N(R) = 2. This response frame acknowledges 0 and 1 and requests the retransmission of 2. However, let us suppose another SREJ frame was sent by Site B before the first SREJ condition cleared. As the frame flow diagram in Figure 3-23 shows, multiple SREJs contradict the idea of the N(R) value acknowledging the preceding frames. In our example, Site A does not know whether the second SREJ of N(R) = 4 acknowledges preceding frames, since it contradicts the previous SREJ of N(R) = 2. Again, the requirement for only one SREJ to be outstanding eliminates any ambiguity, but if the frame error rate is high and its occurrence exceeds the round-trip propagation delay between Sites A and B, then the single SREJ convention can reduce the throughput on the channel. This problem stems from the fact that the channel may go idle while the stations wait for the first SREJ to clear. In our previous example, the SREJ N(R) = 4 could not be sent until Site B had received its response to its first SREJ N(R) = 2. This effect is evident especially on circuits that experience long delays.

One relief to the SREJ dilemma is to use the SREJ N(R) = X only to refuse (NAK) the N(S) = X frame. That is, the SREJ has no acknowledgment functions. In our frame flow diagram, Site A would assume that SREJ N(R) = 2 and SREJ N(R) = 4 only NAK frames 2 and 4. Consequently, channel efficiency is not reduced significantly on (a) error-prone channels or (b) channels with long propagation delays.

However, if the SREJ has no positive acknowledgment, as seen in the previous example, how is frame 3 acknowledged, if SREJ N(R) = 4 does not inclusively acknowledge preceding frames? The acknowledgment is through one of three alternatives. With the first, a subsequent REJ can be used to acknowledge previous frames. A second alternative can use a regular user data frame with the N(R) value acknowledging preceding frames.

The last approach, *selective reject-reject* (SREJ-REJ) has been proposed as an alternative to the other two techniques. SREJ-REJ performs like SREJ, except that once

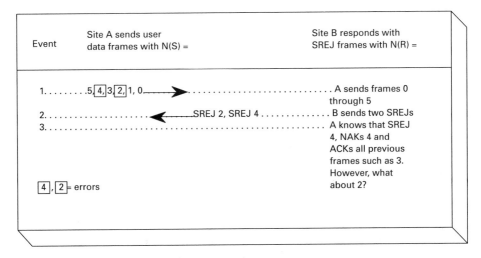

**Figure 3-23.** The Problem with Multiple Selective Rejects

an error is detected, it waits to verify the next frame as correct before sending the SREJ. If the receiver detects the loss of two contiguous data frames, it sends a REJ instead and discards all subsequently received frames until the lost frame is received correctly. Also, if another frame error is detected prior to recovery of the SREJ condition, the receiver saves (stores) all frames received after the first errored frame and discards frames received after the second errored frame until the first errored frame is recovered. Then, a REJ is issued to recover the second frame and the other subsequent discarded frames. SREJ-REJ is depicted in the frame flow diagram in Figure 3-24.

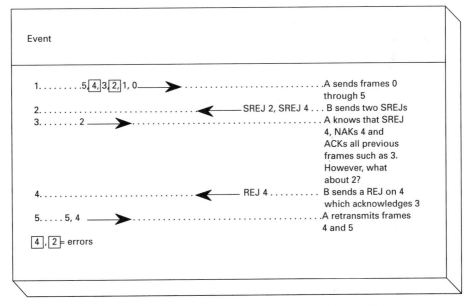

**Figure 3-24.** Using a Combination of Selective Reject and Reject

## LINK EFFICIENCY CONSIDERATIONS

### Window Sizes

Window size is important to link efficiency. A large window requires the receiver to reserve more storage for the incoming frames, yet it also provides a means to keep the channel active because the larger windows allow a greater range of sequence numbers to be used. More numbers simply reduce the possibility of a transmitting site having to close its transmit window because it used all its send sequence number values. In contrast, a small window size decreases the amount of storage required at the receiver for the incoming frames. On the other hand, it increases the possibility of a closed transmit window.

Interestingly, a network that is busy or congested benefits from a small window size, because with the Go-Back-N (REJ) technique, lost frames and all succeeding frames are retransmitted. The best performance by a busy/congested network is obtained by using a small window. Why? Because the large window commits a large number of frames to be outstanding at any one time. Consequently, in the event of an error (with Go-Back-N [REJ]), the errored frame and all those that followed must be retransmitted. Obviously, a small window size limits the number of frames that can be outstanding at any one time, and thus limits the frames that might need to be retransmitted.

Some systems have only one frame on the link at a time. A high-speed, short-distance network is an example, such as a local area network. When a station begins a transmission, the receivers detect it with very little delay. Therefore, as a general rule local networks transmit only one frame on the link at a time. Satellite networks operate at the other extreme. Due to the long propagation delay, satellite channels must have multiple frames on the link at the same time; otherwise, the link goes idle and its efficiency decreases.

Window sizes can be calculated in a number of ways. This discussion examines a relatively simple process entailing three interrelated factors:

    T:    transmission rate of channel (in bit/s)
    D:    round-trip delay of signal (in seconds)
    L:    length of user information frame (the I frame; in bits)

Round-trip delay includes not only the propagation delay on the circuit, but the delay encountered at the receiver with tasks such as error-checking, sequencing, buffer management, frame construction, and so on. Some tasks are performed very rapidly with hardware; others may take more time due to software execution, queue management, and contention for resources at the station. Designers use different factors to determine D, and some factors are more significant than others. For example:

- Propagation delays of frame to receiver and acknowledgment from receiver. The effect of piggybacking (the ACK is returned in a data frame) plays a significant role in link efficiency. Some designers do not factor in the acknowledgment time.

- Time to transmit frame onto the link in both directions.
- Processing time at the receiver for the data frame and the transmitter for the acknowledgment frame. This factor also may be insignificant, unless the stations are busy and queue the frames for a time.

The window size should allow for a sufficient number of outstanding frames (K) to keep the transmit window open. K is the smallest integer not less than r (window size) and is calculated as follows (more detailed equations are presented later):

$$r = \frac{T * D}{L}$$

A higher channel speed or a longer propagation delay requires a larger window. Conversely, a longer frame decreases the window size requirement. Here are some examples:

1. $T = 4,800$;    $D = .7$;    $L = 1,056$;    $r = 3.1$
2. $T = 9,600$;    $D = .7$;    $L = 1,056$;    $r = 6.3$
3. $T = 9,600$;    $D = 1.1$;    $L = 1,056$;    $r = 10$

Example 1 shows a 4,800 bit/s line using a typical frame of 1,056 bits (128 bytes in a packet; 4 bytes in the control frame around the packet: $132 * 8 = 1,056$) with a round-trip delay of .7 seconds. The minimum window requirement is 4. Example 2 illustrates the use of a higher-speed line which necessitates a larger window size of 7. Example 3 shows the effect of a longer round-trip propagation delay (1.1 seconds). Notice the minimum window size is now 10. A round-trip delay of .5 to 1.0 second can occur on a satellite circuit, for example.

A more rigorous analysis is provided here for those seeking more detail. The minimum window size for a reject protocol is defined as:

$$M_I = 2 + \frac{S_I (T_{I-r} + T_{r-I} + T_{rproc} = TI_{proc})}{I_I} + \frac{3 \, I_r S_I}{2 \, I_I S_r}$$

Where: $I_I$ = local station's average I frame length, including flags, address field, control field, and frame check sequence (bits); $I_r$ = remote station's average I frame length, including flags, address field, control field, and frame check sequence (bits); $M_I$ = minimum modulus of sequence number necessary to support continuous I frame transmissions by the local station; $S_I$ = local station's transmission speed (bits per second); $S_r$ = remote station's transmission speed (bits per second); $T_{Iproc}$ = time required by local station to process a received frame (seconds); $T_{I-r}$ = propagation time from local to remote station (seconds); $T_{rproc}$ = time required by remote station to process a received frame (seconds); $T_{r-I}$ = propagation time from remote to local station (seconds).

As an example, assume two stations are operating at 2,400 bit/s with I frames of 2,400 bits in length. The channel experiences a delay of 50 ms. Each station processes a frame in 1 ms. A simple substitution and calculation yields an answer of 3.602, which is rounded to 4. Since a typical sequencing is modulo 8, the window is sufficient for continuous transmission.

For selective reject, the minimum window is:

$$M_I = 5A + 2 + \frac{S_I (A + 1)(T_{I-r} + T_{r-I} + T_{rproc} = T_{Iproc})}{I_I} + \frac{(A + 3)I_rS_I}{2\,I_IS_r} + \frac{ARS_I}{I_IS_r}$$

Where: A = number of transmissions required before I frame is successfully received; R = length of SREJ frame, including flags, address field, control field, and frame check sequence field.

As another example, assume the medium is a satellite channel that experiences a propagation delay of .25 seconds in each direction. In this situation, SREJ is used and one continuous transmission is to occur through at least one retransmission attempt. The SREJ formula reveals that $M_I = 11$. Consequently, the window of seven is insufficient for continuous transmission. The sequence numbers and state variables must be increased.

## Medium Length

Two parameters used in analyzing link performance are T, the transmission rate of the link and D, the propagation delay between the stations on the link (which is proportional to distance). The product of T and D (i.e., T * D) is an important factor in the analysis: efficiency is the same for a 10 Mbit/s, .6 mile link (1 Km) as it is for a 5 Mbit/s, 1.2 mile (2 Km) link!

Of equal importance is the concept of medium length, which is the length of the transmission channel described in bits. It describes the number of bits that can be on the link between two stations at any specific time.

Before we examine the medium length formula, propagation velocity is described. The propagation delay D partially is dependent on the type of medium. Generally, the following equation is used to calculate propagation delay (PV) on a wire medium:

$$PV = 6.6 * 10^8 \text{ feet per second } (2 * 10^8 \text{ meters per second}).$$

## Estimating Link Efficiency

The length of the link (a) is proportional to r and is derived from the same formula of T * D/L. Also, a can be stated as follows because L/T is the time taken by the transmitter to place the frame on the link:

$$a = D / (L/T)$$

In other words, a = propagation time/transmission time.

The following method for determining link efficiency is based on the supposition that a is the single most important factor and others, such as processing line and queue waiting, are relatively insignificant. In most cases, the supposition is correct.

$$u = 1 / (1 + 2d)$$

From this formula, we can determine easily the utilization efficiency of the link.

## COMPARISON OF ARQ SCHEMES

### Conventional ARQ

Earlier discussions in this chapter explained the ARQ schemes. Now the focus shifts to the throughput performance of the following error control schemes:

- Stop-And-Wait ARQ
- Go-Back-N (reject) ARQ
- Selective reject ARQ
- Selective reject/reject ARQ
- Hybrid ARQ

The equations defined herein use the following notations: I = idle time between two successive transmissions; d = data rate of transmitter; $P_c$ = probability that a received n bit word contains no error; K/n = rate of the code word used (K information bits; n code word bits); T = average number of bits that must be transmitted for a code word to be received correctly; N = number of code words.

The throughput for Stop-And-Wait ARQ is calculated as:

$$TP_{sw} = P_c \ (K/n) \ / \ 1 + Id/n.$$

The throughput for Go-Back-N is calculated as:

$$TP_{GBN} = P_c \ (K/n) \ / \ P_c + (1 - P_c) \ N.$$

The throughput for selective reject is is calculated as:

$$TP_{SR} = P_c \ (K/n).$$

Several observations can be made about these equations. The Stop-And-Wait ARQ is quite inefficient for systems with long propagation delays. The Go-Back-N ARQ is acceptable for short propagation delays and relatively low data rates. However, it is inefficient in the other situations, especially if the error rate is high. The selective reject works best because the throughput does not depend upon the round-trip propagation delay. Figure 3-25 compares Go-Back-N and selective reject [LIN84]. The comparison is made on a satellite channel at 1.544 Mbit/s data rate and a round-trip delay of 700 ms.

Since selective reject retains frames until the "earlier" frame is retransmitted, it may require considerable buffering capacity. Indeed, for a very large window, the buffering would be intolerable. It also requires more logic to reinsert the retransmitted frame into the proper place in a queue (that is, in front of its succeeding frame with greater N(S) values). Moreover, most systems utilize circuits with relatively low data rates and propagation delays. Consequently, the Go-Back-N (reject) method is more commonly used than is selective reject.

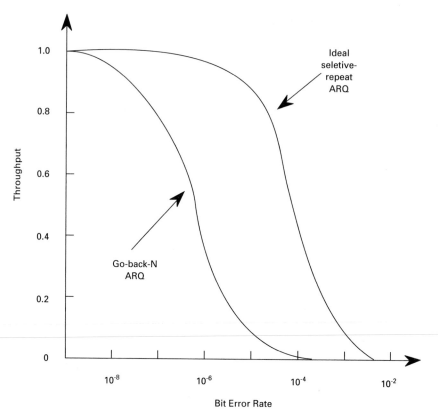

**Figure 3-25.** Throughput Comparison of Selective Reject and Go-Back-N [LIN84]

## Modified ARQ

Other ARQ approaches yield even better results. Earlier in this chapter, the selective reject/reject technique was examined. A variation on this theme (called by the same name) is shown in Figure 3-26. The difference here and in previous scenarios is that the retransmitted frame must be retransmitted again. But the principles are the same: (a) move from selective reject to Go-Back-N reject, and (b) upon executing event (*a*), discard succeeding frames (to preserve buffer) until the errored frame is retransmitted once again (eventually correctly, one hopes).

The throughput for selective reject/reject is as follows:

$$TP_{SR/R} = P_c \, (K/n) \, / \, 1 + (N-1)(1-P_c)^{\,V+1}$$

Where: V = retransmission in the selective reject mode allowed before switching to Go-Back-N reject mode.

Figure 3-27 plots the throughput performance of selective reject/reject against selective reject and reject. As V increases, the throughput performance increases.

## Hybrid ARQ

Systems are available that use a combination of forward error corrections and ARQ. For example, a typical scheme uses a code for simultaneous error detection and correction.

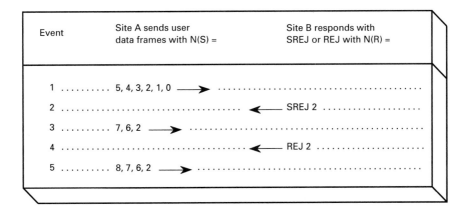

| Event | Site A sends user data frames with N(S) = | Site B responds with SREJ or REJ with N(R) = |
|---|---|---|
| 1 | 5, 4, 3, 2, 1, 0 → | |
| 2 | | ← SREJ 2 |
| 3 | 7, 6, 2 → | |
| 4 | | ← REJ 2 |
| 5 | 8, 7, 6, 2 → | |

**Figure 3-26.** Reject the Same Frame More Than Once

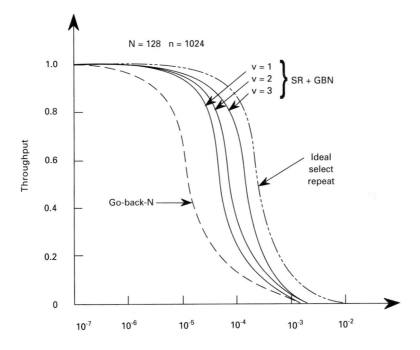

**Figure 3-27.** Throughput Comparison at Selective Reject, Go-Back-N and Others [LIN84]

The system first attempts to correct the errors and deliver the frame to the user. If the errors cannot be corrected, the frame is rejected, and a selective reject or reject is sent to the transmitter.

Another variation also is a combination of FEC and ARQ. With this approach, the system dynamically adds extra error correction bits when the channel is noisy. Otherwise, conventional ARQ methods are employed. This latter approach provides better throughput during periods in which the channel is "behaving."

## SUMMARY

Data link controls employ a wide array of techniques to manage link operations. Primary/secondary protocols usually are employed on wide area multipoint links. Peer-to-peer protocols are more common on local area networks. Polling systems remain a prevalent option for link control.

Error detection is performed with some type of parity check, checksum, or cyclic redundancy check (CRC). (These operations are examined in Chapter 2.) Increasingly, vendors are moving to the use of CRC.

Bit-oriented protocols largely have replaced byte-oriented protocols. Asynchronous protocols remain widespread because of their simplicity and relatively low cost. Almost all newer data link controls now employ inclusive acknowledgment, piggybacking, and sliding window schemes.

# 4

# *Asynchronous Data Link Controls*

## INTRODUCTION

This chapter provides an examination of asynchronous link control protocols. A brief history of these protocols is followed by an example of the reasons that asynchronous protocols are so robust. Five asynchronous protocols are highlighted to indicate their major attributes. These protocols are XMODEM, YMODEM, BLAST, Kermit, and MNP. Finally, the last section of the chapter reviews asynchronous PADs.

## REVIEW OF ASYNCHRONOUS SYSTEMS

Asynchronous communications have existed for many years. They are attractive because the asynchronous components are not complex and are relatively inexpensive.

As discussed in earlier chapters, a synchronous transmission is so named because the characters in a data stream are transmitted without prior timing arrangements. Each character (not a full message) is synchronized. The synchronization occurs by the detection of a start bit at the receiver. The sender and receiver need be synchronized only on a character-by-character basis.

Additionally, the asynchronous operation allows some inaccuracies in synchronization between the sender and the receiver. If properly implemented, asynchronous operations permit some drift in the timing of the character. This drift can be recovered in the next arriving character, because the receiver is resynchronyed with each character.

## HISTORY OF ASYNCHRONOUS DEVELOPMENT

Electronic communications date back to the late 1790s, although the telegraph is credited as the foundation of many of the data communications concepts in use today.

In 1832, Samuel F. B. Morse began work on the development of the first successful telegraph. After several attempts, he and Alfred Vail designed a code in 1838 to represent the letters of the alphabet with spaces (absence of an electric current); dots (an electric current of short duration), and dashes (an electric current of longer duration—three times longer than a dot).

This code is the Morse code. It was cleverly designed, as the most frequently occurring characters were assigned short code symbols. For example, the letter *E* was assigned the symbol value of one dot, while a *Z* was assigned successive dash, dash, dot, dot symbols. This variable length code reduced the number of strokes the operator had to make and decreased the number of signals transmitted across the circuit, as well.

Using common sense, Morse and Vail determined the code structure by counting the number of letters in the bins of a printer's character type box. Modern information theory tells us the code could be improved only by some 15 percent!

One of the major problems encountered by the pioneers was intersymbol interference. The DC current does not build up or decay on the line in an abrupt and clean manner. When the telegraph sent a space (no current), the decay of the signal also took time. Intersymbol interference occurred when the dots and dashes followed each other so closely they "ran together" at the receiving end, thus becoming indistinguishable. Although we are discussing some historical events to provide a background for more complex topics, intersymbol interference remains a problem today.

The earlier telegraphers devised several methods to ameliorate the undesirable effects of intersymbol interference and signal distortion. One approach had unfortunate consequences. To overcome the effects of noise on the first trans-Atlantic cable and to increase the intelligibility of the code, unduly high voltages were placed on the line. The high voltages eventually destroyed the insulation and rendered the cable useless.

Other approaches were more successful. Since a dash takes three times longer to send than a dot, double-current telegraphy was implemented to reduce the longer dash time period. A current in one direction represented a dash and a current in the other direction represented a dot. No current represented a space. Double-current telegraphy improved the speed of the transmission considerably.

Thomas Edison also contributed to the field of communications. In 1874 he developed the novel idea of the quadraplex telegraph. It represented more than one symbol per signal. This idea is known today as multiple-level signaling and is an integral part of modern communications.

The quadraplex telegraph used two intensities of current and two directions of current. The two states were independent and thus provided four different conditions of current flow. This technique further increased the speed of transmissions because more information could be transmitted in a given time.

Early communications systems employed a transmitter and a teleprinting system, which acted as the receiver for the traffic. These early machines printed onto a drum of paper, which rotated and recorded the incoming signals by printing onto the paper with a stylus—thus, the term *mark* came to be used. The lifting of the stylus was called the *space*.

In later systems, the paper was printed based on receiving electrical impulses consisting of the fixed-length character code (a fixed number of binary bits to represent a character). These signals set a circumferential type wheel in a particular position (to a desired character) and the printing occurred by contacting the character with the paper tape.

Because of its variable length, the Morse code proved to be too complex for data communications systems. As stated previously, the industry adopted a fixed-length code devised, supposedly, by John Maurice Emile Baudot. He developed the Baudot code while working in the French telegraph service in the 1870s. Baudot's code now is known as International Telegraph Alphabet #1. However, the code most people associate with Baudot code actually is the International Telegraph Alphabet #2, which was devised by Donald Murray.

The Baudot code is a five-bit code (although during the development of this code the term bits was not in use) with $2^5$ characters (32). Two characters are used to shift the printer into letters or figures to provide for more character variation (see Figure 4-1). Although this five-bit code has very limited use today, it will be employed in this chapter to explain some of the properties of asynchronous systems.

## THE START AND STOP BITS

The idea of using a signal at the beginning of each character to synchronize the receiving machine with the transmission is an elegantly simple way to solve a problem. It was developed over seventy years ago and still is the key component in asynchronous systems. Since the synchronization occurs between the transmitting and receiving devices

| Hex | Binary | LETTERS Shift | FIGURES Shift | Hex | Binary | LETTERS Shift | FIGURES Shift |
|-----|--------|---------------|---------------|-----|--------|---------------|---------------|
| 0 | 00000 | Blank | Blank | 10 | 10000 | T | 5 |
| 1 | 00001 | E | 3 | 11 | 10001 | Z | + |
| 2 | 00010 | LF | LF | 12 | 10010 | L | ) |
| 3 | 00011 | A | - | 13 | 10011 | W | 2 |
| 4 | 00100 | Space | Space | 14 | 10100 | H | reserved |
| 5 | 00101 | S | ' | 15 | 10101 | Y | 6 |
| 6 | 00110 | I | 8 | 16 | 10110 | P | 0 |
| 7 | 00111 | U | 7 | 17 | 10111 | Q | 1 |
| 8 | 01000 | CR | CR | 18 | 11000 | O | 9 |
| 9 | 01001 | D | WRU | 19 | 11001 | B | ? |
| 0A | 01010 | R | 4 | 1A | 11010 | G | reserved |
| 0B | 01011 | J | BELL | 1B | 11011 | FIGS | FIGS |
| 0C | 01100 | N | , | IC | 11100 | M | . |
| 0D | 01101 | F | reserved | 1D | 11101 | X | / |
| 0E | 01110 | C | : | 1E | 11110 | V | = |
| 0F | 01111 | K | ( | 1F | 11111 | LTRS | LTRS |

**Figure 4-1.** International Alphabet #2

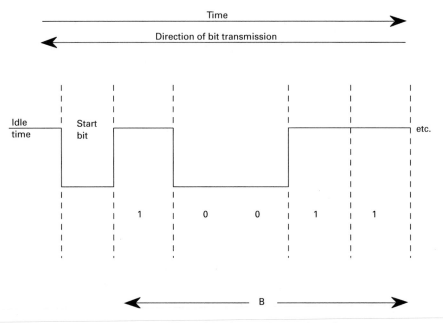

**Figure 4-2.** The Asynchronous Start Bit

on a character-by-character basis, some allowance can be made for inaccuracies, because the inaccuracy can be corrected with the next arriving character. In other words, a "looser" timing tolerance is allowed, which translates to lower component costs.

A decision to use a start bit to synchronize a teleprinter with the incoming transmission stream required some modifications to existing teleprinters, but it formed the basis for many communications systems that still exist today.

As shown in Figure 4-2, an asynchronous communications channel is said to be in an idle state with high voltage. This also is known as the MARK condition and is represented with a logical 1. A negative pulse is represented as logical zero and is known as a SPACE. Asynchronous traffic is sent from the least to the most significant bit. In this figure, the international alphabet character "B" is sent as bits 10011.

While the start bit adds a significantly enhanced feature to data communications systems, it does not solve one very vexing problem: bit corruption on the communications channel. Is this an important problem? In many communications systems it is (because the communications channel is not designed for data, but rather for voice, which has a high tolerance for errors such as impulse noise and crosstalk).

The problem with asynchronous systems (discussed thus far) is illustrated in Figure 4-3. The character B is transmitted without problems, but the succeeding synchronization signal (the start bit) is distorted on the communications channel. Consequently, the next zero bit is interpreted as the start bit, when, in fact, it is the first bit of the second character of the transmission from the letter L. Consequently, the receiver assumes that the first bit of the letter L begins with 1, when, in fact, that is the second bit. Consequently, it interprets four bits of the letter L and the next space incorrectly as the letter D.

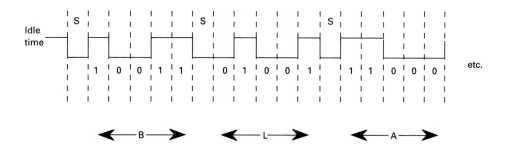

Sending the name "Black"

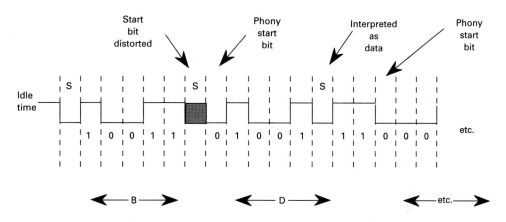

**Figure 4-3.** An Error in the Start Bit

The problem occurs because the data are transmitted without any intervening idle time. Indeed, without remedial action such as that shown in Figure 4-4, subsequent characters would be damaged without any method of correcting them. Thus, in order to prevent this, asynchronous systems use an end-of-character signal (an end-of-character bit). This bit is known in the industry as the *stop bit* (see Figure 4-4). With this addition, an asynchronous system reads the character (which, in our example, is the five-bit code) and the stop bit. If bits become misaligned, the receiver is required to check that each arriving character begins with a start bit and ends with a stop bit; otherwise, the character is discarded. The addition of the stop bit, while enhancing asynchronous operations considerably, was introduced *before* it was realized it solved this problem. In the early days, a period of idle time was inserted between characters to allow for the relatively slow teleprinter's mechanical gear to align itself and await the next character. These idle times became known as *bit times.* Today, they range between 1, 1-1/2, and 2 bit times.

The robustness of asynchronous transmission may not be evident from a superficial

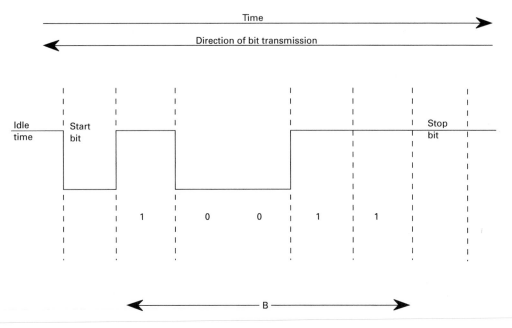

**Figure 4-4.**  Adding the Stop Bit

examination. However, consider the example in Figure 4-5. The data stream transmitted across the communications channel is: "The quick brown fox jumped over..." The five-bit coding for this phrase is shown in the figure. In Figure 4-5(a), the bits are transmitted across from the right-hand side of the page to the left. The underlined numbers indicate the start and stop bits that are placed around each character.

In Figure 4-5(b), the start bit of the character T is distorted. Therefore, the receiver assumes the next zero bit is the start bit. It then counts the next successive five bits, assuming these bits constitute a character. Upon receiving these five bits, it examines the next bit, assuming it to be a stop bit (a value of 1). However, this bit is the start bit for the letter H. Consequently, the receiver has not received a valid start/stop combination and it discards this erroneous character. It searches until it finds a 1 bit, then assumes the next 0 bit is the start. It then counts five more bits. Once again, it encounters a bad stop bit and continues the examination until it finds the next 1, which happens to be the legitimate stop bit of the letter E. Consequently, the next bit is the legitimate start bit for the space character. Now it is resynchronized on the data stream.

While this example shows resynchronization occurring quite rapidly, with only the loss of the word *The,* by no means is it unusual. Indeed, you might try an experiment by jotting down a phrase and showing a distortion occurring either at the stop or the start bit. It will be evident that resynchronization occurs rapidly.

Even though the start and stop bits provide a powerful combination for getting the characters resynchronized, they provide no mechanism for recovering from the distortions that occurred from the initial loss of the synchronization. Therefore, a wide array of link layer protocols have been developed to recover the errored data. The remainder of this chapter examines several of these protocols.

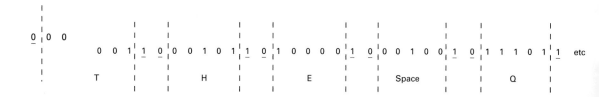

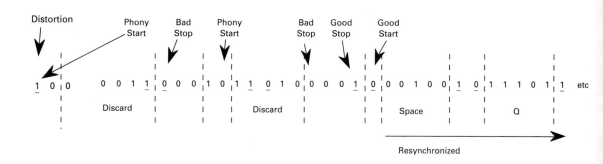

(a) Sending "THE QUICK BROWN FOX...."

(b) An error and error recovery

**Figure 4-5.** Error and Error Recovery

With variations, the XMODEM and Kermit examples are from Joe Campbell's *C Programmer's Guide to Serial Communications,* published by Howard W. Sams & Company. This book goes beyond our overview, but is recommended highly for those wishing to know the detailed operations of asynchronous protocols.

## XMODEM

During the infant days of data communications and computing, the field was populated primarily by hobbyists and other individuals who wished to experiment with this interesting new technology. One of the major problems during this time was exchanging data between the computers. Ward Christiansen solved this problem in 1977 by writing a program that addressed the dual problems of (a) incompatible PC software and (b) incompatible telephone channel-oriented protocols. Christiansen based his program on the fact that the telephone line usually was the only media available to exchange data between computers and the PC. At that time PCs almost always utilized the simple 300 bit/s modem. Most of these modems used identical modulation techniques. Christiansen wrote a file-transfer program and placed it in the public domain by donating it to various user groups. Today several versions of the now famous program exist. Two of the better-known programs are MODEM7 and XMODEM. XMODEM is described next, since it is a very widely used personal computer file transfer protocol.

XMODEM is found in practically all vendor products today. Typically, it comes as a standard package when one purchases a communications product from a PC store. It is rare today to see any communications packages for asynchronous devices that do not include an XMODEM offering, or one of the XMODEM "derivatives."

## The XMODEM Packet (Frame)

XMODEM is a stop-and-wait (half-duplex), code-dependent, automatic-request- for-repeat (ARQ) protocol. It uses a fixed-length data field of 128 bytes (see Figure 4-6). Its other fields are all one byte each. The XMODEM PDU often is referred to as a packet; however, this discussion will use the term *frame* because it correctly defines the link layer PDU.

The SOH, a one-byte start-of-header indicator, signifies the beginning of the frame. The next field contains the sequence number. After initialization, sequencing begins with the first frame with a value of 1. The next field contains the 1's complement of the sequence number. This field is used to check the validity of the sequence number. The approach at the receiver for handling this operation is to complement one of these fields and XOR it at the other. If the result is zero, it signifies that neither field is in error. If the fields are not valid, XMODEM will send a negative acknowledgment (NAK) to the originating device to request retransmission.

The data field is a fixed-length field of 128 bytes. It may contain any type of syntax (binary, ASCII, Boolean, text, etc.). The last field is the one-byte checksum field. This field is used to determine whether an error exists in the data field. It does not check for errors in other parts of the protocol data unit.

As depicted in Figure 4-7, the XMODEM sending process is quite simple. Interestingly, the operations begin on the receiver side (often referred to as a *receiver-driven protocol*). The receiver must begin the data transfer by sending a NAK to the transmitter. Upon receipt of the NAK, the transmitter understands that it must send its first frame. The data transfer operation begins by the transmitter forming a 128-byte frame, sending the traffic, and waiting for an acknowledgment. If the last frame has been sent, the transmitter sends an EOT, receives an acknowledgment, and ends the communications process. If it is not the last transmission, it waits for an acknowledgment or a NAK.

Additionally, the transmitter also may receive a cancel signal (CAN). This rather simple protocol has no method of recovering from a sequence error. Consequently, the receiver will send a CAN to indicate a sequencing problem. This requires that the transmission process be aborted. For example, if a transmitting device retransmits a message unsuccessfully nine times, it performs a time-out and sends the Cancel (CAN) control character. This technique is found in the N1 (retry) and T1 (timer) functions of

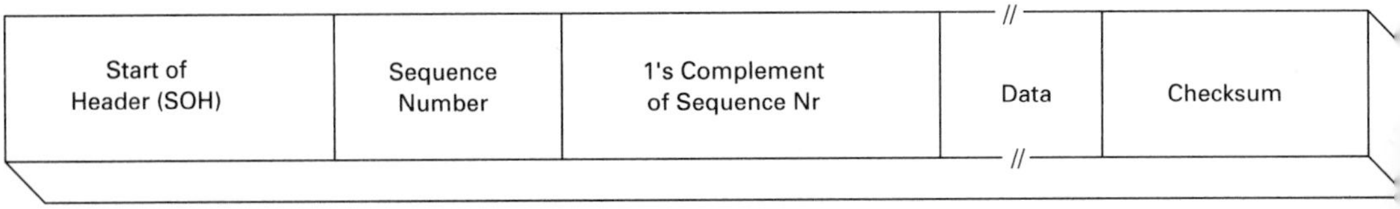

| Start of Header (SOH) | Sequence Number | 1's Complement of Sequence Nr | Data | Checksum |
|---|---|---|---|---|

**Figure 4-6**  The XMODEM Protocol Data Unit

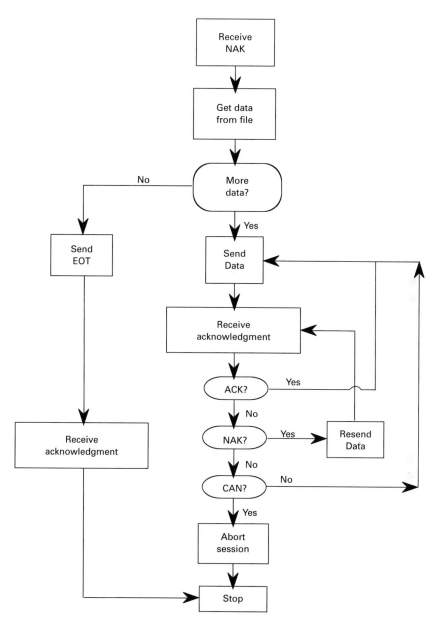

Certain retries and time-outs are not shown.

**Figure 4-7.** XMODEM Sender Logic

the High-Level Data Link Control (HDLC) family. Likewise, if the sender does not hear a receiver's response, it waits a period of ten seconds (or another specific time) before attempting another retransmission. The logic provides the ability for the receiving computer to ignore the duplicate message.

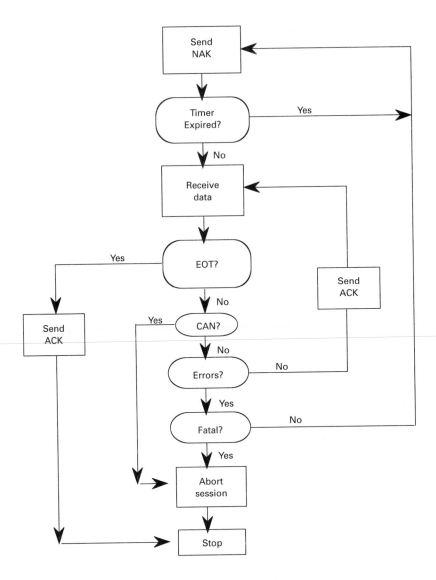

Certain timeouts are not shown

**Figure 4-8.** XMODEM Receiver Logic

This process proceeds with the software looping through the various *if* statements and the various conditional statements until an EOT or a CAN is received.

As shown in Figure 4-8, the receiver's job is not much more complex than that of the sender's. Upon sending a NAK to inform the sender that it is ready to receive data, the receiver waits for incoming traffic. XMODEM uses a timer at the receiver to control when to inform the transmitter that it is not receiving traffic. If a frame does not arrive within a specific period of time (earlier implementations were 10 seconds), the receiver sends a NAK to the sender.

Upon receiving a valid frame with a SOH byte, the receiver checks for a valid packet sequence number using the second and third fields of the protocol data unit. It then edits the sequence number to determine whether it is the correct sequence number. If not, it sends back a CAN to the transmitter. It then checks for the integrity of the data field by using the checksum. If all goes well, it accepts the traffic by sending an ACK. Finally, if it receives an EOT, it sends an acknowledgment of the EOT and ends the transfer operation.

The XMODEM protocol is implemented in some versions with a two-byte cyclic redundancy check (CRC) instead of the original single-byte checksum. The CRC algorithm for this version of XMODEM uses the CCITT polynomial $X^{16} + X^{12} + X^5 + 1$.

The only difference in using a checksum and the CRC sum is that the receiver and transmitter must exchange an initial signal to indicate whether they are using the CRC implementation of XMODEM. Instead of sending the NAK signal to the sender, the receiving modem sends the character C.

Be aware that some packages that use MODEM7 may employ both CRC and checksum operations in their protocol. Certain timing operations are implemented during start-up to determine whether the sender will respond to the C character within a certain period. It is advisable to consult with your vendor to learn how the specific implementation of your protocol uses the checksum/CRC operation.

The XMODEM is a widely used protocol. It is simple, easy to understand, and easy to use. Perhaps its major weakness is the use of an 8-bit field for the checksum, which can cause some undetected errors. However, other versions of XMODEM are available that use the more sophisticated CRC error-checking technique and provide better integrity to the traffic flow. The XMODEM protocol requires the receiver to notify the sender that the CRC option is to be used by sending the C character instead of the NAK.

## YMODEM

YMODEM is quite similar to XMODEM; however, it has some additional features. As examples, it aborts a file transfer with two consecutive ASCII Cancel (CAN) characters. It uses the CCITT CRC-16 algorithm for error-checking. It uses 1-Kbyte blocks (1,024 bytes) instead of XMODEM's 128 bytes, and it permits mixed modes by sending STX for 1-Kbyte blocks and SOH for 128-byte blocks. In addition, it allows multiple files to be sent simultaneously by the use of additional control characters.

## BLAST

Another popular package for the personal computer is BLAST. This product is available for most widely sold personal computers. The BLAST protocol is more powerful than XMODEM. It uses a two-way, full-duplex procedure with the sliding-window concept discussed in Chapter 3. In addition, the error-checking technique utilizes CRC. BLAST allows data (binary files) as well as text files to be transferred to another computer.

## KERMIT

The Kermit protocol is an asynchronous protocol designed for transferring files. It was developed at Columbia University and is one of the most widely used link protocols in the industry.

The protocol is a very robust system providing for many options in the transferring of files between two computers. Insofar as possible, Kermit remains transparent to the specific operating systems and mainframes. Indeed, Kermit was designed to support file transfer between IBM and DEC computers.

Information on Kermit may be obtained from: Kermit Distribution, Columbia University Center for Computing Activities, 7th Floor, Watson Laboratory, 612 West 115th Street, New York, NY 10025.

The transfer procedures for Kermit are somewhat similar to XMODEM (see Figure 4-9). The file transfer process begins after the sender receives a NAK packet. It then sends a *send initiate* packet, which is used to begin the negotiation for the file transfer. After this process, the sender sends a file header packet containing the name of the file and its characteristics. The successful reception of the file header enables the sender to begin sending data. Each data unit is acknowledged by the receiver. After the file transfer process is over, the sender sends an *end of file (EOF)* packet, determines whether it has more files to send, and, if not, stops the process.

During the transfer operation, Kermit sees that the characters transmitted are kept transparent to any network software or operating system by ensuring that control fields are properly identified and that control-like fields are recoded in the data field until presented to the end-user file.

One of the most attractive features of Kermit is the logic devoted to the support of transferring any type of data, including ASCII, binary files, Boolean fields, decimal fields, etc.

Before transmitting the user data, Kermit makes certain that the ASCII control characters inserted by the user are recoded during the transmission process to prevent any system from acting upon them or absorbing them mistakenly.

It performs this support operation by the CHAR function, in which a control character has the value of 20 HEX added to it. The effect of this operation is to "move" this character into the printable string column of the ASCII table. The UNCHAR function reverses the process.

It is possible (likely) that control-like values could be placed in the user data field (after all, we have no control over what the user places in these fields). If actions are not taken on these values, a system mistakenly could assume these are legitimate control characters. Kermit handles this process by appending these fields with a # sign and XORing with 40 HEX. The XORing is used instead of simply adding 40H because it keeps the high-order bit intact.

In addition, Kermit supports several operations to ensure that 7-bit and 8-bit files operate properly.

These operations consume considerable overhead in the creation of additional control characters. Consequently, Kermit provides a simple compression scheme to reduce the amount of traffic on the communications channel.

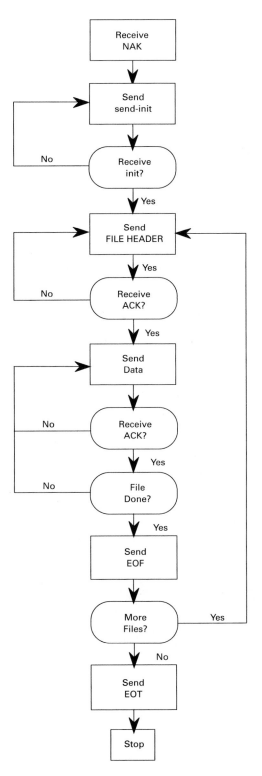

**Figure 4-9.** The Kermit File Transfer Procedure

## The Packet

As depicted in Figure 4-10, the Kermit packet consists of six major fields. The *mark* field is coded as an ASCII SOH (Value 1). This signifies the beginning of the packet.

The *LEN* field is a length field that defines the number of bytes in the packet following the LEN field. The maximum total packet length is restricted to no greater than 96 bytes.

The *SEQ* field is used to sequence each packet. It is a wraparound counter in that once it reaches the maximum value of 63, it returns to 0 and continues to count.

The *type* field defines the type of packet. It could contain a number of characters to define such packet types as data, ACKs, NAKs, EOTs, EOFs, and so on.

The *data* field contains user data, control information regarding the file transfer, or nothing.

The *check* field is used to determine whether the packet was damaged on the transmission. Kermit permits several options for the use of the check field. One option uses a simple checksum, another uses a cyclic redundancy check (CRC).

The type field in the Kermit packet is coded to provide information about end data or control fields (see Figure 4-11). If coded with a D, this packet contains traffic from a file being transmitted. The Y code is used to acknowledge the successful transmission of a packet. The Y packet also is sent in response to a send initiate packet. The NAK packet is used to reject a packet that would require a retransmission from the sender. The *send initiate* packet is used to inform the receiver of this packet about the parameters to be used during the file transfer operation. The *file header* packet must contain the name of the file to be transmitted. The *error* packet is sent when an unrecoverable error (a fatal error) has been encountered. The *EOT* packet is sent when all files have been transmitted and the *EOF* is sent when one file has been transmitted completely. The *display text on screen* is used to signify that the transmitted information is to be displayed. The *attribute* packet is used to send additional information about the file, such as administrative data (date, time, password information, security information, and so on).

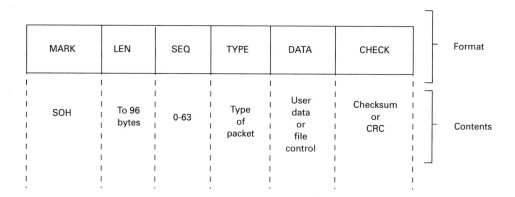

**Figure 4-10.** The Kermit Packet

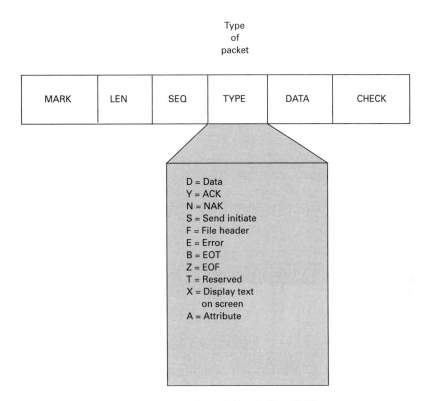

**Figure 4-11.** The Type Field

Figure 4-12 illustrates the S(SEND-INT) packet. It is the most complex packet because it is used for the sender and receiver to define their operating parameters during the file transfer. The *MAXL* field defines the maximum permissible packet size that can be received. The *TIME* field specifies a time-out value that the receiver waits before taking a time-out and taking remedial action. The *NPAD* parameter defines the number of padding characters to be sent in front of each packet. This technique is widely used in half-duplex protocols to allow devices to switch from transmitter to receiver modes. Upon detecting the PAD the receiver can change its mode of operation. The *PADC* identifies the padding character to be used for the process. The *EOL* is used to terminate the packet field itself. The *QCTL* is used for the control character escape. Its value defaults to # sign. The *OPT* represents other optional fields. The *CAPAS* field is one of several options that have been added to Kermit in the last few years. This field can be coded to define that sliding window protocols are to be used, to provide other information about file attributes, and to permit an extended length for a Kermit packet. The extended length field permits the Kermit packet to range up to 9,024 bytes.

## MNP

Yet another popular PC package is Microcom MNP. It is available as a point-to-point protocol and supports a wide variety of computers. MNP is somewhat different from the

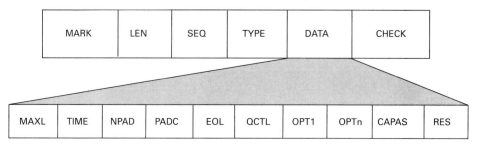

|        | | | | | | | | | |
| MAXL | TIME | NPAD | PADC | EOL | QCTL | OPT1 | OPTn | CAPAS | RES |

MAXL    = Max packet size
TIME    = Time-out value
NPAD    = Number of padding characters
PADC    = Id of padding character
EOL     = End of packet id
QCTL    = Prefix for control characters
OPT     = Other optional fields
CAPAS   = Advanced capability option

**Figure 4-12.**  Example of the S Packet

other systems in that it uses a layered protocol approach very similar to that of the OSI model. At the physical layer, it uses the 8-bit asynchronous start/stop approach. The data link level provides for error detection using a CRC 16-bit field; also it provides for continuous ARQ error correction and for sliding window systems, as well. It has options for half or full duplex and provides other features, such as link disconnect. In addition to these lower-level procedures, MNP provides for file-transfer capabilities similar to those of the systems discussed previously in this chapter. The full frame structure of MNP product is similar to the binary synchronous control protocol (BSC or BISYNC), except that each character within the frame is surrounded by the asynchronous start/stop bits. The start/stop bits provide the clocking signals across the interface between the devices, which enables the PCs to utilize the conventional asynchronous board.

## ASYNCHRONOUS PADS

### The CCITT X.3 Asynchronous PAD

Many data networks in operation today use synchronous link control protocols. Therefore, some means must be devised to allow the large population of asynchronous devices to access these networks. This service is provided with a packet assembler/disassembler (PAD). The job of the PAD is to provide protocol conversion for an asynchronous device to a synchronous data network and a complementary protocol conversion at the receiving end of the network. The goal is to provide a transparent service to user DTEs through the network.

The asynchronous-oriented PAD performs the following functions:

- Assembly of characters into packets
- Disassembly of user data field at other end

- Handling virtual call set-up, clearing, resetting, and interrupt packets
- Generation of service signals
- Mechanism for forwarding packets (a full packet, or when a timer expires)
- Editing PAD commands
- Automatic detection of data rate, code, parity, and operational characteristics

The CCITT X.3 PAD Recommendation is the prevalent standard in use today for defining the operating procedures between an asynchronous device and the PAD. The term *X.3* defines a set of 22 parameters the PAD uses to identify and control each terminal communicating with it. When a DTE connection is established to the PAD, the PAD parameters are used to determine how the PAD communicates with the user DTE and vice versa. The user DTE also has the option of altering the parameters after the logon to the PAD device is complete.

Refer to the actual CCITT recommendation for more detailed information on the use of these parameters.

## The TELNET Protocols

The TELNET family of protocols permit host computers to learn about the characteristics of terminals attached to other hosts with which they communicate. Equally important, TELNET provides conventions for the negotiation of a number of functions and services for a terminal-based session between two machines. This approach ameliorates the protocol conversion problem, because the negotiating machines have the option of not using a service that cannot be supported by either machine.

TELNET does not perform any protocol conversion between different machines. Rather, it provides a mechanism to determine the characteristics of the machines and a means to negotiate the manner in which the machines will internetwork to exchange data.

The TELNET protocol allows a program on a host machine (called the "TELNET client") to access the resources of another machine (called the "TELNET server") as if the client were attached locally to the server. Although TELNET provides a variety of features, some people call the standard a *remote login* protocol because it supports a remote device's login with a host machine.

The TELNET standard is based on the idea of a network virtual terminal (NVT). The term "virtual" is used because a NVT actually does not exist; it is an imagined device that provides a standard means of representing a terminal's characteristics. The idea is to relieve the host computers from the tasks of maintaining characteristics about every terminal with which they are communicating.

With the TELNET standard, both the user and server devices are required to map their terminal characteristics into the virtual terminal description. The end result is that the devices appear to be communicating with the network virtual terminal because they are assuming that both parties are providing a complementary mapping.

The TELNET protocol, like other virtual terminal protocols, allows the communicating machines to *negotiate* a variety of options to be used during the session. The server and client are required to use a standard set of procedures to establish these options.

The use of negotiated options takes into consideration the possibility that host machines may provide services beyond those in a virtual terminal. Moreover, the TELNET model does not restrict the negotiated options to those stipulated solely in the protocols. Rather, TELNET allows the negotiation of different conventions beyond the TELNET specifications.

Interested readers can obtain more information about the TELNET capabilities from the following address:

SRI International
Network Information Systems Center
333 Ravenswood Ave. Room EJ291
Menlo Park, CA 94025

## SUMMARY

Asynchronous communication, with all its shortcomings, remains one of the prevalent techniques for transferring data between computers. With the extraordinary growth of personal computers and their use of asynchronous ports, asynchronous protocols will be prominent for many years

# 5

# Binary Synchronous Control (BSC)

## INTRODUCTION

This chapter examines character-oriented link protocols. The emphasis is on a family of protocols known as binary synchronous control (BSC). The BSC frame formats are shown, as well as the functions provided by the fields in the frames. BSC line modes, control modes, and timers also are examined. Several ISO character-oriented protocols are reviewed at the end of the chapter.

## BSC CHARACTERISTICS

In the mid-1960s, IBM introduced the first general-purpose data link control to support multipoint or point-to-point configurations. This product, the binary synchronous control protocol (BSC, also known as simply BISYNC), found widespread use throughout the world in the 1970s and 1980s. Indeed, it became one of the most commonly used synchronous line protocols in existence. IBM's product families, designated as 3270 and 3780, originally were based on BSC. Practically every vendor has some version of BSC implemented in a product line, and the standards organizations publish specifications on the protocol.

Despite this, it should be understood that link control products that use BSC gradually are being phased out of most organizations' systems. Replacements either are an HDLC-type protocol or a local area network protocol.

BSC is a half-duplex protocol, in that transmissions are provided two ways, but a station alternates the use of the link with another station. The protocol supports point-to-point and multipoint connections, as well as switched and nonswitched channels. BSC is a code-sensitive protocol, and every character transmitted across a channel must be decoded at the receiver to determine whether it is a control character or a data character. Code-dependent protocols also are called *byte* or *character protocols*.

## BSC FORMATS AND CONTROL CODES

The BSC frame formats and control codes are shown in Figure 5-1. Although the figure does not show all the possibilities for the format of a BSC frame, it offers a sampling of some of the major implementations of the BSC frame format.

Since BSC is a character-oriented protocol, it is possible that a code recognized as BSC control could be created by the user application process. For instance, assume a user program creates a bit sequence that is the same as the ETX (end of text) control code. The

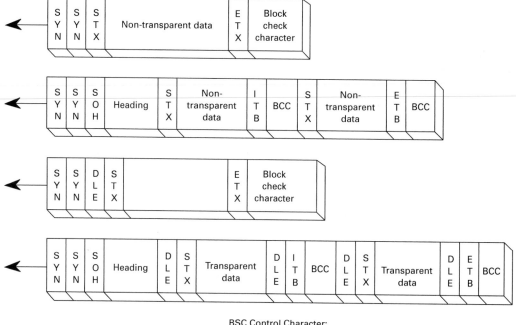

BSC Control Character:

| Character | Function |
|-----------|----------|
| SYN | Synchronous idle (keeps channel active) |
| DLE | Data link escape (used to achieve code transparency |
| ENQ | Enquiry (used with polls/selects and bids |
| SOH | Start of heading |
| STX | Start of text (puts line in text mode) |
| ITB | End of intermediate block |
| ETB | End of transmission block |
| ETX | End of text |
| EOT | End of transmission (puts line in control mode) |
| BCC | Block check count |

**Figure 5-1.** BSC Formats and Control Codes

receiving station, upon encountering the ETX inside the user data, would assume that the end of the transmission is signified by the user-generated ETX. BSC would then accept the ETX as a protocol control character and would attempt to perform an error check on an incomplete BSC frame. This situation would result in an error.

Control codes must be excluded from the text and header fields, and BSC addresses the problem with the DLE control code. This code is placed in front of the control codes to identify these characters as valid line control characters. The DLE is not placed in front of user-generated data. Consequently, if bit patterns resembling any of these control characters are created in the user text and encountered by the receiving station, the receiving station assumes they are valid user data because the DLE does not precede them. The DLE places the line into a transparent text mode, which allows the transmission of any bit pattern.

The DLE presents a special problem if it is generated by the end-user application process, since it could be recognized as a control code. BSC handles this situation by inserting a DLE next to a data DLE character. The receiver discards the first of two successive DLEs and accepts the second DLE as valid user data.

The headers illustrated in Figure 5-1 are optional. If they are included, the SOH code is placed in front of the header.

## LINE MODES

The BSC channel or link operates in one of two modes. The control mode is used by a master station to control the operations on the link, such as the transmission of polling and selection frames. The message or text mode is used for the transmittal of an information block or blocks. Upon receiving an invitation to send data (a poll), the slave station transmits user data either with an STX or an SOH in front of the data or heading. These control characters place the channel in the message or text mode. Thereafter, data are exchanged under the text mode until an EOT is received, which changes the mode back to control. During the time the channel is in text mode, it is dedicated to the exchange of data between two stations only. All other stations must remain passive.

The polls and selects are initiated by a frame with the contents: Address.ENQ (where address is the address of the station). The control (master) station is responsible for sending polls and selects.

BSC provides for contention operation on a point-to-point circuit, as well. In this situation one of the stations can become the master by "bidding" to the other station. The station accepting the bid becomes the slave. A point-to-point line enters the contention mode following the transmission or reception of the EOT.

The ENQ code plays an important role in BSC control modes. To summarize its functions:

- Poll: Control station sends with an address prefix.
- Select: Control station sends with an address prefix.
- Bid: Point-to-point stations send to contend for control station status.

BSC uses several EBCDIC or ASCII values to indicate whether a frame is a poll or a select. For example, one approach for the 3274 control unit is to use EBCDIC hex 7F as a poll to a device and EBCDIC C4 as a select.

## LINE CONTROL

The transmitting station knows the exact order of frames it transmits, and it expects to receive ACKs to its transmissions. The receiving site transmits the ACKs with sequence numbers. Only two numbers are used. The ACK0 is represented as 1070 in EBCDIC hexadecimal notation and 1030 in ASCII hexadecimal notation. The ACK1 is represented as 1061 in EBCDIC hexadecimal notation and as 1031 in ASCII hexadecimal notation.

This sequencing technique is sufficient, since the channel inherently is half duplex. Only one frame can be outstanding at one time. An ACK0 indicates the correct receipt of even-numbered frames; an ACK1 indicates the receipt of odd-numbered frames.

In addition to the frame-format control codes in Figure 5-1, BSC uses several other line control codes:

ACK0    Positive acknowledgment to even-sequenced blocks of data or a response to a select or bid.

ACK1    Positive acknowledgment to odd-sequenced blocks of data.

WACK    (Wait Before Transmit—Positive Acknowledgment) Receiving station temporarily unable to continue to process or receive transmissions. Signifies a line reversal. Also used as a positive acknowledgment of a transmission. Station will continue to send WACK until it is ready to receive.

RVI     (Reverse Interrupt) Indicates station has data to send at the earliest opportunity. This causes an interrupt of the transmission process.

TTD     (Temporary Text Delay) Indicates sending DTE cannot send data immediately, but wishes to maintain control of line (for examples: its buffer is being filled or its card hopper is empty).

## BSC TIMERS AND TIME-OUTS

Like other line protocols, BSC uses timers and time-outs to manage errors and unusual conditions. A receiving station usually will time-out after three seconds of no activity from a transmitting station (receive time-out). On a switched line, a station will disconnect if it is inactive for a specified period, usually twenty seconds (disconnect time-out). In the event of a delay, a station must issue a WACK or TTD (continue time-out). The continue time-out value must be less than the value of the receive time-out and usually is set to two seconds. The transmitting station transmits periodically SYN SYN to maintain synchronization between stations.

Box 5-1 provides several examples of BSC control traffic flow on the link:

---

**BOX 5-1.** EXAMPLES OF BSC LINK ACTIVITY

---

Transmission: ENQ SYN SYN →
Meaning: A point-to-point station seeks a connection establishment and acquires control of the line. If both stations transmit this signal at the same time, a predesignated primary station is allowed to retry.

---

Transmission: ENQ Station Address SYN SYN EOT SYN SYN →
Meaning: With a multipoint link, the primary station uses this format to send a poll (station address is uppercase) or a select (station address is lowercase).

---

Transmission: ACK0 SYN SYN →
Meaning: Station is ready to receive traffic.

---

Transmission: ACK0/1 SYN SYN →
Meaning: Station ACKs transmission and/or is ready to receive traffic.

---

Transmission: NAK SYN SYN →
Meaning: Station NAKs transmission and/or is not ready to receive traffic.

---

Transmission: WACK SYN SYN →
Meaning: Station requests other station to try again since it is temporarily not ready. This format also is used to acknowledge previous traffic.

---

Transmission: RVI SYN SYN →
Meaning: ACKs previous traffic and requests other station to suspend transmissions since receiving station needs the link itself.

---

Transmission: ENQ STX SYN SYN →
Meaning: Sending station is experiencing a temporary delay but does not wish to relinquish the line. Also used when a polled station is not ready to transmit but wants the polling station to wait. This format is called a temporary text delay (TTD).

---

Transmission: EOT SYN SYN →
Meaning: This is a negative response to a poll and also is used when a sending station has completed its transmission.

## OTHER "BSC-LIKE" SPECIFICATIONS

### ISO 2111, ISO 1745, and ISO 2628

While BSC probably is the best known character-oriented protocol, other similar products and standards are used widely. The ISO protocols are examples. ISO 2111, ISO 1745, and ISO 2628 are complementary protocols.

ISO 2111 describes the transmission control characters to manage the data link. These codes are the same as BSC codes (STX, DLE, ETB, etc.), so they are not explained again here. The other rules for ISO 2111 are summarized in Box 5-2.

The ISO 1745 (1975) specification defines the actual link operations, that is, the functions of the control codes. ISO 1745 allows either asynchronous start/stop or

---

### BOX 5-2. RULES FOR THE ISO 2111 PROTOCOL

1. The first occurrence of DLE.SOH or DLE.STX initiates code independent information procedures. Code independent procedures are terminated by DLE.ETB or DLE.ETX.

2. DLE.SYN may be used for "filler" within the code independent portion of the message, provided it never is inserted between two characters of a DLE sequence or ahead of the error-check sequence. Filler is discarded by the receiver.

3. Code independent information shall consist of an integer number of octets (8-bit groups).

4. For each occurrence of the 8-bit combination corresponding to DLE within the original text, an additional DLE is inserted adjacent to it. This inserted DLE is discarded by the receiver.

5. Error calculation is initiated by, but does not include, the first occurrence of SOH, DLE.SOH, DLE.STX.

6. Error calculation does not include DLE.SYN or the first DLE of any DLE sequence (e.g., DLE.DLE, DLE.STX, DLE.ETX).

7. The sender divides the information to be sent by the generating polynomial $(x^{16} + x^{12} + x^5 + x^0)$ and the 16-bit remainder is sent as the block check sequence (BCS) immediately after the terminating DLE.ETB or DLE.ETX.

8. The block check sequence is sent high-order bit first.

9. The receiver divides the transmission, including BCS, by the same generating polynomial. If no transmission errors occurred, the remainder will be zero.

synchronous transmission. Duplex or half-duplex links are allowed. The link is actually managed by the "states" of the attached stations: master, slave, or neutral.

Master stations can select other stations that become slaves, and receive information messages. They must respond to the master, which has sole responsibility for information transfer. A data link can have only one master at a time, but may have several slaves. Any station on a multipoint network (other than the control station) is called a *tributary station*. Both point-to-point and multipoint links may have a control station. The standard allows switched connections and contention procedures on multipoint data links.

The ISO 1745 control codes are almost identical to those of BSC. For that reason, they are listed here and not described again:

|         |         |
|---------|---------|
| - SOH   | - STX   |
| - ETX   | - EOT   |
| - ENQ   | - ACK   |
| - DLE   | - NAK   |
| - SYN   | - ETB   |

ISO 2628 specifies the recovery, abort, and interrupt procedures to complement ISO 2111 and ISO 1745. The standard defines the following timers and recovery procedures.

**A: No Response Timer.** Stations employ Timer A to protect against an invalid response or no response. The A timer starts after transmitting an ending character (ENQ, ETB, ETX) and stops on receipt of a valid reply (EOT, ACK, NAK, STX). The recovery alternatives are:

    **a.** retransmit the same data (up to n times),

    **b.** abort by sending EOT (if abort procedures are used), and

    **c.** transmit something else (poll, message, etc.).

**B: Receive Timer.** Station(s) employ Timer B to protect against loss of a message block-terminating character, e.g., buffer overflow. Timer B starts on receipt of a message-framing character (SOH, STX). Timer B stops on receipt of a terminating character (ETB, ETX, ENQ). The recovery requires that the station:

    **a.** remain in slave status,

    **b.** discard the incomplete block,

    **c.** prepare to receive another transmission, and

    **d.** initiate search for character synchronization signals.

**C: No Activity Timer (Dial-Up Lines).** All dial-up stations employ this timer to assure a disconnect in the event of an error. Timer C starts on receipt of an indication that the circuit is connected or on receipt (or transmission) of each asynchronous character or (SYN) synchronizing sequence. Timer C stops on receipt (or transmission) of DLE.EOT or loss-of-circuit indication. The recovery requires:

    **a.** the circuit be disconnected, and

    **b.** the station return to control mode (if applicable).

**D: No Activity Timer (Dedicated Lines).** All stations employ this timer to recover from loss of activity. D starts on receipt (or transmission) of each asynchronous character or (SYN) synchronizing sequence (in synchronous systems). D stops on receipt or transmission of EOT. The recovery requires that the station return to control mode (if applicable).

## SUMMARY

Character-oriented link control protocols were the pervasive technology for managing data links in the 1960s and 1970s. BSC was offered practically in all vendors' link layer products. With some exceptions, they have been replaced by bit-oriented protocols due to the relative inefficiency of their half-duplex operations and the awkward nature of code-dependent operations.

# 6

# HDLC

## INTRODUCTION

This chapter examines the operations of the High-Level Data Link Control (HDLC) standard, certainly the most widely used synchronous data link control protocol in existence. We examine the architecture of the protocol from the standpoint of operating line modes and link configuration options. The many features of HDLC are contrasted and compared. Because HDLC has so many features, one should check with specific vendors for their actual implementation of HDLC. Most vendors have a version of HDLC available, although the protocol often is renamed by the vendor or designated by different initials.

## CHARACTERISTICS OF HIGH-LEVEL DATA LINK CONTROL (HDLC) SPECIFICATIONS

HDLC is a bit-oriented line protocol specification published by the International Standards Organization (ISO). It has achieved wide use throughout the world. The recommended standard provides for many functions and covers a broad range of applications. Frequently, it serves as a foundation for other protocols that use specific options in the HDLC repertoire. The Advanced Data Communication Control Procedures (ADCCP) are published as ANSI X3.66. With minor variations, they are identical to HDLC. However, to keep matters simple, we examine only HDLC, since its use is more widespread.

The following list summarizes the HDLC specifications published by the ISO. The summary titles are the author's. The actual title of each document is not listed here. This chapter represents a summary of several of these specifications. Subsequent chapters complete the analysis.

| | |
|---|---|
| 3309 (two documents): | HDLC frame structure and addendum |
| 4335 (three documents): | HDLC elements of procedures |
| 7448 (one document): | Multilink procedures (MLP) |
| 7776 (one document): | HDLC-LAPB compatible link control procedures |
| 7809 (five documents): | HDLC-consolidation of classes of procedures; list of standard HDLC protocols that use HDLC procedures |
| 8471 (one document): | HDLC-balanced link address information |
| 8885 (one document): | HDLC-additional specifications describing use of an XID frame and multilink operations |

## THE HDLC FAMILY

The HDLC protocol has been used as a basis for the development of a number of other widely used link layer protocols. Figure 6-1 provides an illustration of how pervasive HDLC is in the industry. This figure is not all-inclusive, but it represents some of the major implementations of HDLC. These protocols are shown at the node of the tree of the figure. The terms in parentheses indicate the technologies (usually, upper-layer protocols, and most often a network layer) that the data link protocol supports. The exception to this statement is the node labeled *Frame Relay*. It supports no overlying network layer. This will become more evident in the Chapter 13 discussion of frame relay.

While many systems use the HDLC protocol, it does not mean that these systems are compatible. Indeed, often they are not compatible. We shall see in this chapter that HDLC has a broad range of options that can be implemented in different vendors' products.

The link access procedure balanced (LAPB) protocol is a link layer protocol used on X.25 interfaces. It operates within an X.25 three-layer stack of protocols at the data link layer and is used to ensure that the X.25 packet is delivered safely between the user device and the packet network.

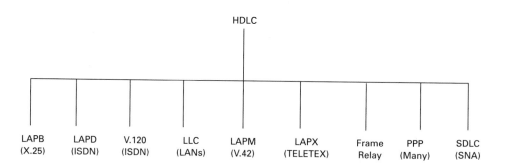

**Figure 6-1.** The HDLC Family

The link access procedure for the D channel (LAPD) is employed on ISDN interfaces. Its purpose is to deliver ISDN messages (and perhaps, user data) safely between user devices and the ISDN node.

The V.120 recommendation published by the CCITT contains an HDLC protocol. It is used on ISDN terminal adapters for multiplexing operations. It uses many of the concepts of LAPD for addressing and it allows the multiplexing of multiple users across one link.

The logical link control (LLC) protocol is employed on IEEE 802 and ISO 8802 local area networks (LANs). It is configured in a variety of ways to provide different types of HDLC services. It rests atop any 802 or 8802 LAN.

The link access procedure for modems (LAPM) protocol is relatively new and gives modems a powerful HDLC capability. It operates within V.42 modems and, as one might expect, it is responsible for the safe delivery of traffic across communications links between two modems.

The link access procedure for half-duplex links (LAPX) is, as its name suggests, a half-duplex link control protocol. It is used in the teletex technology.

The frame relay protocol uses an HDLC procedure for its link operations. Indeed, frame relay is so named because its purpose is to relay an HDLC-type frame across a network. Frame relay was derived from many of the operations of LAPD and V.120.

The point-to-point protocol (PPP) also is a derivation of HDLC. It is employed on a number of internet point-to-point links. Its primary purpose is to encapsulate network PDUs and to identify the different types of network protocols that may be carried in the I field of the PPP frame.

The synchronous data link control (SDLC) protocol is the Layer 2 protocol for IBM's Systems Network Architecture (SNA), which is a multilayer protocol stack. It also is responsible for the safe delivery of traffic. As an aside, be careful not to use SNA and SDLC synonymously. SDLC resides only in Layer 2 of SNA's protocol suite.

You may understand now how important it is to understand the features of HDLC and its basic operations. By knowing, one also comprehends the operation of many widely used protocols. The good news, then, is that if one learns HDLC, one learns about other protocols, as well. The bad news is that each of these protocols is a derivation of HDLC. The protocols use various combinations of HDLC features and, in many instances, add their own protocol-specific operations. While learning HDLC is very valuable, it does not ensure knowledge concerning the specific features of the other protocols. Therefore, to learn about a specific protocol, there is no substitute for the actual source document.

## HDLC CHARACTERISTICS

HDLC provides a number of options to satisfy a wide variety of user requirements. It supports both half-duplex and full-duplex transmission, point-to-point and multipoint configuration, and switched or nonswitched channels. One should study Figure 6-2 while reading the following section.

An HDLC station is classified as one of three types. The primary station is in control of the data link. This station acts as a master and transmits command frames to the secondary stations on the channel. In turn, it receives response frames from those stations. If the link is multipoint, the primary station is responsible for maintaining a separate session with each station attached to the link. It uses poll commands to solicit data from the secondary stations.

HDLC does not need a *select* command because it establishes windows and buffers during link setup, thereby ensuring that the receiving station has adequate resources to handle the traffic (within the negotiated window size).

The secondary station acts as a slave to the primary station. It responds to the command frames from the primary station in the form of response frames. It maintains only one session, that being with the primary station, and it has no responsibility for control on the link. On a multipoint link, secondary stations cannot communicate directly with each other; they must first transfer their frames to the primary station.

The combined station transmits both commands and responses and receives both commands and responses from another combined station. It maintains a session with the other combined station. The stations are peers on the link.

HDLC provides three methods to configure the channel for primary, secondary, and combined station use. An unbalanced configuration provides for one primary station and one or more secondary stations to operate as point-to-point or multipoint, half-duplex, full-duplex, switched or nonswitched. The configuration is called *unbalanced* because the primary station is responsible for controlling each secondary station and for establishing and maintaining the link.

The symmetrical configuration is used very little today. The configuration provides for two independent, point-to-point unbalanced station configurations. Each station has a primary and secondary status; therefore, each station is considered logically to be two stations—a primary and a secondary station. The primary station transmits commands to the secondary station at the other end of the channel and vice versa. Even though the stations have both primary and secondary capabilities, the actual commands and responses are multiplexed onto one physical channel.

A balanced configuration consists of two combined stations connected point-to-point only, half-duplex or full-duplex, switched or nonswitched. The combined stations have equal status on the channel and may send unsolicited frames to each other. Each station has equal responsibility for link control. Typically, a station uses a command in order to solicit a response from the other station. The other station can send its own command, as well.

The terms *unbalanced* and *balanced* have nothing to do with the electrical characteristics of the circuit. In fact, data link controls should not be aware of the physical circuit attributes. The two terms are used in a completely different context at the physical and link levels.

While the stations are transferring data, they communicate in one of the three modes of operation:

Normal response mode (NRM) requires the secondary station to receive explicit permission from the primary station before transmitting. After receiving permission, the secondary station initiates a response transmission that may contain data. The transmission may consist of one or more frames while the channel is being used by the secondary station. After the last frame transmission, the secondary station must again wait for explicit permission before it can transmit again.

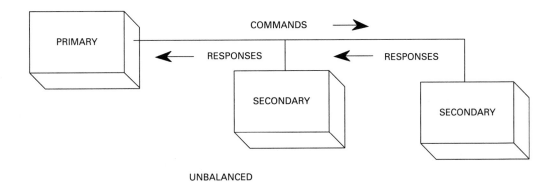

UNBALANCED

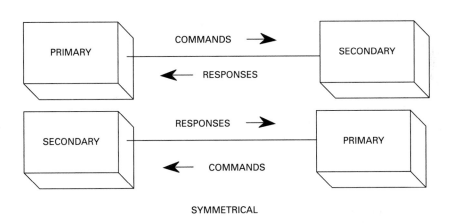

SYMMETRICAL

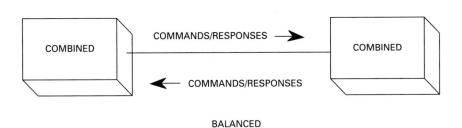

BALANCED

**Figure 6-2.** HDLC Link Configurations

Asynchronous response mode (ARM) allows a secondary station to initiate transmission without receiving explicit permission from the primary station. The transmission may contain data frames or control information reflecting status changes of the secondary station. ARM can decrease overhead because the secondary station does not need a poll sequence in order to send data. A secondary station operating in ARM can transmit only when it detects an idle channel state for a two-way alternate (half-duplex) data flow, or at any time for a two-way simultaneous (duplex) data flow. The primary station maintains responsibility for tasks such as error recovery, link setup, and link disconnections.

Asynchronous balanced mode (ABM) uses combined stations. The combined station may initiate transmissions without receiving prior permission from the other combined station.

Normal response mode (NRM) is used frequently on multipoint lines. The primary station controls the link by issuing polls to the attached stations (usually terminals, personal computers, and cluster controllers). The asynchronous balanced mode (ABM) is a better choice on point-to-point links, since it incurs no overhead and delay in polling. The asynchronous response mode (ARM) is used very little today.

The term *asynchronous* has nothing to do with the physical interface of the stations. It is used to indicate that the stations need not receive a preliminary signal from another station before sending traffic. HDLC uses synchronous formats in its frames.

## FRAME FORMAT

HDLC uses the term *frame* (as does the book) to indicate the independent entity of data (protocol data unit) transmitted across the link from one station to another. Figure 6-3 shows the frame format. The frame consists of four or five fields:

- Flag fields (F)                          8 bits
- Address field (A)                        8, or multiples of 8 bits
- Control field (C)                        8, or multiples of 8 bits
- Information field (I)                     variable length; not used in some frames
- Frame check sequence field (FCS)         16 or 32 bits

All frames must start and end with the flag (F) sequence fields. The stations attached to the data link are required continuously to monitor the link for the flag sequence. The flag sequence consists of 01111110. Flags are continuously transmitted on the link between frames to keep the link in an active condition.

Other bit sequences also are used. At least seven, but fewer than fifteen, continuous 1s (abort signal) indicates a problem on the link. Fifteen or more 1s keep the channel in an idle condition. One use of the idle state is in support of a half-duplex session. A station can detect the idle pattern and reverse the direction of the transmission.

Once the receiving station detects a nonflag sequence, it is aware it has encountered the beginning of the frame, an abort condition, or an idle channel condition. Upon encountering the next flag sequence, the station recognizes it has found the full frame. In summary, the link recognizes the following bit sequences as follows:

| | | |
|---|---|---|
| 01111110 | = | Flags |
| At least 7, but fewer than 15 1s | = | Abort |
| 15 or more 1s | = | Idle |

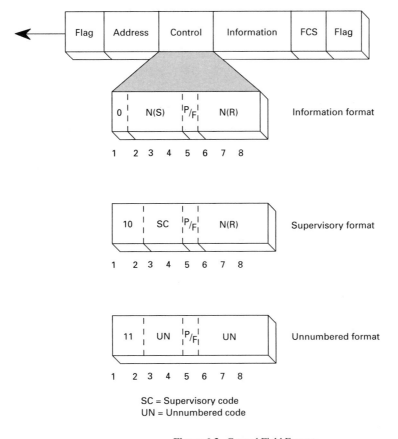

**Figure 6-3.** Control Field Formats

The time between the actual transmissions of the frames on the channel is called *interframe time fill.* This time fill is accomplished by transmitting continuous flags between the frames. The flags may be 8-bit multiples, and they can combine the ending 0 of the preceding flag with the starting 0 of the next flag.

HDLC is a code-transparent protocol. It does not rely on a specific code (ASCII/IA5, EBCDIC, etc.) for the interpretation of line control. For example, bit position n within an octet has a specific meaning, regardless of the other bits in the octet. On occasion, a flaglike field 01111110 may be inserted into the user data stream (I field) by the application process. More frequently, the bit patterns in the other fields appear "flaglike." To prevent "phony" flags from being inserted into the frame, the transmitter inserts a zero bit after it encounters five continuous 1s anywhere between the opening and closing flags of the frame. Consequently, zero insertion applies to the address, control, information, and FCS fields. This technique is called *bit stuffing.* As the frame is stuffed, it is transmitted across the link to the receiver.

The procedure to recover the frame of the receiver is a bit more involved (no pun intended). The "framing" receiver logic can be summarized as follows: The receiver continuously monitors the bit stream. After it receives a 0 bit with five continuous, succeeding 1 bits, it inspects the next bit. If it is a 0 bit, it pulls this bit out; in other words, it unstuffs the bit. However, if the seventh bit is a 1, the receiver inspects the eighth bit. If it is a 0, it recognizes that a flag sequence of 01111110 has been received. If it is a 1, then it knows an abort or idle signal has been received and counts the number of succeeding 1 bits to take appropriate action.

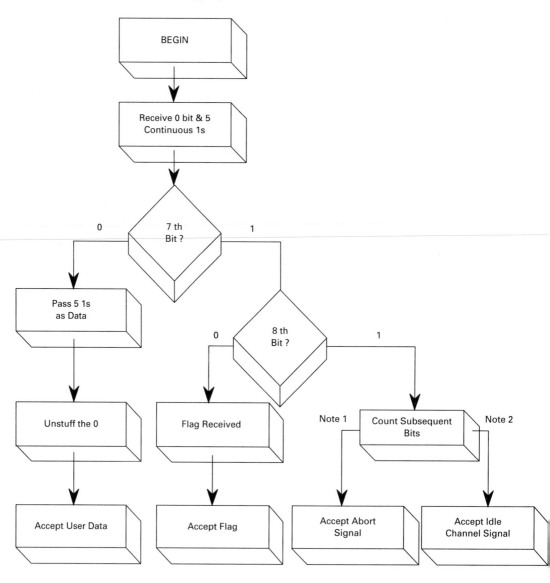

Note 1: Detect at least 7 but < 15 continuous 1s.
Note 2: Detect 15 or more continuous 1s.

**Figure 6-4.** Framing Operations at the Receiver

In this manner, HDLC achieves code and data transparency. The protocol is not concerned about any particular bit code inside the data stream. Its main concern is to keep the flags unique. Figure 6-4 summarizes the framing operations of HDLC at the receiver.

Many systems use bit stuffing and the non-return-to-zero-inverted (NRZI) encoding technique to keep the receiver clock synchronized. With NRZI, binary 1s do not cause a line transition, but binary 0s do cause a change. It might appear that a long sequence of 1s could present synchronization problems, since the receiver clock would not receive the line transitions necessary for the clock adjustment. However, bit stuffing ensures a 0 bit exists in the data stream at least every 5 bits. The receiver can use them for clock alignment.

The address (A) field identifies the primary or secondary station involved in the frame transmission or reception. A unique address is associated with each station. In an unbalanced configuration, the address field in both commands and responses contains the address of the secondary station. In balanced configurations, a command frame contains the destination station address and the response frame contains the sending station address.

The control (C) field contains the commands, responses, and sequence numbers used to maintain the data flow accountability of the link between the primary stations. The format and the contents of the control field varies, depending on the use of the HDLC frame.

The information (I) field contains the actual user data. The information field resides only in the frame under the Information frame format. It usually is not found in the Supervisory or Unnumbered frame, although one option of HDLC allows the I field to be used with an Unnumbered frame.

The frame check sequence (FCS) field is used to check for transmission errors between the two data link stations. The FCS field is created by a cyclic redundancy check described in Chapter 2. We summarize it here. The transmitting station performs modulo 2 division (based on an established polynomial) on the A, C, and I fields plus leading zeros and appends the remainder as the FCS field. In turn, the receiving station performs a division with the same polynomial on the A, C, I, and FCS fields. If the remainder equals a predetermined value, the chances are quite good the transmission occurred without any errors. If the comparisons do not match, it indicates a probable transmission error, in which case the receiving station sends a negative acknowledgment, requiring a retransmission of the frame.

## The Control Field

Let us return to a more detailed discussion of the control field (C), because it determines how HDLC controls the communications process (see Figure 6-3). The control field defines the function of the frame and therefore invokes the logic to control the movement of the traffic between the receiving and sending stations. The field can be in one of three formats (Unnumbered, Supervisory, and Information transfer).

The Information format frame is used to transmit end-user data between the two devices. The Information frame also may acknowledge the receipt of data from a transmitting station. It can perform certain other functions as well, such as a poll command.

The Supervisory format frame performs control functions such as the acknowledgment of frames, the request for the retransmission of frames, and the request for the temporary suspension of the transmission frames. The actual usage of the supervisory frame is dependent on the operational mode of the link (normal response mode, asynchronous balanced mode, asynchronous response mode).

The Unnumbered format also is used for control purposes. The frame is used to perform link initialization, link disconnection, and other link control functions. The frame uses five bit positions, which allow for up to 32 commands and 32 responses. The particular type of command and response depends on the HDLC class of procedure.

The actual format of the HDLC determines how the control field is coded and used. The simplest format is the Information transfer format. The N(S) (send sequence) number indicates the sequence number associated with a transmitted frame. The N(R) (receive sequence) number indicates the sequence number that is expected at the receiving site.

## PIGGYBACKING, FLOW CONTROL, AND ACCOUNTING FOR TRAFFIC

HDLC maintains accountability of the traffic and controls the flow of frames by state variables and sequence numbers. These concepts are described in Chapter 3. To briefly summarize, the traffic at both the transmitting and receiving sites are controlled by these state variables. The transmitting site maintains a send state variable (V[S]), which is the sequence number of the next frame to be transmitted. The receiving site maintains a receive state variable (V[R]), which contains the number that is expected to be in the sequence number of the next frame. The V(S) is incremented with each frame transmitted and placed in the send sequence field in the frame.

Upon receiving the frame, the receiving site checks the send sequence number with its V(R). If the CRC passes and if V(R)=N(S), it increments V(R) by one, places the value in the sequence number field in a frame, and sends it to the original transmitting site to complete the accountability for the transmission.

If the V(R) does not match the sending sequence number in the frame (or the CRC does not pass), an error has occurred, and a reject or selective reject with a value in V(R) is sent to the original transmitting site. The V(R) value informs the transmitting DTE of the next frame that it is expected to send, that is, the number of the frame to be retransmitted.

### The Poll/Final Bit

The fifth bit position in the control field is called the P/F or poll/final bit. It is recognized only when set to 1 and is used by the primary and secondary stations to provide a dialogue with each other:

- The primary station uses the P bit = 1 to solicit a status response from a secondary station. The P bit signifies a poll.
- The secondary station responds to a P bit with data or a status frame, and with the F bit = 1. The F bit also can signify end of transmission from the secondary station under Normal Response Mode (NRM).

The P/F bit is called the P bit when used by the primary station and the F bit when used by the secondary station. Most versions of HDLC permit one P bit (awaiting an F-bit response) to be outstanding at any time on the link. Consequently, a P set to 1 can be used as a checkpoint. That is, the P = 1 means, "Respond to me, because I want to know your status." Checkpoints are quite important in all forms of automation. It is the machine's technique to clear up ambiguity and, perhaps, to discard copies of previously transmitted frames. Under some versions of HDLC, the device may not proceed further until the F-bit frame is received, but other versions of HDLC (such as LAPB) do not require the F-bit frame to interrupt the full-duplex operations.

How does a station know if a received frame with the fifth bit= 1 is an F or P bit? After all, it is in the same bit position in all frames. HDLC provides a simple solution: The fifth bit is a P bit and the frame is a command if the address field contains the address of the receiving station; it is an F bit and the frame is a response if the address is that of the transmitting station. Some implementations of HDLC, such as LAPD, have expanded the address or control field to permit the use of a command/response bit. Later chapters explain this technique.

This use of a command or response frame can be quite important because a station may react very differently to the two types of frames. For example, a command (P = 1) usually requires the station to send back specific types of frames.

## HDLC COMMANDS AND RESPONSES

Table 6-1 shows the HDLC commands and responses. They are summarized briefly here.

The Receive Ready (RR) is used by the primary or secondary station to indicate that it is ready to receive an information frame and/or to acknowledge previously received frames by using the N(R) field. The primary station also may use the Receive Ready command to poll a secondary station by setting the P bit to 1.

The Receive Not Ready (RNR) frame is used by the station to indicate a busy condition. This informs the transmitting station that the receiving station is unable to accept additional incoming data. The RNR frame may acknowledge previously transmitted frames by using the N(R) field. The busy condition can be cleared by sending the RR frame.

The Selective Reject (SREJ) is used by a station to request the retransmission of a single frame identified in the N(R) field. As with inclusive acknowledgment, all information frames numbered up to N(R)–1 are acknowledged. Once the SREJ has been transmitted, subsequent frames are accepted and held for the retransmitted frame. The SREJ condition is cleared upon receipt of an I frame with a N(S) equal to V(R).

An SREJ frame must be transmitted for each errored frame; each frame is treated as a separate error. Only one SREJ frame can be outstanding at a time, since the N(R) field in the frame inclusively acknowledges all preceding frames. To send a second SREJ would contradict the first SREJ, because all I frames with N(S) lower than N(R) of the second SREJ would be acknowledged.

The Reject (REJ) is used to request the retransmission of frames starting with the frame numbered in the N(R) field. Frames numbered N(R)–1 all are acknowledged. The REJ frame can be used to implement the Go-Back-N technique.

**TABLE 6-1.**  HDLC CONTROL FIELD FORMAT

| Format | Encoding | | | | | | | | Commands | Responses |
|---|---|---|---|---|---|---|---|---|---|---|
| | 1 | 2 | 3 | 4 | 5 | 6 | 7 | 8 | | |
| Information | 0 | - | N(S) | - | | - | N(R) | - | I | I |
| Supervisory | 1 | 0 | 0 | 0 | • | - | N(R) | - | RR | RR |
| | 1 | 0 | 0 | 1 | • | - | N(R) | - | REJ | REJ |
| | 1 | 0 | 1 | 0 | • | - | N(R) | - | RNR | RNR |
| | 1 | 0 | 1 | 1 | • | - | N(R) | - | SREJ | SREJ |
| Unnumbered | 1 | 1 | 0 | 0 | • | 0 | 0 | 0 | UI | UI |
| | 1 | 1 | 0 | 0 | • | 0 | 0 | 1 | SNRM | |
| | 1 | 1 | 0 | 0 | • | 0 | 1 | 0 | DISC | RD |
| | 1 | 1 | 0 | 0 | • | 1 | 0 | 0 | UP | |
| | 1 | 1 | 0 | 0 | • | 1 | 1 | 0 | | UA |
| | 1 | 1 | 0 | 1 | • | 0 | 0 | 0 | NR0 | NR0 |
| | 1 | 1 | 0 | 1 | • | 0 | 0 | 1 | NR1 | NR1 |
| | 1 | 1 | 0 | 1 | • | 0 | 1 | 0 | NR2 | NR2 |
| | 1 | 1 | 0 | 1 | • | 0 | 1 | 1 | NR3 | NR3 |
| | 1 | 1 | 1 | 0 | • | 0 | 0 | 0 | SIM | RIM |
| | 1 | 1 | 1 | 0 | • | 0 | 0 | 1 | | FRMR |
| | 1 | 1 | 1 | 1 | • | 0 | 0 | 0 | SARM | DM |
| | 1 | 1 | 1 | 1 | • | 0 | 0 | 1 | RSET | |
| | 1 | 1 | 1 | 1 | • | 0 | 1 | 0 | SARME | |
| | 1 | 1 | 1 | 1 | • | 0 | 1 | 1 | SNRME | |
| | 1 | 1 | 1 | 1 | • | 1 | 0 | 0 | SABM | |
| | 1 | 1 | 1 | 1 | • | 1 | 0 | 1 | XID | XID |
| | 1 | 1 | 1 | 1 | • | 1 | 1 | 0 | SABME | |

LEGEND:

| | | | |
|---|---|---|---|
| I | Information | NR0 | Non-Reserved 0 |
| RR | Receive Ready | NR1 | Non-Reserved 1 |
| REJ | Reject | NR2 | Non-Reserved 2 |
| RNR | Receive Not Ready | NR3 | Non-Reserved 3 |
| SREJ | Selective Reject | SIM | Set Initialization Mode |
| UI | Unnumbered Information | RIM | Request Initialization Mode |
| SNRM | Set Normal Response Mode | FRMR | Frame Reject |
| DISC | Disconnect | SARM | Set Async Response Mode |
| RD | Request Disconnect | SARME | Set ARM Extended Mode |
| UP | Unnumbered Poll | SNRM | Set Normal Response Mode |
| RSET | Reset | SNRME | Set NRM Extended Mode |
| XID | Exchange Identification | SABM | Set Async Balanced 3 Mode |
| DM | Disconnect Mode | SABME | Set ABM Extended Mode |
| • | The P/F Bit | | |

The Unnumbered Information (UI) format allows for transmission of user data in an unnumbered (i.e., unsequenced) frame. The UI frame actually is a form of connectionless-mode link protocol in that the absence of the N(S) and N(R) fields precludes flow-controlling and acknowledging frames. The IEEE 802.2 logical link control (LLC) protocol uses this approach with its LLC Type 1 version of HDLC.

The Request Initialization Mode (RIM) format is a request from a secondary station for initialization to a primary station. Once the secondary station sends RIM, it can monitor frames, but it can respond only to SIM, DISC, TEST, or XID.

The Set Normal Response Mode (SNRM) places the secondary station in the Normal Response Mode (NRM). The NRM precludes the secondary station from sending any unsolicited frames. This means the primary station controls all frame flow on the line.

The Disconnect (DISC) places the secondary station in the disconnected mode. This command is valuable for switched lines; the command provides a function similar to hanging up a telephone. UA is the expected response.

The Disconnect Mode (DM) is transmitted from a secondary station to indicate it is in the disconnect mode (not operational).

The Test (TEST) frame is used to solicit testing responses from the secondary station. HDLC does not stipulate how the TEST frames are to be used. An implementation can use the I field for diagnostic purposes, for example.

The Set Asynchronous Response Mode (SARM) allows a secondary station to transmit without a poll from the primary station. It places the secondary station in the information transfer state (IS) of ARM.

The Set Asynchronous Balanced Mode (SABM) sets mode to ABM, in which stations are peers with each other. No polls are required to transmit, since each station is a combined station.

The Set Normal Response Mode Extended (SNRME) sets SNRM with two octets in the control field. This is used for extended sequencing and permits the N(S) and N(R) to be seven bits in length, thus increasing the window to a range of 1-127.

The Set Asynchronous Balanced Mode Extended (SABME) sets SAMB with two octets in the control field for extended sequencing.

The Unnumbered Poll (UP) polls a station without regard to sequencing or acknowledgment. Response is optional if the poll bit is set to 0. This provides for one response opportunity.

The Reset (RSET) is used as follows: the transmitting station resets its N(S) and receiving station resets its N(R). The command is used for recovery. Previously unacknowledged frames remain unacknowledged.

## HDLC TIMERS

The vendors vary in how they implement link level timers in a product. HDLC defines two timers T1 and T2. Most implementations use T1 in some fashion. T2 is used, but not as frequently as T1. The timers are employed in the following manner:

T1:  A primary station issues a P bit and checks whether a response is received to the P bit within a defined time. This function is controlled by the timer T1 and is called the "wait for F" time-out.

T2:  A station in the ARM mode that issues I frames checks whether acknowledgments are received within a timer period. This function is controlled by timer T2 and is called "wait for N(R)" time-out.

Since ARM is not used much today, timer T1 typically is invoked to handle the T2 functions.

To examine T1 further, refer to Figure 6-5. The state diagram for a primary station time-out function is illustrated (with a normal response mode [NRM]). Box 6-1 explains the use of the timer for NRM.

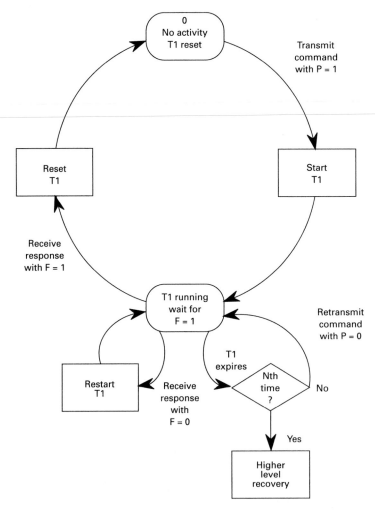

**Figure 6-5.** HDLC T1 Activity [ECMA 79]

---

**BOX 6-1.** T1 ACTIVITY AT PRIMARY STATION

| Action | Reason |
|---|---|
| Start T1 from 0 | When a command is sent with P = 1 |
| Restart T1 from 0 | When a response is received with F = 1 |
| Reset T1 to 0 | When a response is received with F = 1 |
| Retransmit command with P = 1 | T1 expires |

---

## SUMMARY OF THE MAJOR HDLC OPERATIONS

Figure 6-6 shows the operations of several of the major HDLC/LAPB entities' operations within the data link layer. Using the concepts of encapsulation and decapsulation (discussed in Chapter 1), the fields of the HDLC frame are constructed at the transmit side and used at the receive side to invoke the desired operations. The order of the operations is important. For example, it makes no sense to perform the bit- stuffing operations at the transmit side until all bits in the frame have been constructed. Also, the last event at the transmit side is the placement of the flags in front of, and behind the frame. This operation occurs after the bit stuffing, since it makes no sense to bit-stuff the flags.

## THE HDLC SCHEMA

The overall HDLC schema is shown in Figure 6-7. Two options are provided for unbalanced links (Normal Response Mode [UN] and Asynchronous Response Mode [UA]) and one for balanced (Asynchronous Balanced Mode [BA]).

In order to classify a protocol conveniently, the terms *UN, UA,* and *BA* are used to denote which subset of HDLC is used. In addition, most subsets use the functional extensions. For example, a protocol classified as UN 3,7 uses the unbalanced normal response mode option and the selective reject and extended address functional extensions.

### Examples of HDLC Link Operations

Figures 6-8 through 6-11 are provided as examples of several HDLC link operations. Each figure is accompanied with a short explanation of the events taking place on the link. Note that the figures are drawn with the frames occupying the link in nonvarying time slots. Although usually not the case, this approach keeps the illustrations relatively

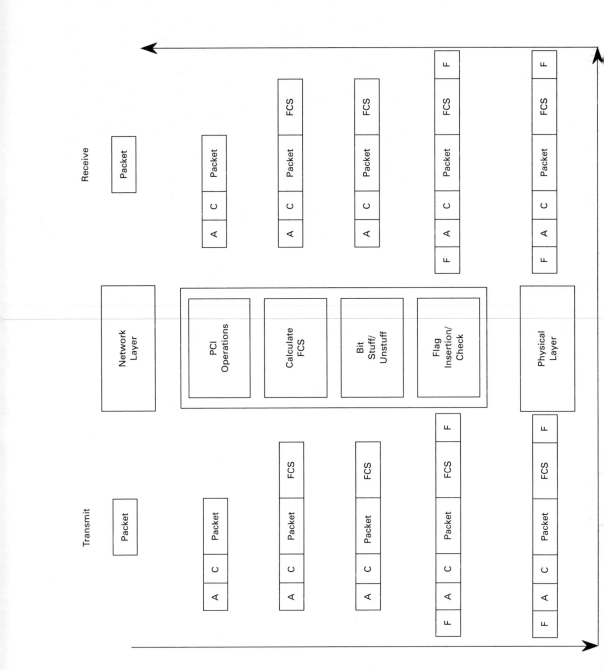

**Figure 6-6.** Major HDLC Operations

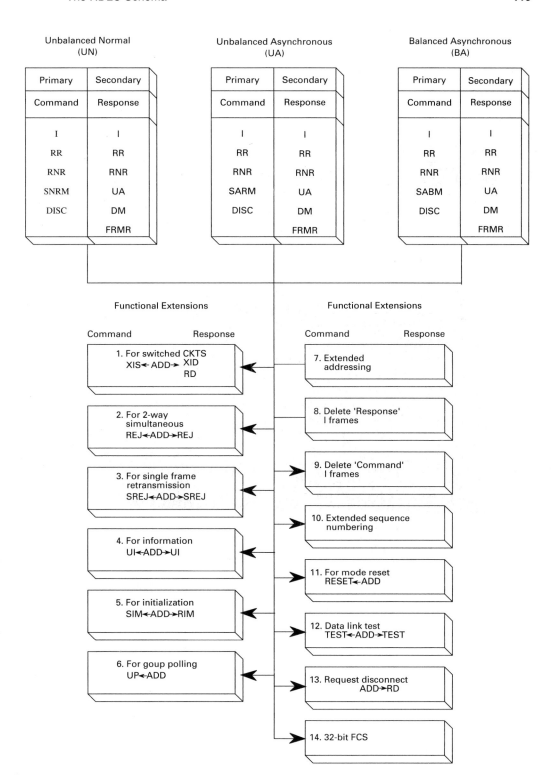

**Figure 6-7.** HDLC Schema/Set

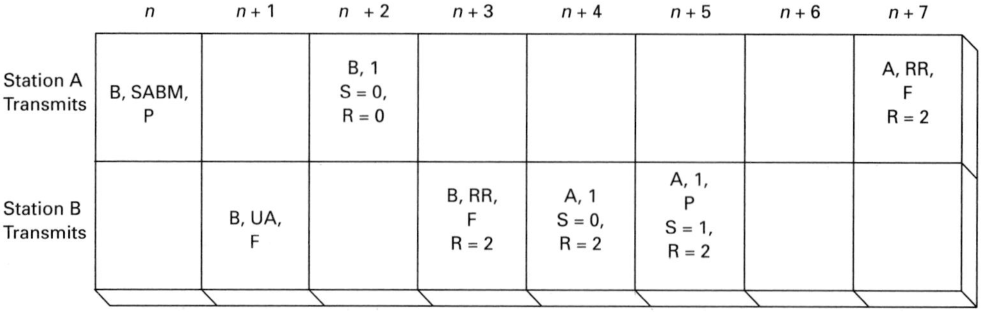

| | n | n + 1 | n + 2 | n + 3 | n + 4 | n + 5 | n + 6 | n + 7 |
|---|---|---|---|---|---|---|---|---|
| Station A Transmits | B, SABM, P | | B, 1, S = 0, R = 0 | | | | | A, RR, F, R = 2 |
| Station B Transmits | | B, UA, F | | B, RR, F, R = 2 | A, 1 S = 0, R = 2 | A, 1, P S = 1, R = 2 | | |

Legend (1 means 1 field present):

n: Station A transmits *Set Asynchronous Balanced Mode* (SABM) command with P bit set.

n + 1: Station B responds with an *Unnumbered Acknowledgment* (UA) response with F bit set.

n + 2, 3: Station A sends information frames 0 and 1, sets P bit.

n + 4, 5, 6: Station B acknowledges A's transmission by sending 2 in the receive sequence number field. Station B also transmits information frames 0 and 1, and sets P = 1.

n + 7: Station B acknowledges A's frames of 1 and 2 with N(R) = 2 and responds to P = 1 with F = 1.

**Figure 6-8.** Asynchronous Balanced Mode with Half-Duplex Data Flow (using P/F for checkpointing)

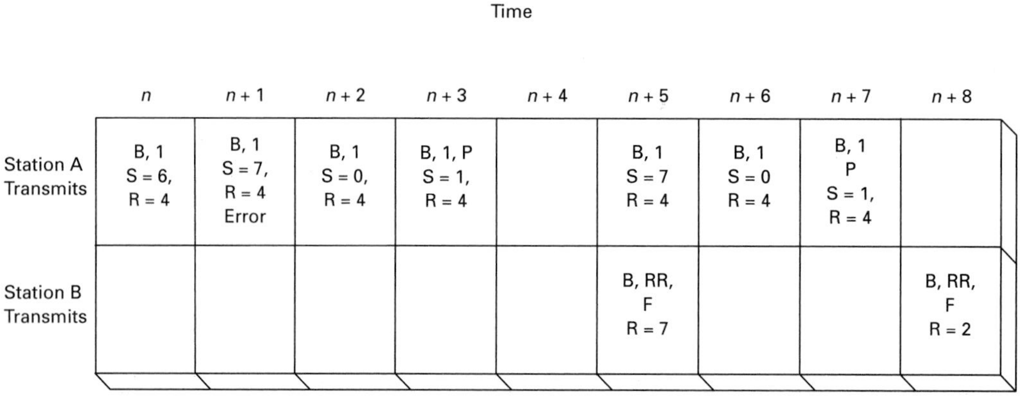

Time

| | n | n + 1 | n + 2 | n + 3 | n + 4 | n + 5 | n + 6 | n + 7 | n + 8 |
|---|---|---|---|---|---|---|---|---|---|
| Station A Transmits | B, 1, S = 6, R = 4 | B, 1, S = 7, R = 4 Error | B, 1, S = 0, R = 4 | B, 1, P, S = 1, R = 4 | | B, 1 S = 7 R = 4 | B, 1 S = 0 R = 4 | B, 1 P S = 1, R = 4 | |
| Station B Transmits | | | | | | B, RR, F, R = 7 | | | B, RR, F, R = 2 |

Figure illustrates an Ongoing Session

Legend (1 means 1 field present):

n, n + 1, 2, 3: Station A sends information frames 6, 7, 0, and 1

n + 4: Station returns a *Receive Ready* (RR) with a send sequence number of 7 and a final bit. This means station B is expecting to receive frame 7 again (and all frames transmitted after 7).

n + 5, 6, 7: Station A retransmits frames 7, 0 and 1 and sets the P bit for a checkpoint.

n + 8: Station B acknowledges frames 7, 0, and 1 with a *Receive Ready* (RR) and a receive sequence number of 2, and sets the F bit.

**Figure 6-9.** An SDLC Error-Recovery Operation

Time

| | $n$ | $n + 1$ | $n + 2$ | $n + 3$ | $n + 4$ | $n + 5$ | $n + 6$ |
|---|---|---|---|---|---|---|---|
| Station A Transmits | B, 1<br>S = 6,<br>R = 4 | B, 1<br>S = 7,<br>R = 4<br>(Error) | B, 1<br>S = 0,<br>R = 4 | B, RR<br>F<br>R = 4 | B, 1<br>S = 7<br>R = 4 | B, 1<br>S = 0<br>R = 4 | |
| Station B Transmits | | | A, REJ,<br>P<br>R = 7 | | | | B, RR,<br>R = 1 |

Figure illustrates an Ongoing Session

Legend (1 means 1 field present)
$n$, $n + 1$, 2: Station A sends information frames 6, 7 and 0. Station B defects an error in frame 7, and immediately sends a *Reject* frame with a receive sequence number of 7. Notice the use of the address field and P bit to depict a command frame.

$n + 3$, 4, 5: Station A returns an RR and retransmits the erroneous frames.

$n + 6$: Station B acknowledges the retransmission.

**Figure 6-10.** An LAPB Error-Recovery Operation

simple. The illustrations are accurate conceptually. The figures depict the following link configurations:

Figure 6-8:     Link setup with SABM and half-duplex operations
Figure 6-9:     A typical error recovery with a NRM link
Figure 6-10:    A typical error recovery with an ABM link
Figure 6-11:    A multipoint operation

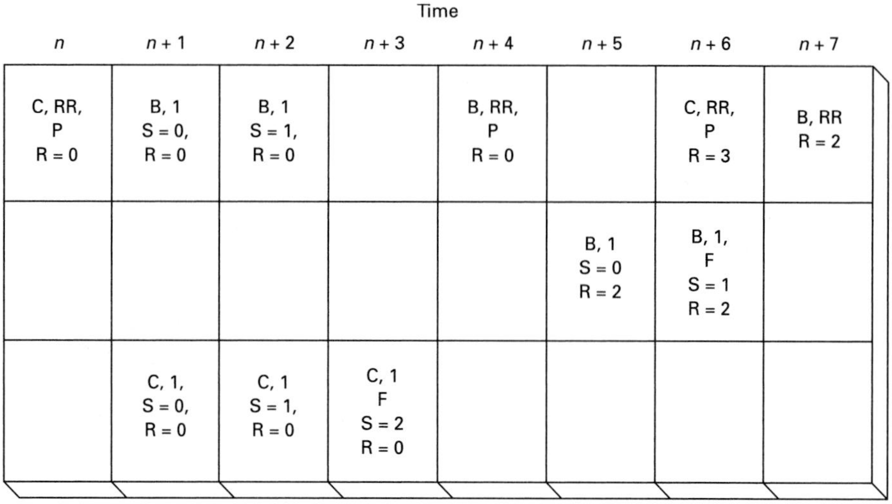

Time

| | $n$ | $n+1$ | $n+2$ | $n+3$ | $n+4$ | $n+5$ | $n+6$ | $n+7$ |
|---|---|---|---|---|---|---|---|---|
| | C, RR, P R = 0 | B, 1 S = 0, R = 0 | B, 1 S = 1, R = 0 | | B, RR, P R = 0 | | C, RR, P R = 3 | B, RR R = 2 |
| | | | | | | B, 1 S = 0 R = 2 | B, 1, F S = 1 R = 2 | |
| | | C, 1, S = 0, R = 0 | C, 1, S = 1, R = 0 | C, 1 F S = 2 R = 0 | | | | |

Figure illustrates an Ongoing Session

Legend (1 means 1 field present)

*n:* Station A uses *Receive Ready* command to poll station C with bit set.

*n* + 1, 2: Station A sends frames 0 and 1 to B, which station C responds to the previous poll and sends frames 0 and 1 to A on the other subchannel of the full-duplex circuit.

*n* + 3: Station C sends information frame 2 and sets final bit.

*n* + 4: Station A polls B for a checkpoint (confirmation).

*n* + 5: Station B responds by acknowledging A's 0 and 1 frames with a receive sequence of 2.

*n* + 6: Station A acknowledges C's frames 0, 1 and 2 with a *Receive Ready* (RR) and a receive sequence of 3. Station B sends frame 1, and sets F to 1 in response to the P bit in n + 4.

n + 7: Station A acknowledges B's frames 0 and 1 with a *Receive Ready* (RR) and a receive sequence of 2.

**Figure 6-11.** An SDLC Multipoint Operation

## SUMMARY

HDLC serves as a foundation for many widely used data link protocols. Its features of asynchronous balanced mode and normal response mode provide a flexible means of configuring point-to-point, peer-to-peer operations or multipoint master/slave operations. The HDLC family has spread into the inventory of practically every vendor offering a data link control product.

# 7

# *LAPB*

## INTRODUCTION

This chapter examines balanced protocol, the link access procedure more commonly known as LAPB. The relationship of LAPB and HDLC is explained. The LAPB frame is analyzed, as well as the rules for coding the address field in the frame. LAPB acts as the link control protocol for X.25-based networks; therefore, the relationship of LAPB and X.25 is explored.

## OVERVIEW OF X.25

In the late 1960s and early 1970s, many data communications networks using packet switching technology were created by companies, government agencies, and other organizations. The design and programming of these networks were performed by each organization to fulfill specific business needs. During this time, an organization had no reason to adhere to any common convention for its data communications network interface protocols, since the organization's private network provided services only to itself. Consequently, these networks used specialized protocols tailored to satisfy the organization's unique requirements.

The public network vendors were faced with answering a major question—how can the network best provide the interface for a user's terminal or computer to the network? X.25 came about largely because these networks recognized that a common data communications network interface protocol was needed, especially from the perspective of the network owners.

The following list summarizes the main tasks of X.25:

- The management of virtual circuits between the network and the user
- The creation and use of headers for the control and data packets
- The exchange of packets between the local DTE and DCE and the remote DTE and DCE, with extensive rules for flow control, sequencing, and error-checking
- The provision of certain network services (called facilities in X.25) between the communicating DTEs

X.25 operates with logical channels. A logical channel is one in which a user perceives the existence of a dedicated physical circuit between the DTE and the DCE. However, the physical circuit usually is allocated to multiple users. Through the use of statistical multiplexing techniques, different users' packets are interleaved onto one physical channel. Ideally, the channel performance is good enough to ensure that each user does not notice degraded service from other traffic on the channel.

X.25 uses logical channel numbers (LCNs) to identify each DTE X.25 session with its local DCE. As many as 4,095 logical channels and user sessions can be assigned to a physical channel, although not all numbers actually are assigned at one time, due to performance considerations.

X.25 connects a user to the packet network either with a permanent virtual circuit or a switched virtual call. *A permanent virtual circuit* (PVC) is analogous to a leased line in a telephone network. The transmitting DTE is assured of obtaining a session (connection) with the receiving DTE through the packet network. X.25 requires a permanent virtual circuit be established before the session begins. Consequently, an agreement must be reached by the two users and the packet network carrier before a permanent virtual connection will be allocated. Among other things, this includes the reservation of an LCN for the PVC user.

Thereafter, when a transmitting DTE sends a packet into the packet network, the identifying logical channel number in the packet indicates that the requesting DTE has a permanent virtual circuit connection to the receiving DTE. Consequently, services will be provided by the network and the receiving DTE without further session negotiation. PVC requires no call setup or clearing procedures, and the logical channel continuously is in a data transfer state.

A *switched virtual call* resembles some of the procedures associated with telephone dial-up lines, because call setup and breakdown procedures are employed. The *calling* DTE issues a special X.25 packet called a *Call Request packet* to the network with a logical channel number and the address of the *called* DTE. The network uses the address to route the Call Request packet to the DCE that is to support the call at the remote end. This DCE then sends an *Incoming Call packet* to the proper DTE.

Logical channel numbering is done on each side of the network, and the logical channel number at the local DTE/DCE most likely is a different value than the logical channel number at the remote DTE/DCE. The critical requirement is to keep the specific DTE-to-DTE session identified at all times with the same pair of LCNs. Inside the network, the intermediate packet-switching nodes also may perform their own LCN numbering, but X.25 does not require LCN identification within a network. Remember, the activities within the network are beyond the scope of the X.25 Recommendation.

If the receiving DTE chooses to acknowledge and accept the call request, it transmits a *Call Accepted packet* to the network. The network then transports this packet to the requesting DTE in the form of a *Call Connected packet.* The channel enters a data transfer state after the call establishment. This action has created an end-to-end virtual circuit.

After a session has been created, X.25 provides strict rules on the manner in which the user's data can "enter" and "exit" the packet network. Many procedures are invoked to take care of the user data, such as flow control, sequencing, ACKs, resets, diagnostics, and so on.

## The X.25 Layers

The X.25 Recommendation is divided into three layers (see Figure 7-1). It consists of entities that reside in the lower three layers of the OSI model. The physical layer provides the physical signaling and connections between the user DTE and the DCE. At this layer, standards such as X.21, X.21bis, EIA-232-D, and V.35 are used. This layer also is called X.25, Layer 1.

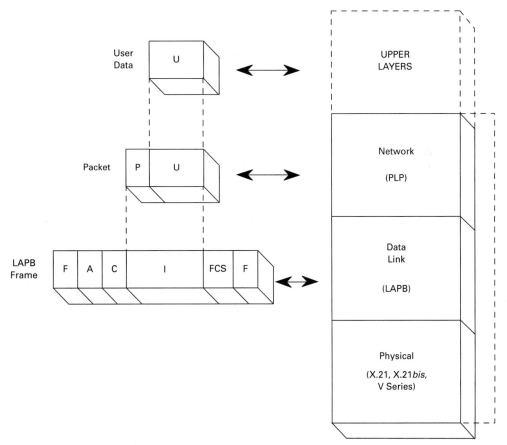

**Figure 7-1.** The Layers of X.25

As one might expect, the data link layer is responsible for the management of the flow of data between the user DTE and the network DCE. It performs error checking and retransmits the data if they are distorted during the transfer on the link. It is responsible for the error-free transmission of the X.25 packet across the link. This layer uses the LAPB protocol (link access procedure, balanced). It also is called the *frame level,* because it creates and uses the LAPB frame.

The network layer is responsible for creating the X.25 packet and managing the connection with the network through the exchange of packets with the DCE. It relies on the data link layer to transport the packet safely between the DTE and the DCE. It also is called packet layer procedures (PLP) and X.25, Layer 3. Notice from Figure 7-1 that the packet is encapsulated into the frame for transmission to/from the DTE and the DCE.

## THE ROLE OF LAPB IN AN X.25-BASED NETWORK

The role of LAPB in the X.25-based network is to deliver safely the X.25 packet between the user device (DTE) and the packet network (DCE). Since X.25 is a network interface protocol and does not define the actions within the packet network, LAPB also resides only at the X.25 interface between the DTE and the network. This interface is shown in Figure 7-2.

Therefore, the LAPB functions are quite restricted in relation to the entire packet network. This is not to say that LAPB could not be used inside the network; however, that option is for the network administrator to consider.

## MAJOR FEATURES OF LAPB

LAPB is aligned closely with HDLC. Readers not familiar with HDLC should read Chapter 6 before proceeding further into this chapter. The focus now is on some of the more detailed aspects of LAPB.

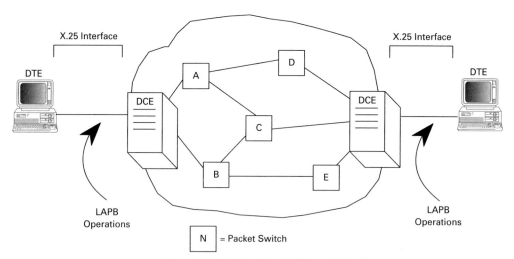

**Figure 7-2.** LAPB and the X.25 Network Interface

## THE LAPB SUBSET CLASSIFICATION

LAPB is classified as a BA 2,8 or BA 2,8,10 subset of HDLC. Figure 7-3 depicts these subsets. The shaded boxes show which HDLC procedures LAPB uses. Option 2 provides for simultaneous rejection of frames in a two-way transmission mode. Option 8 does not permit the transmitting of information in the response frames. This restriction presents no problem, since in the asynchronous balanced mode, the information can be transferred in command frames. Because both stations are combined stations, both can transmit commands at any time. Moreover, with LAPB, the sending of a command frame with the

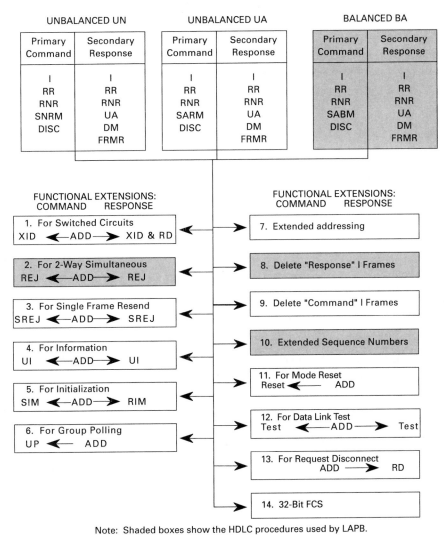

Note: Shaded boxes show the HDLC procedures used by LAPB.

**Figure 7-3.** The LAPB Subset

P bit = 1 occurs when the station wants a "status" frame (unnumbered or supervisory) and not an information frame. Consequently, the responding station is not expected to return an I field.

Option 10 provides for extended sequencing, which permits the N(S) and N(R) fields to be extended from the default length of 3 bits to 7 bits. The next section explains the use of extended sequencing, as well as the associated format.

## EXTENDED SEQUENCING

In 1984 LAPB was modified to allow extended sequencing. The effect of this change provides seven bits each for N(S) and N(R). Prior to the 1984 change, the 3-bit sequence space did not support a sequence number large enough to prevent a station from shutting itself down after all the sequence numbers had been used to sequence each outgoing frame. This problem became evident as LAPB was placed on links of higher speed and on links with longer propagation delay. For example, with geosynchronous satellite links (when the distance from the transmitter to the receiver is approximately 22,300 miles), the small 3-bit sequence number of 0 through 7 was exhausted before the receiver of the traffic had an opportunity to return an acknowledgment and slide the transmitter's windows forward to allow the reuse of the sequence numbers. The solution was to increase the number of bits in the sending and receiving fields, as depicted in Figure 7-4.

While the implementation of extended sequencing was initiated to satisfy circuits with long propagation delays, the use of these sequence numbers also is useful on links that have very high bit-transfer rates. For example, high-speed local area networks and optical fiber lines that operate in the megabit per second rate will exhaust quickly the possible numbers for a three-bit sequence field. For this reason, extended sequence numbering is used frequently with the LAPB protocol.

## TIMERS AND PARAMETERS

HDLC defines three timers, T1, T2, and T3. Most implementations use T1 in some fashion. T2 is used, though not as frequently as T1. LAPB also defines a third timer, T3, which is relatively new and is not implemented in all vendors' products. The timers are used in the following manner:

T1:     A primary station sends a frame and checks whether a response is received to the P-bit within a defined time. This function is controlled by the timer T1 and is called the "wait for F" time-out.

T2:     T2 is set to the amount of time available at the DTE or DCE before an acknowledging frame must be sent.

T3:     In LAPB, this timer is used to signify to the network level that an excessively long idle time is occurring on the link. LAPB requires that T3 > T1.

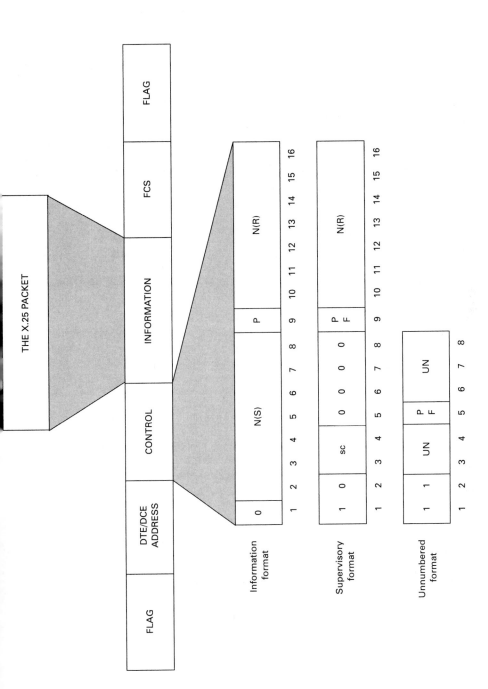

**Figure 7-4.** LAPB Extended Sequencing

SC: Supervisory Codes
UN: Unnumbered Codes

125

N2:          HDLC also defines this parameter. It is set to the number of times a frame
             will be retransmitted. If this parameter is exceeded, the link is considered
             out of order.

## LINK SETUP CONVENTIONS

Table 7-1 shows the commands and responses in the LAPB Recommendation. It is
evident that LAPB uses the HDLC commands/responses. This table shows the two LAPB
sequencing options established with SABM and SABME frames. The use of a modulo 8
operation uses the N(S) and N(R) fields of three bits to make up the sequence numbers
1–7. This option is established with SABM and is explained in the HDLC chapter
(Chapter 6) with some illustrations, so it is not repeated here. Figure 7-4 depicts the
modulo 128 operation, which uses a sequence number range between 1 and 127 [seven
bits in N(R) and N(S)]. This option is established with SABME. Using modulo 8, the
stations can send up to 7 frames without receiving an acknowledgment (also called a
transmit window of 7). With modulo 128, the window ranges from 1 to 127.

As discussed earlier, extended sequencing using SABME was added to LAPB in
1984 because certain links, such as satellite circuits and optical fibers, exhaust the
numbers of 1–7 before an acknowledgment is transmitted back to the transmitting station.
Larger transmit windows allow a greater range of sequence numbers to be used, which
reduces the possibility of a transmitting site having to close its transmit window due to
using all its send sequence number values.

## LAPB LINK ESTABLISHMENT

The LAPB link is set up by the user device (DTE) or the packet exchange DCE. The
SABM/SABME commands set up the link and turn on its T1 timer in order to determine
when it should expect a reply. Figure 7-5 illustrates how a link is established.

**TABLE 7-1.** LAPB AND THE CONTROL FIELD (MODULO 8)

| Format Responses | Control Field Bit Encoding | | | | | | | | Commands | |
|---|---|---|---|---|---|---|---|---|---|---|
|  | 1 | 2 | 3 | 4 | 5 | 6 | 7 | 8 |  |  |
| Information | 0 | - | N(S) | - | P | - | N(R) | - | I | I |
| Supervisory | 1 | 0 | 0 | 0 | P/F | - | N(R) | - | RR | RR |
|  | 1 | 0 | 0 | 1 | P/F | - | N(R) | - | REJ | REJ |
|  | 1 | 0 | 1 | 0 | P/F | - | N(R) | - | RNR | RNR |
| Unnumbered | 1 | 1 | 0 | 0 | P | 0 | 1 | 0 | DISC |  |
|  | 1 | 1 | 0 | 0 | F | 1 | 1 | 0 |  | UA |
|  | 1 | 1 | 1 | 0 | F | 0 | 0 | 1 |  | FRMR |
|  | 1 | 1 | 1 | 1 | F | 0 | 0 | 0 |  | DM |
|  | 1 | 1 | 1 | 1 | P | 1 | 0 | 0 | SABM |  |

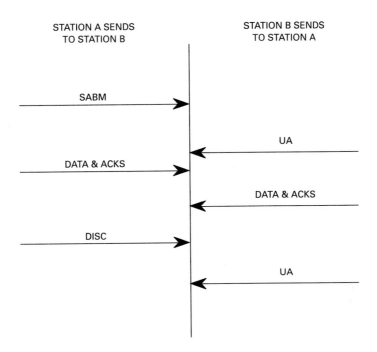

STATION A SENDS
TO STATION B

STATION B SENDS
TO STATION A

SABM

UA

DATA & ACKS

DATA & ACKS

DISC

UA

**Figure 7-5.** LAPB Link Setup and Disconnect (SABM Operations)

Either station may perform link establishment. A station indicates it is able to set up the link by transmitting continuous flags. Prior to link setup, either station can send DISC to make certain all traffic and modes are cleared. If the link cannot be set up, DM must be returned.

If the receiving station accepts the SABM/SABME, it sends back a UA frame. Upon receipt of the UA frame, the station resets its send and receive state variables to zero and stops the T1 timer. The link is then ready for the transmission of traffic. The link will not accept any other frames after issuing the link setup commands except another SABM/SABME, UA, or DM.

A station can disconnect the link at any time by issuing the DISC command. A UA is the expected response. After entering the disconnect phase, a station may initiate link setup again with a SABM or a SABME. If the initiation is successful, the UA is returned.

It is possible that the two stations may receive frames that are inconsistent logically. For example, both stations simultaneously could issue a SABM command. This problem is called a *frame collision*. LAPB requires that if a collision of the same unnumbered commands occurs, both stations shall send a UA response as soon as possible. If the commands are different, both stations must enter the disconnected phase and issue a DM response as soon as possible. The purpose of these rules is to bring the link back to a state that permits the reinitialization for link setup.

Even though the SABM/SABME frames are link setup commands, they also can be used to clear any busy signal that was established by an earlier RNR frame. Upon acceptance of the SABM/SABME frame, the state variables must be set to zero, and any previously transmitted I frames that are unacknowledged will remain unacknowledged. In other words, this operation causes the loss of outstanding frames. LAPB does not recover from the loss of these frames, and a higher-level protocol is responsible for recovery actions.

## LAPB ADDRESSING CONVENTIONS

X.25 requires that the LAPB address field designate the DTE as A and DCE as B (where A = 00000011 and B = 00000001, with low-order bits shown to the right). The address field actually is used to identify the frame as a command or response. The command frame contains the address of the receiving DTE or DCE. The response frame contains the address of the sending DTE or DCE.

In summary:

- DTE issues:  Command frames with address B/Response frames with address A
- DCE issues:  Command frames with address A/Response frames with address B

## LAPB USE OF P/F BIT

LAPB has specific procedures for the use of the P/F bit. The station, upon receiving a SABM/SABME, DISC, Supervisory, or I frame with the P = 1, must set the F to 1 in the next response it transmits. The following conventions apply:

| FRAME SENT WITH P-BIT SET TO 1 | RESPONSE REQUIRED WITH F-BIT SET TO 1 |
|---|---|
| SABM/SABME,DISC. | UA, DM |
| I (Information transfer) | RR, REJ, RNR, FRMR |
| I (Disconnected mode) | DM |
| Supervisory (RR,RNR,REJ) | RR, REJ, RNR, FRMR |

## THE POLL/FINAL BIT

The fifth bit position in the control field is called the P/F or poll/final bit. It is recognized only when set to 1 and is used by the primary and secondary stations to provide dialogue with each other. To amplify from Chapter 6:

- The primary station uses the P bit = 1 to solicit a response frame from a secondary station. The P bit signifies a poll. The P bit = 1 is used with LAPB to request a status frame and not an I frame.
- The secondary station responds to a P bit with data or a status frame and with the F bit = 1. LAPB sends back only a status frame with an unnumbered or supervisory format. It does not permit an information frame to be returned in the response. The F bit also can signify end-of-transmission from the secondary station under Normal

Response Mode (NRM). With LAPB, it means the polled station has fulfilled its responsibility to respond, and the station can continue to transmit frames.

The P/F bit is called the P bit when used by the primary station and the F bit when used by the secondary station. LAPB permits one P bit (awaiting an F bit response) to be outstanding at any time on the link. Consequently, a P set to 1 can be used as a checkpoint. That is, the P = 1 means, "Respond to me, because I want to know your status."

How does a station know if a received frame with the fifth bit = 1 is an F or P bit? After all, it is in the same bit position in all frames. HDLC uses the address field for the following purpose. The fifth bit is a P bit and the frame is a command if the address field contains the address of the *receiving* station; it is an F bit and the frame is a response if the address is that of the *transmitting* station. This distinction is quite important, because

**TABLE 7-2.** LAPB REQUIRED ACTIONS FOR COMMANDS AND RESPONSES

| | | |
|---|---|---|
| RR | (1) | Clears a busy condition set with RNR. |
| | (2) | With P = 1, asks station for its status. |
| RNR | (1) | With P = 1, asks station for its status. |
| | (2) | A station is not allowed to transmit I frames upon receiving RNR. |
| REJ | (1) | Requests a retransmission of frames beginning with N(R). |
| | (2) | Only one REJ can be outstanding at a time. |
| | (3) | Condition is cleared when an I frame is received with its N(S) equal to the N(R) in the initial REJ frame. |
| | (4) | With P = 1, asks station for its status. |
| | (5) | Can clear a busy condition that was set by RNR. |
| SABM | (1) | Clears any busy condition. |
| | (2) | Clears values in V(S) and V(R). |
| | (3) | Previously unacknowledged frames remain unacknowledged. |
| | (4) | Expects a UA in response. |
| DISC | (1) | Terminates previous mode. |
| | (2) | Notifies receiver that transmitting station is suspending operation. |
| | (3) | Expects a UA in response. |
| | (4) | Previously unacknowledged frames remain unacknowledged. |
| UA | (1) | Clears a busy condition. |
| | (2) | Received mode-setting commands are not acted upon until UA is transmitted. |
| DM | (1) | Used to report status. |
| | (2) | Can be sent with or without a preceding DISC command. |
| | (3) | Monitors received commands; if it receives an SABM and it cannot act, then it sends DM. |
| FRMR | (1) | Received a command or response field that is not used by LAPB. |
| | (2) | I field is too long. |
| | (3) | Invalid N(R) received. |
| | (4) | I field is in a frame other than an I frame. |
| | (5) | Supervisory or unnumbered frame received with incorrect length. |
| | (6) | An error condition noted that is not recoverable by retransmission of the identical frame. |

a station may react differently to the two types of frames. For example, a command (address of receiver, P = 1) requires the station to send back specific types of frames.

## LAPB Actions with Commands and Responses

LAPB requires exact actions with the command and response frames. These rules are essential to the operation of an unambiguous protocol between the DTE and the DCE. If a station issues a frame that is not acceptable to the receiving station, the frame usually is rejected, with the frame control field coded as a reject. These rules are summarized in Table 7-2.

## LAPB EXCEPTION CONDITIONS

LAPB provides several procedures for the recovery of the following exception conditions:

> Busy condition
> N(S) sequence error condition
> Invalid frame condition
> Frame rejection condition
> Excessive idle channel time condition

A *busy condition* occurs when a station is unable to receive I frames due to internal problems. The RNR frame must be transmitted from the busy station. When a busy condition is to be cleared, a transmission of UA, SABM, SABME, RR, or REJ is permitted.

If LAPB encounters the *N(S) sequence error condition*, it discards the out-of-sequence frames. This condition occurs when an I frame is received in which the value of N(S) does not equal the receive state variable V(R). LAPB is very clever in this regard. When any problem with a frame is detected by the receiver, it does not increment its receive state variable. As a consequence, when it returns the value of an acknowledge frame [in the N(R) field] back to the transmitter, this value is different from the transmitter's send state variable. This condition alerts the transmitter that it must go back to the value contained in the N(R) field and begin the retransmission of the frames from that point forward.

Be aware that LAPB does not allow the N(R) field, unto itself, to mean any type of negative acknowledgment. Some link protocols, such as SDLC, do allow implicit rejection of frames. With LAPB, a negative acknowledgment can occur only with the use of the N(R) field with the reject frame.

The *invalid frame condition* occurs because of the conditions listed in the FRMR. The *frame rejection condition* occurs because of the conditions discussed earlier.

Finally, the *excessive idle time condition* occurs because the station waits for a specified period within the value of T3 without taking any action. It must wait for a detection of a return-to-active channel state. However, if T3 expires, a higher level of protocol is notified of the excessive idle channel state condition. LAPB does not attempt any remedial actions.

LAPB handles the frame check sequence error with a series of actions. Table 7-3 describes these actions.

**TABLE 7-3.**  LAPB CONVENTIONS FOR AN FCS ERROR

1. A frame with an FCS error is discarded and no action is taken as a result of that frame.
2. This means V(R) is not incremented.
3. Therefore, the next valid frame will have a N(S) that does not equal the receiver's V(R).
4. The REJ frame will be used to initiate a recovery. (The REJ is a command. If an acknowledged transfer of the retransmission request is required, P = 1; otherwise, it can be a response.)
5. The received REJ will require the sending station to set its V(S) to equal the N(R) in the REJ and:
   (a) In all cases, if other unacknowledged I frames already had been transmitted following the one indicated in the REJ, then those frames will be retransmitted by this station following the requested I frame. The "rejecting" station will then discard the I field of all I frames until the expected I frame is correctly received.
   (b) If the REJ frame is a P = 1, the station first will transmit RR, RNR, or REJ with F = 1, before sending the corresponding I frame.
6. X.25 further requires the packet exchange DCE to handle the received REJ in the following manner:
   (a) If the DCE is transmitting a supervisory command or response when it receives the REJ frame, it will complete that transmission before commencing transmission of the requested I frame.
   (b) If the DCE is transmitting an unnumbered command or response when it receives the REJ frame, it will ignore the request for retransmission.
   (c) If the DCE is transmitting an I frame when the REJ frame is received, it may abort the I frame and commence transmission of the requested I frame immediately after abortion.
   (d) If the DCE is not transmitting any frame when the REJ frame is received, it will commence transmission of the requested I frame immediately.

## INFORMATION TRANSFER STATES

Like many communications protocols, LAPB is state-driven. While executing a specific state, it: (a) accepts certain types of frames for action, (b) rejects other frames that are logically inconsistent with the state, and (c) ignores frames that have no bearing on the state and the activities on the link. An example of the actions pertaining to one state (the information transfer state) is shown in Table 7-4.

Finally, a few more words are in order regarding the disconnect commands and responses. LAPB uses the disconnect command to terminate previous mode settings. This action is used infrequently because modes usually are static with either SABM or SABME. The disconnect also can be used to inform the other station that a station is suspending operations. The UA is the expected response to the disconnect command. Be aware that disconnect commands will cause unacknowledged I frames to be discarded and lost. As stated before, higher-level protocols are responsible for any lost frames.

The disconnect mode response can be used by either station to indicate that it has entered a disconnect phase, even though it may not have received the disconnect command. It also can be a response to the receipt of a mode-setting command to inform the station that it is in a disconnected phase and cannot accept the command.

**TABLE 7-4.** LAPB ACTIONS IN THE INFORMATION TRANSFER STATE

| Frame Received or an Event Occurs | Frame Sent | Change State To: |
|---|---|---|
| I, P=1 | RR, F=1 | - |
| RR, P=1 | RR, F=1 | - |
| REJ, P=1 | RR, F=1 | - |
| RNR, P=1 | RR, F=1 | Remote Station Busy |
| RNR, P=0 | RR, F=0 | Remote Station Busy |
| SABM, P=0 or 1 | UA, F=P | - |
| DISC, P=0 or 1 | UA, F=P | Disconnected |
| RR, F=1 | SABM, P=1 | Link Setup |
| REJ, F=1 | SABM, P=1 | Link Setup |
| RNR, F=1 | SABM, P=1 | Link Setup |
| RNR, F=0 | - | Remote Station Busy |
| UA, F=0 or 1 | SABM, P=1 | Link Setup |
| DM, F=1 or 0 | SABM, P=1 | Link Setup |
| FRMR, F=1 or 0 | SABM, P =1 | Link Setup |
| Local Start | SABM, P=1 | Link Setup |
| Local Stop | DISC, P=1 or 0 | Disconnect Request |
| Station Becomes Busy | RNR, F=P | Station Busy |
| T1 Expires | RR, P=1 | Waiting Acknowledgment |
| N2 Exceeded | SABM, P=1 | Link Setup |
| Invalid N(S) Received | REJ, F=P | REJ Frame Sent |
| Invalid N(R) Received | FRMR, P=1 | Frame Reject |
| Unrecognized Frame Received | FRMR, P=1 | Frame Reject |

## LAPB SERVICE DEFINITIONS

Until 1988, the CCITT did not publish an OSI-based protocol specification for the data link layer. However, link access procedure, balanced (LAPB) is indeed a protocol specification.

In the 1988 *Blue Books,* the CCITT has added an appendix to the X.212 service definition recommendation (Appendix III). The purpose of X.212 Appendix III is to establish how to define (through service definitions) the connection-mode data link services with the use of LAPB.

X.212 is a service definition recommendation. As such, it describes the primitives that are transferred between the network layer and the data link layer which define the services the data link layer is to perform for the network layer. From the context of LAPB, the X.212 primitives are mapped into LAPB frames in accordance with Table 7-5.

As can be seen from an examination of this table, the purpose of X.212 Appendix III is to provide a mapping function of the OSI X.212 service definitions to the LAPB protocol.

**TABLE 7-5.**  X.212 AND LAPB MAPPING

| X.212 Primitives | LAPB Frames |
|---|---|
| DL-CONNECT request | SABM or SABME |
| DL-CONNECT indication | SABM or SABME |
| DL-CONNECT response | UA |
| DL-CONNECT confirm | UA |
| DL-DISCONNECT request | DISC or DM |
| DL-DISCONNECT indication | DISC or DM |
| DL-DATA request | I Frame |
| DL-DATA indication | I Frame |
| DL-RESET request | SABM or SABME |
| DL-RESET indication | SABM or SABME |
| DL-RESET response | UA |
| DL-RESET confirm | UA |

| Primitive Parameters | Fields in the LAPB Frame |
|---|---|
| Called Address | Address Field (Note 1) |
| Calling Address | Address Field (Note 1) |
| Responding Address | Address Field (Note 1) |
| QOS Parameters | None (Note 2) |
| Originator & Reason | None (Note 2) |
| User Data | Information (I) field |

Note (1):   Contents are mapped according to LAPB's rules on identifying a command or a response.
Note (2):   Only one option is available to LAPB, so OSI options are not used in LAPB.

## EXAMPLES OF DATA LINK OPERATIONS

Figures 7-6 through 7-8 are provided as examples of LAPB link operations. Each figure shows the transmission of frames from station A to station B or from station B to station A. The term *station* refers to any type of machine that uses HDLC, such as a computer, a terminal, and so on.

Each figure is accompanied by an explanation of the activities on the link. The arrows depict the time sequences of the frame transmissions. The notation of "I" means the frame is carrying the information field, which contains user data and/or control information from the upper layers (typically, the X.25 packet, which is created in the network layer). The P/F indicator is used to show whether the poll/final (P/F) bit is set to 0 or 1. The N(S) and N(R) notations are used to show the values of the send and receive sequence numbers, respectively. The position of the fields in these figures does not show the order of field or bit transmission on the LAPB link. The fields are drawn to help in following the sequence of operations. The figures depict these link configurations:

Figure 7-6:    Normal data transfer;
Figure 7-7:    Timer operations; and
Figure 7-8:    An error recovery with REJ.

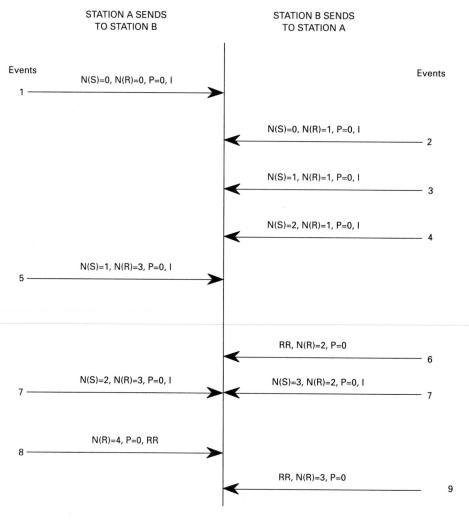

**Figure 7-6.** Normal Data Transfer

## Legend to accompany Figure 7-6

| Event(s) | Operation |
| --- | --- |
| 1 | Station A sends an information frame and sequences the frame with N(S) = 0. The N(R) = 0 means station A is expecting to receive a frame with its field of N(S) = 0. The P bit is set to 0, which means station A does not require station B to send any nondata frames. |
| 2–4 | Station B sends frames numbered N(S) = 0 through N(S) = 2. Its N(R) field is set to 1, which acknowledges station A's frame sent in Event 1( it had an N(S) value of 0). Remember, the N(R) value states that the station acknowledges all previously transmitted frames. The N(R) value also identifies the N(S) value that is expected from the other station. |
| 5 | Station A sends an I frame sequenced with N(S) = 1, which is the value station B expects next. Station A also sets the N(R) field to the value of 3, |

which inclusively acknowledges station B's previously transmitted frames numbered N(S) 0, 1, and 2.

6        Station B has no data to transmit. However, to prevent station A from "timing-out" and resending data, station B sends a receive ready (RR) frame with the N(R) = 2 to acknowledge station A's frame with N(S) = 1 (sent in Event 5).

7        The arrows depicting the frame flow from the two stations are aligned vertically with each other. This depiction means the two frames are transmitted from each station at about the same time and are exchanged almost simultaneously across the full-duplex link. The values of the N(R) and N(S) fields reflect the sequencing and acknowledgment frames of the previous events.

8–9      Stations A and B send RR frames to acknowledge the frames transmitted in Event 7.

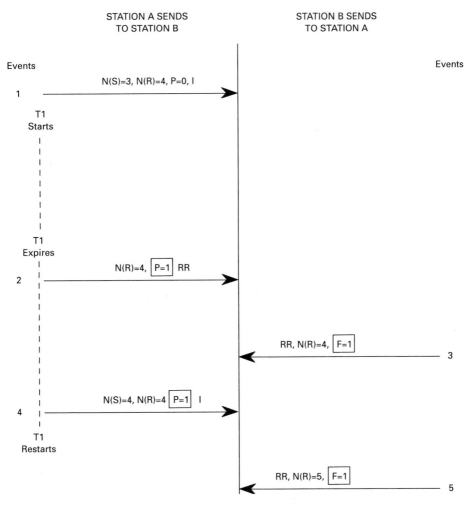

**Figure 7-7.** Timer Operations

## Legend to accompany Figure 7-7

Figure 7-7 illustrates how LAPB uses its transmit (T1) timer. In addition, it depicts how the P/F bit can be utilized to manage the flow of traffic between two stations.

| Event(s) | Operation |
| --- | --- |
| 1 | Station A sends an I frame and sequences it with N(S) = 3. |
| 2 | Station B does not respond within the bounds of the T1 timer, so station A times out and sends a receive ready (RR) command frame with the P bit set to 1. |
| 3 | Station B responds with F = 1 and acknowledges station A's frame by setting N(R) = 4. |
| 4 | Station A resets T1 and sends another I frame. It keeps the P bit set to 1 to force station B to respond (which is optional). |
| 5 | Station B responds with an RR frame with N(R) = 5 and F = 1. |

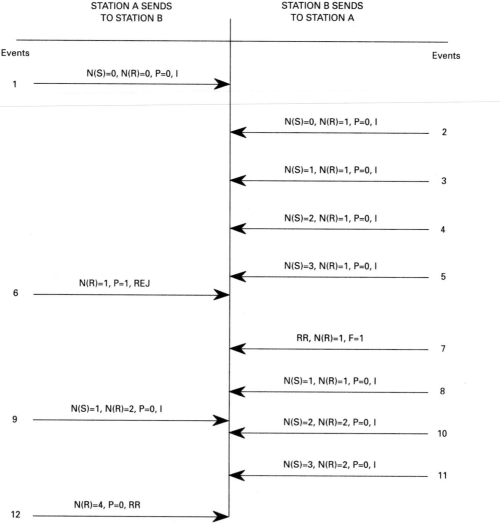

**Figure 7-8** Error Recovery with Reject

## Legend to accompany Figure 7-8

Figure 7-8 depicts the use of the reject frame to recover damaged frames.

| Event(s) | Operation |
|---|---|
| 1 | Station A sends an I frame and sequences it with N(S) = 0. The N(R) = 0 means it expects station B to send an I frame with a send sequence number of 0. |
| 2 – 5 | Station B sends four frames numbered N(S) = 0, 1, 2, and 3. The N(R) value is set to 1 to acknowledge station A's previous frame. Notice the N(R) value does not change in any of these frames because station B is indicating that it still is expecting a frame from station A with a send sequence number of 1. During these frame transmissions, we assume that the frame with N(S) = 1 is distorted. |
| 6 | Station A issues a reject (REJ) frame with N(R) = 1 and P = 1. This means that it is rejecting station B's frame that was sequenced with the N(S) = 1, as well as all succeeding frames. |
| 7 | Station B must first clear the P-bit condition by sending a non-I frame with the F-bit set to 1. |
| 8 – 11 | Station B then retransmits Frames 1, 2, and 3. During this time (in Event 9), Station A sends an I frame with N(S) = 1. This frame has its N(R) = 2 to acknowledge the frame transmitted by station B in Event 8. |
| 12 | Station A completes the recovery operations by acknowledging the remainder of station B's retransmissions. |

## MULTILINK PROCEDURES (MLP)

In recent years, many manufacturers have developed link level protocols to manage more than one link. The advantages are obvious. First, additional throughput can be achieved, and second, a faulty link can be replaced easily by a predefined backup link.

In 1984, LAPB was amended to include provisions for multilink procedures (MLP). The MLP protocol is quite similar to SNA's transmission groups. It is layered on top of LAPB single-link procedures, as shown in Figure 7-9

Each single link behaves as a conventional LAPB, and MLP adds a sequence number for all the multilinks. This sequence number is used to manage the windows and control the flow of traffic across all the links that are identified to the MLP. The multilink sequence numbers range from 0 to 4,095 in order to accommodate many links operating at high data transfer rates.

Figure 7-10 shows the relationships of the multilink and single link layers and control fields.

The flow control, sequencing, and window management of MLP closely follow the concepts of individual single links. The main difference is MLP's management of the multiple physical links as if they were one logical link. MLP uses the following sequence numbers and state variables to accomplish multilink management:

Multilink send state variable MV(S)
Multilink send sequence number MN(S)

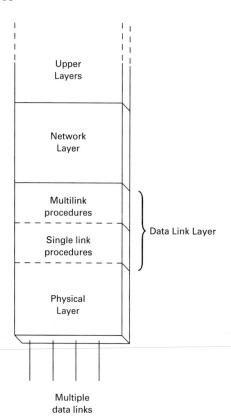

Upper
Layers

Network
Layer

Multilink
procedures

Single link
procedures

Data Link Layer

Physical
Layer

Multiple
data links

**Figure 7-9.** Relationship of Multilink and
Single Link Procedures

Multilink transmitted frame acknowledgment state variable MV(T)
Multilink receive state variable MV(R)
Multilink window size MW
Multilink receive window guard region MX
Multilink system parameter MV

MV(S) identifies the sequence number of the next send sequence number [MN(S)] to be given to a SLP. It is incremented by 1 with each frame assignment.

MN(S) contains the value of the sequence number of the multilink frame. Note that it is not the same as the N(S) in the SLP control field. The two values perform independent functions. The N(S) sequences the frame on the single link and the MN(S), acting as a higher-level sequence number, sequences the frame traversing the multiple links. The MN(S) is used at the receiver to resequence incoming frames that may have arrived out of order across the multiple links (due to SLP retransmission) and to check for duplicate frames (due to the transmitting MLP placing a copy of the frame on more than one SLP to increase the probability of delivery).

MV(T) is maintained at the transmitting station. It identifies the oldest multilink frame that has not yet been acknowledged from the remote station. Due to the existence of more than one link at the interface, it is possible that multilink frames with sequence numbers higher than MV(T) may have been acknowledged.

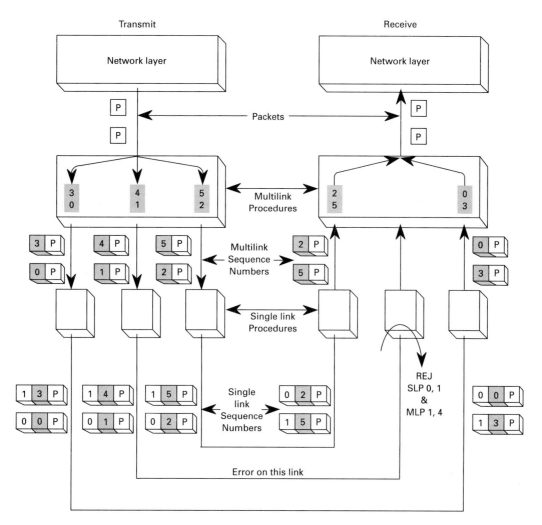

Note: Shaded Boxes Represent MLP Sequence Numbers

**Figure 7-10.** Multilink Operations

MV(R) is maintained at the receiving station to identify the next expected in-sequence frame to be delivered to the next layer (usually, X.25, X.75, or a vendor's proprietary network layer). As previously stated, multilink frames with sequence numbers higher than MV(R) may have been received.

MW is the window of frames that the transmitting site can give to its SLPs and the receiving site can give to its next higher level. The MW window parameter is significant for both the transmit and receive sites. Its value is affected by factors such as propagation delay, frame lengths, the number of links, the SLP T1 timer, and the N2 retry parameter. The multilink MW is defined as:

Transmit MW  =       MV(T) Æ M(V)T + MV–1 inclusive

Receive  MW  =       MV(R) Æ M(V)R + MV–1 inclusive

MLP permits any received multilink frame whose MN(S) is within the window to be released to the upper level. Of course, the MN(S) also must equal the multilink receive state variable MV(R).

The MX parameter identifies a range of multilink sequence numbers beginning at MV(R) + MW. The parameter permits the receiving station to accept multilink frames that are outside its receive window.

The MV is a parameter to denote the maximum number of sequentially numbered frames that the transmitting station can give to the SLPs beyond the value of MV(T) (the oldest multilink frame awaiting an acknowledgment). The value is established at both sites on the link and is the same value for a given direction of transmission. Its purpose is to prevent overrunning the receiver's window guard region. Therefore, it is not allowed to exceed maximum MN(S) value less the value of the window guard region: MV £ 4,095 - MX.

These numbers and variables can be quite perplexing to the uninitiated. So, let us develop a practical example of MLP operations. Figure 7-10 shows two stations (computers, switches, front-ends, etc.) connected with three physical links. Each link is controlled by a single-link protocol, such as LAPB. The receiving single-link protocols deliver the protocol data units (PDUs, or frames) to the MLP sublayers only when the FCS error-check passes and all edits on the control fields are satisfactory. Then, the MLP sublayer resequences the data before sending them to their next upper layer (usually, the network layer).

In Figure 7-10, we assume Link 2 experiences some problems (such as noise) and the transmitting SLP retransmits its SLP frames 0 and 1, which are MLP frames 1 and 4. In the meantime, SLP frames 2 and 3 have been delivered to MLP. However, it may hold these data units until it receives a frame with an MLP sequence of 1. Upon receipt of this unit, it passes MLP 1, then 2, then 3 to its next layer. In this example, it resequences the traffic from the single links.

## SUMMARY

LAPB is responsible for managing the traffic on the X.25 link. It provides for flow control mechanisms and retransmits the data if they are distorted during the transmission. The vast majority of X.25 products use some type of HDLC-based link control technique, and most manufacturers have adopted the LAPB standard. However, in the past few years, a number of X.25 systems have been implemented on other data link controls, such as LAPD and LLC. This trend will continue as users acquire more ISDN circuits (LAPD links) and local area networks (LLC).

# 8

# LAPD and V.120

## INTRODUCTION

This chapter examines a widely used protocol named LAPD—link access procedure for the D channel. The protocol is used on an integrated services digital network (ISDN) for out-of-band (control) signaling. We review the functions of ISDN in the introductory part of this chapter and analyze the operations of LAPD, as well as the contents of the LAPD frame, later in the chapter. Comparisons are made to other protocols, as well, such as LAPB and HDLC.

We also examine another protocol that was derived from LAPD. This protocol is called V.120 and is used in ISDN terminal adapters (TAs).

## OVERVIEW OF ISDN

The purpose of ISDN is to provide digital connectivity for the end user. Presently, almost every subscriber local loop is analog. This loop is too slow and unreliable for data communications, however. Thus, ISDN is intended to extend digital technology over the subscriber loop to the end-user terminal by using common telephone wiring and a standard interface plug. Ideally, the numerous diverse interfaces that exist today will be reduced (or eliminated) with a limited set of common conventions.

An integrated services digital network (ISDN) provides end-to-end digital connectivity to support a wide range of services. In essence, all images (voice, data, television, facsimile, etc.) are transmitted with digital technology.

ISDN is centered on three main areas: (1) the standardization of services offered to subscribers in order to foster international compatibility; (2) the standardization of user-to-network interfaces in order to foster independent terminal equipment and network equipment development; and (3) the standardization of network capabilities in order to foster user-to-network and network-to-network communications.

## The ISDN Terminals and Channels

To begin the analysis of ISDN, consider the end-user ISDN terminal in Figure 8-1. This device (called a DTE in this book) is identified by the ISDN term *TE1* (terminal equipment, Type 1). The TE1 connects to the ISDN through a twisted pair 4-wire digital link. This link uses time division multiplexing (TDM) to provide three channels, designated as the B, B, and D channels (or 2B+D).

The B channels are intended to carry user information streams. They provide for several different kinds of applications support. For example, Channel B can provide for voice at 64 Kbit/s, data transmission for packet-switch utilities at bit rates less than or equal to 64 Kbit/s, and compressed video by using both B channels.

The D channel is intended to carry control and signaling information, although in certain cases ISDN allows for the D channel to support user data transmission, as well. The B channel does not carry signaling information.

ISDN describes signaling information as s-type, packet data as p-type, and telemetry as t-type. The D channel may carry all these types of information through multiplexing operations.

The B channels operate at a speed of 64 Kbit/s; the D channel operates at 16 Kbit/s. The 2B+D is designated as the basic rate interface. ISDN also allows up to eight TE1s to share one 2B+D channel.

Figure 8-2 illustrates other ISDN options. In this scenario, the user DTE is called a TE2 device. It is the equipment currently in use, such as IBM 3270 terminals, telex devices, etc. The TE2 connects to the terminal adapter (TA), which is a device that allows non-ISDN terminals to operate over ISDN lines. The user side of the TA typically uses a conventional physical level interface, such as EIA-232, or the CCITT V-Series Recommendations. It is packaged like an external modem, or as a board that plugs into an expansion slot on the TE2 devices. The EIA or V-series interface is called the R reference point in ISDN terminology.

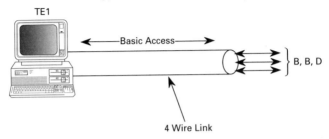

TE1: Terminal Equipment Type 1

**Figure 8-1.** An ISDN Terminal and Basic Access Interface (2B+D)

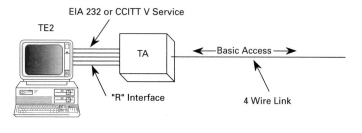

TA: Terminal Adapter
TE2: Terminal Equipment Type 2

**Figure 8-2.** ISDN Terminal Adapter and the R Interface

## Basic Access and Primary Access

The TA and TE2 devices are connected through the basic access to either an ISDN NT1 or a NT2 device. (NT is *network termination*). Figure 8-3 shows several of the options. The NT1 is a customer premise device that connects the 4-wire subscriber wiring to the conventional 2-wire local loop. ISDN allows up to eight terminal devices to be addressed by NT1.

The NT1 is responsible for the physical layer functions (of OSI), such as signaling synchronization and timing. It provides a user with a standardized interface.

The NT2 is a more intelligent piece of customer premise equipment. It is found typically in a digital PBX. The NT2 device is capable of performing concentration services. It multiplexes 23 B+D channels onto the line at a combined rate of 1.544 Mbit/s. This function is called the *ISDN primary rate access.*

The NT1 and NT2 devices may be combined into a single device called *NT12.* This device handles the physical, data link, and network layer functions.

In summary, the TE equipment is responsible for user communications and the NT equipment is responsible for network communications.

## Other ISDN Channels

The most common ISDN interface supports a bit rate of 144 Kbit/s and is called the *basic rate interface* (BRI). The rate includes two 64 Kbit/s B channels, and one 16 Kbit/s D channel. In addition to these channels, ISDN provides for framing control and other overhead bits, which total to a 192 Kbit/s bit rate. The 144 Kbit/s interface operates synchronously in the full-duplex mode over the same physical connector. The 144 Kbit/s signal provides time division multiplexed provisions for the two 64 Kbit/s channels and one 16 Kbit/s channel. The standard allows the B channels to be further multiplexed in the subchannels. For example, 8, 16, or 32 Kbit/s subchannels can be derived from the B channels. The two B channels can be combined or broken down as the user desires.

## The ISDN Layers

The ISDN approach is to provide an end user with full support through the seven layers of the OSI model. In so doing, ISDN is divided into two kinds of services. The bearer

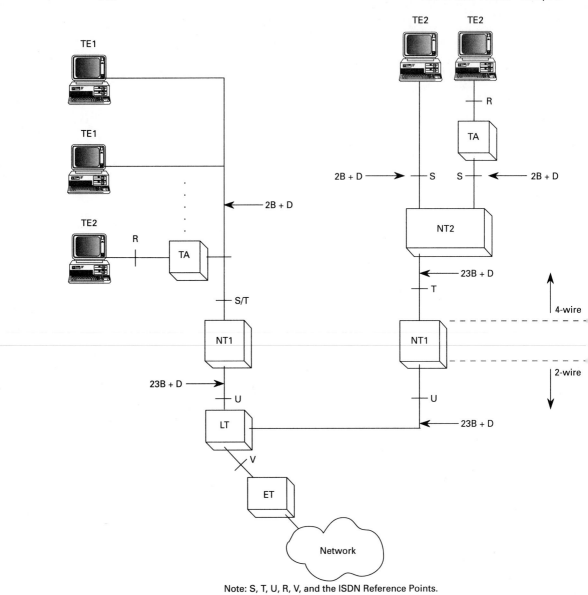

Note: S, T, U, R, V, and the ISDN Reference Points.

**Figure 8-3.** An ISDN Configuration

services are responsible for providing support for the lower three levels of the seven-layer standard. Teleservices (for example, telephone, Teletex, Videotex message handling) are responsible for providing support through all seven layers of the model and generally for making use of the underlying lower-level capabilities of bearer services. The services are referred to as low-layer and high-layer functions, respectively (see Figure 8-4). The ISDN functions are allocated according to the layering principles of the OSI and CCITT standards. Various entities of the layers are used to provide a full end-to-end capability. These layered capabilities may be supplied by PTTs, telephone companies, or other suppliers.

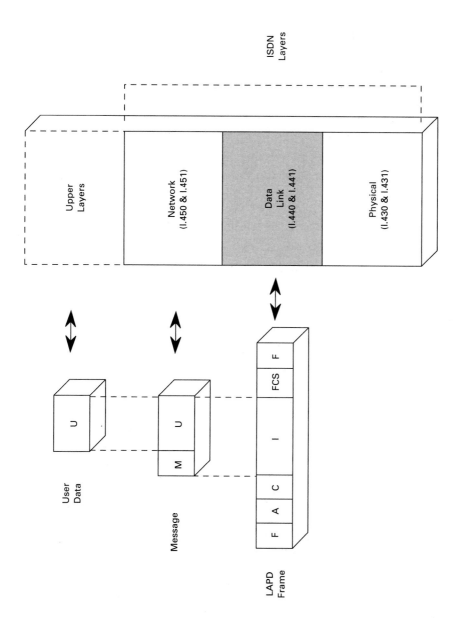

**Figure 8-4.** ISDN Bearer Layers

The operations of the lower layers are of interest to us here. The ISDN physical layer is responsible for providing physical signaling and synchronization on the ISDN channels. Also, this layer defines the electrical characteristics of the signals, the connectors between the terminals, and the ISDN components. The physical layer supports the basic rate interface (I.430) and the primary rate interface (I.431).

The data link layer contains the D channel. The purpose of this channel is to serve the network layer by protecting the messages transmitted through the D channel. If any packet-type data (user data) are passed on the D channel, this layer also is responsible for protecting this information.

The network layer is the user-to-network interface signaling protocol. It supports circuit switch connections, packet switch connections, and user-to-user connections. I.450 and I.451 specify the procedures to establish, manage, and clear a network connection at the ISDN user-network interface (see Figure 8-5). The more widely used Level 3 messages are summarized below.

The SETUP message is sent by the user or the network to indicate a call establishment. The message contains several parameters to define and identify the connection.

The SETUP ACKnowledge message is sent by the user or the network to indicate the call establishment has been initiated. The parameters for the SETUP ACK message are similar to the SETUP message.

The CALL PROCeeding message is sent by the network or the user to indicate the call is being processed. The message also indicates the network has all the information it needs to process the call.

The CONNect message and the CONNect ACKnowledge messages are exchanged between the network and the network user to indicate the call is accepted between either the network or the user. These messages contain parameters to identify the session and the facilities and services associated with the connection.

To clear a call, the user or the network can send a RELease or DISConnect message. Typically, the RELease COMplete is returned, but the network may maintain the call reference for later use, in which case, the network sends a DETach message to the user.

A call may be suspended temporarily. The SUSPend message is used to create this action. The network can respond to this message with either a SUSPend ACKnowledge or a SUSPend REJect.

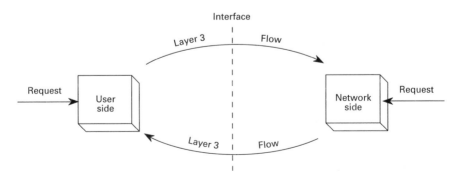

**Figure 8-5.** ISDN Interface

During an ongoing ISDN connection, the user or network may issue CONgestion CONtrol messages to flow-control USER INFOrmation messages. The message simply indicates whether the receiver is ready or not ready to accept messages.

The USER INFOrmation message is sent by the user or the network to transmit information to a (another) user.

If a call is suspended, the RESume message is sent by the user to request the resumption of the call. This message can invoke a RESume ACKnowledge or a RESume REJect.

The STATUS message is sent by the user or the network to report on the conditions of the call.

## The ISDN Bus Configuration

ISDN devices can be attached through the basic rate interface, either through a point-to-point or multipoint topology. For the multipoint topology, the channel is configured as a passive bus. With a passive bus configuration, the terminal equipment can be connected at any point on the bus and can transmit simultaneously. A local area protocol (discussed later) is used to manage the traffic on this multipoint bus.

Each terminal on the multipoint bus must have a unique identifier so that traffic is sent to the proper devices. This address is called the *terminal end point identifier* (TEI) and, as we shall see shortly, it is incorporated into the LAPD PDU. The TEI is used by the system in the following manner. When an outgoing call is made from a terminal, the TEI is identified in the frame of the calling terminal. Conversely, for calls going to the terminals, the network uses the TEI to send the traffic to the proper terminal. It is possible for addressing to pertain to more than one terminal, in which case more than one TE may respond to connection requests.

# LAPD FUNCTIONS

The ISDN provides a data link protocol to allow ISDN devices to communicate with each other across the D channel. This protocol is Link Access Procedure for the D channel (LAPD). LAPD operates at the data link layer of the OSI architecture. The protocol is independent of channel transmission rate and requires a full-duplex bit transparent channel.

LAPB is used on an ISDN D channel for the purposes of controlling ISDN sessions on B channels. LAPD's role for ISDN is similar to that of LAPB's role for X.25: to convey Level 3 messages between machines. The ISDN Level 3 message resides in the I field of the LAPD frame. Although LAPD transports ISDN Level 3 messages, LAPD and the D channel also can support user traffic. The rationale for this concept is that the D channel is not utilized fully by the control signaling procedures. Consequently, during latent periods the idle bandwidth can be utilized to carry user traffic.

# THE LAPD FRAME

The coding of the LAPD frame complies with the HDLC standards published in ISO 4335 and ISO 7809. The unnumbered frame operations are in compliance with ISO 4335.

Figure 8-6 depicts the LAPD frame format. LAPD has a frame format similar to HDLC. Moreover, like HDLC, it provides for unnumbered, supervisory, and information transfer frames. Table 8-1 shows the LAPD commands and responses as well as a modulo 128 operation. The control octet to distinguish among the information format, supervisory format, or unnumbered format is identical to HDLC. The LAPD unacknowledged information frames (UI) provide no flow control, windowing, or error recovery, but do give faster data transfer.

Table 8-1 shows two commands and responses that do not exist in the HDLC standard. These are sequenced information 0 (SI0) and sequenced information 1 (SI1). The purpose of the SI0/SI1 commands is to transfer information fields provided by Layer 3. The information commands are verified by means of the end (SI) field. The P bit is set to 1 for all SI0/SI1 commands. The SI0 and SI1 responses are used during single frame operation to acknowledge the receipt of SI1 and SI0 command frames and to report the loss of frames or any synchronization problems. LAPD does not allow information fields to be placed in the SI0 and SI1 response frames. Obviously, information fields are in SI0 and SI1 command frames.

LAPD provides for two octets for the address field. This is necessary for multiplexing multiple sessions onto the D channel. The address field contains the address

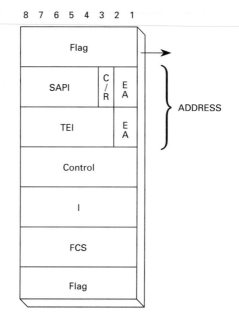

FLAG = 01111110
EA = Address Field Extension Bit
C/R = Command/Response Bit
SAPI = Service Access Point Identifier } Data Link Connection
TEI = Terminal Endpoint Identifier      } Identification (DLCI)
I = Information Field
FCS = Frame Check Sequence

**Figure 8-6.** The LAPD Frame

**TABLE 8-1.** LAPD COMMANDS AND RESPONSES

| Format | Commands | Responses | 8 | 7 | 6 | 5 | 4 | 3 | 2 | 1 |
|--------|----------|-----------|---|---|---|---|---|---|---|---|
| | | | | | | Control Field | | | | |
| Information Transfer | I (information) | | __N(R)__ | | | P | __N(S)__ | | | 0 |
| Supervisory | RR (receive ready) | RR (receive ready) | __N(R)__ | | | P/F | 0 | 0 | 0 | 1 |
| | RNR (receive not ready) | RNR (receive not ready) | __N(R)__ | | | P/F | 0 | 1 | 0 | 1 |
| | REJ (reject) | REJ (reject) | __N(R)__ | | | P/F | 1 | 0 | 0 | 1 |
| Unnumbered | SABM (set asynchronous balanced mode) | | 0 | 0 | 1 | P | 1 | 1 | 1 | 1 |
| | SABME (set asynchronous balanced mode extended) | | 0 | 1 | 1 | P | 1 | 1 | 1 | 1 |
| | | DM (disconnect mode) | 0 | 0 | 0 | F | 1 | 1 | 1 | 1 |
| | SI0 (sequenced information 0) | SI0 (sequenced information 0) | 0 | 1 | 1 | P/F | 0 | 1 | 1 | 1 |
| | SI1 (sequenced information 1) | SI1 (sequenced information 1) | 1 | 1 | 1 | P/F | 0 | 1 | 1 | 1 |
| | UI (unnumbered information) | | 0 | 0 | 0 | P | 0 | 0 | 1 | 1 |
| | DISC (disconnect) | | 0 | 1 | 0 | P | 0 | 0 | 1 | 1 |
| | | UA (unnumbered acknowledge) | 0 | 1 | 1 | F | 0 | 0 | 1 | 1 |
| | | FRMR (frame reject) | 1 | 0 | 0 | F | 0 | 1 | 1 | 1 |

field extension bits, a command/response indication bit, a service access point identifier (SAPI), and a terminal end point identifier (TEI), which was introduced earlier in this chapter. The SAPI and TEI fields are known collectively as the data link control identifier (DLCI). These entities are discussed in the following paragraphs.

The purpose of the address field extension is to provide more bits for an address. The presence of a 1 in the first bit of an address field octet signals that it is the final octet of the address field. Consequently, a two-octet address would have a field address extension value of 0 in the first octet and a 1 in the second octet. The address field extension bit allows the use of both the SAPI in the first octet and the TEI in the second octet, if desired.

The command/response (C/R) field bit identifies the frame as either a command or a response. The user side sends commands with the C/R bit set to 0. It commands with the C/R set to 1 and responds with the C/R set to 0. The network side uses the opposite values for commands and responses.

## SAPIs AND TESIs

The service access point identifier (SAPI) identifies the entity where the data link layer services are provided to the layer above (that is, Layer 3). These SAPIs are defined in the ISDN:

| SAPI VALUE | FRAME CARRIES |
|:---:|:---:|
| 0 | Signaling Information (S-type) |
| 16 | Packet Data (P-type) |
| 63 | Management Information |

The terminal end point identifier (TEI) identifies a connection end point within a service access point. It is implemented to identify either a single terminal (TE) or multiple terminals. The TEI is assigned automatically by a separate assignment procedure. A TEI value of all 1s identifies a broadcast connection.

Figure 8-7 shows the relationship of the terminals to the multipoint bus and the P and S SAPIs. The terminal passes traffic to control entities or packet entities based on the value of the SAPI field. The S-type frames are used to process signaling information from Layer 3 of the ISDN protocol. The P-type frames contain end user data and are passed to the appropriate end user entity for processing.

## Accessing Link Layer Management Through a SAPI

The data link layer for ISDN is modeled differently from several of the other HDLC-type protocols. The principal difference is that the ISDN link layer model contains management functions. Two management entities are available. The layer management entity (LME) provides management support for any type of operation that affects the entire layer. For example, operations dealing with a TEI (assignment, removal, diagnostics, etc.) are handled by the LME. The LME is accessed through a SAPI.

Individual connections within the layer are handled by the connection management entity (CME). This service is not provided with a SAPI, but is made available through a specific LAPD frame. Functions provided by the CME include connection flow control management, operating on errors, and the optional initialization of parameters.

## TEI Management

LAPD provides a procedure to manage terminal end point identifiers (TEI). This procedure is important because each terminal on the bus must be identified uniquely with a TEI. The TEI management procedure assigns a TEI value for the data link layer entities within the TEI (the user equipment) to use during a session. The TEI management procedures also allow the ISDN network to check and remove TEI values. In addition, these procedures provide for operations in which the ISDN node can verify that a TEI value has or has not been assigned. The TEI may be assigned on an automatic basis, in which case the operations described in this section will not be necessary.

The ISDN network node provides a service called the *assignment source point* (ASP), which is used to coordinate the management, assignment, and deletion of the TEIs. The process of TEI assignments is depicted in Figure 8-8. The user device sends a LAPD unnumbered information (UI) frame to the ISDN ASP. This message is conveyed to ASP with the I field of the UI frame containing a message type to identify an identity request, a reference number (Ri), and an action indicator (Ai). The purpose of the reference number is to distinguish between multiple user equipment which may request at the same time an assignment value for TEI. This is simply a random number which ranges from 0 to 65,535 that is generated by the device. The action indicator is a single octet value that is used to indicate a request to the ASP for the assignment of the TEI.

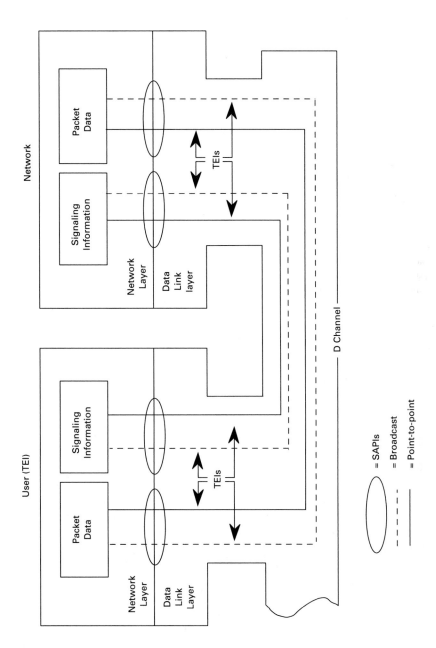

**Figure 8-7.** SAPI and TEI Operations

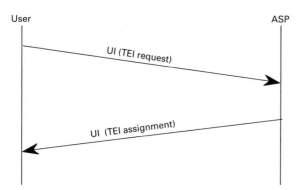

User             ASP

UI (TEI request)

UI (TEI assignment)

**Figure 8-8.** TEI Management

Upon the initiation of the UI frame, LAPD starts a timer designated as T202. The frame is sent to the ASP, which is required to select the TEI value or to deny this request because of previous requests received which contain an identical Ri, or because the request has editing problems in discerning the intelligibility of the message. If all goes well, the ASP returns another UI frame to the user device containing a message type identified as identity assigned, the reference number Ri, and the actual assigned value (TEI) in the Ai field. After these operations have occurred, there is an unambiguous TEI identified for the user device to perform its operations.

LAPD supports several procedures to manage the TEI, as well. For example, a TEI check procedure is used to audit proper assignments of the TEI to ensure that the TEI value is in proper use or to verify that a multi-TEI assignment has proceeded correctly. The process occurs much like the initial assignment procedure with the exchange of UI frames between the user device and ASP. The contents of the LAPD frame are changed slightly where a message type contains an identity check request and the Ai field contains a TEI value that is to be checked. Additionally, the TEI check procedure uses Timer 201, in which the user device sends out the TEI check procedure frame.

TEIs also may be removed. In this situation, the ASP is responsible for transmitting the message back to the user device, wherein the message type is identified as *message remove* and the TEI value is identified in the Ai field.

## PARAMETERS FOR LAPD OPERATIONS

Like most HDLC implementations, LAPD uses a number of parameters to support its operations. The principal parameters used are summarized as follows:

- Modulo 128
- Interframe time, contiguous 1s
- Maximum I field length, 260 octets
- Window size, 1 for s and 3 for p
- Acknowledgment time, 1 second
- Retry for transmissions, up to 3

## LAPD SERVICE DEFINITIONS

Since LAPD was published during the development of the OSI model, the CCITT developed its architecture around the architecture of OSI. Consequently, layer-to-layer communications in one machine are defined through service definitions (or the more commonly known term *primitives*). The primitives are established between LAPD and the upper (network) layer, the lower (physical) layer, and the layer management entity.

A description of the primitives and an overview of their functions are presented in Table 8-2.

**TABLE 8-2.** LAPD PRIMITIVES

| Primitive Name | Primitive Function |
|---|---|
| DL-ESTABLISH | Establishes and confirms a frame operation |
| DL-RELEASE | Used to request and report on the procedures for terminating a multiple frame operation |
| DL-DATA | Provides connection-oriented services for sending and receiving messages between Layers 2 and 3 |
| DL-UNIT DATA | Provides for connectionless services for sending and receiving messages between Layers 2 and 3 |
| MDL-ASSIGN | Used by LME to request LAPD to associate a TEI with a specified connection end point value and used by data link layer to notify LME of the need for a TEI value to be assigned |
| MDL-REMOVE | Used by LME to request LAPD to remove a TEI value with a specified connection end point value |
| MDL-ERROR | Used by the CME and LAPD to report on problems |
| MDL-UNIT DATA | Used to exchange management entity messages between LME and LAPD using the UI transfer service |
| MDL-XID | Used to support the LAPD XID procedures |
| PH-DATA | Used between LAPD and the physical layer to transfer traffic between these layers |
| PH-ACTIVATE | Used between the physical layer and LAPD to initiate a physical layer connection |
| PH-DEACTIVATE | Used to indicate that the physical layer connection has been deactivated |

## CONTENDING FOR USE OF THE D CHANNEL

The user devices (TE1) can be multidropped onto one basic rate interface. With this configuration, it is possible that the terminals transmit at approximately the same time, which results in collisions. ISDN provides several features to determine whether other devices are using the link at the same time (refer to Figure 8-9 during this discussion).

When the NT receives a D bit from the TE, it echoes back the bit in the next E-bit position. The TE expects the next E bit to be the same as its last transmitted D bit. Under normal conditions, the TE continues to detect its own D bits in the E bits.

A terminal cannot transmit into the D channel until after it has detected a specific number of ones (no signal) corresponding to a preestablished priority. If the number is reached, the TE then can send its D channel data.

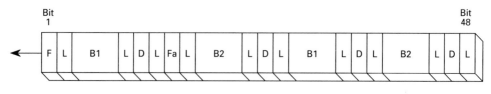

(a) TE Frame (Terminal to Network)

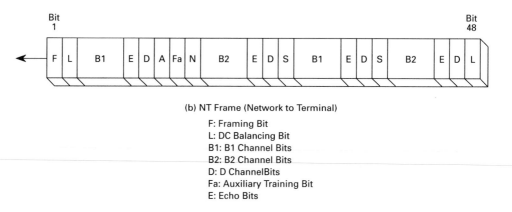

(b) NT Frame (Network to Terminal)

F: Framing Bit
L: DC Balancing Bit
B1: B1 Channel Bits
B2: B2 Channel Bits
D: D ChannelBits
Fa: Auxiliary Training Bit
E: Echo Bits

**Figure 8-9.** Basic Rate Frame Format

If the TE detects a bit in the echo channel (E channel) that is different from its D bits, it must stop transmitting immediately. This indicates that another terminal has begun transmitting at the same time.

This simple technique ensures that only one terminal can transmit its D message at one time. After the successful transmission of the D message, the terminal has its priority reduced by requiring it to detect more continuous 1s before transmitting. A terminal is not allowed to raise its priority back to its previous value until all other devices on the multidrop line have had an opportunity to send a D message.

A telephone connection on the line has a higher priority and precedence over all user services. Signaling information is a higher priority than nonsignaling information. Presently, the TE must detect 10 E bits of 1 before sending nonsignaling information, but only 8 E bits before sending signaling information.

## V.120

The CCITT also has published the V.120 Recommendation. Its purpose is to support an ISDN interface with a DTE and its associated physical layer interface. The DTE is assumed to be operating with the CCITT V Series interfaces (modems that employ analog signaling). In addition, V.120 also supports the multiplexing of multiple user data links onto the ISDN S/T interface.

V.120 uses a link level protocol based on the modification of LAPD (Q.921). Since LAPD provides a multiplexing capability with its TEI field, the V.120 standards group applied the LAPD operations to V.120.

V.120 describes the use of a terminal adaptor (TA) for the ISDN-to-V Series DTE internetworking. However, this TA performs more functions than a conventional TA. It must perform the following:

- Electrical and mechanical interfaces conversions,
- adaptation of bit transfer rate (as in V.110),
- end-to-end synchronization of traffic,
- call management between the two end users, and
- a variety of maintenance functions.

The scheme for V.120 is depicted in Figure 8-10. Notice that the ISDN network sits between the TAs and TEs. V.120 establishes the protocols that are to be used between the TAs. The term *TA-V* means the TA supports a V-Series interface.

Three modes of operations are supported with the V.120 terminal adapter: (a) asynchronous mode, (b) synchronous mode, and (c) transparent mode.

You probably are aware that asynchronous mode terminals (async TE2s) use start/stop bits and parity checks. The TA accepts the asynchronous stream from the user device and removes the start and stop bits. As an option, parity may be checked by the TA. In either case, the user data characters are placed in a frame for transmission to a peer entity. The peer entity is another TA or a TE1.

With the synchronous mode, the transmission from the user TE2 is an HDLC-type frame. The HDLC flags and any zero-stuffed bits are removed at the TA. The TA performs an error check using the FCS. In the event an FCS check indicates the frame was damaged during transmission, an FCS error information signal is relayed to the peer entity. It has the option of discarding the frame, generating an incorrect FCS for handling at the other side, or causing an abort at its interface (at the R-reference point).

The user device's address, control, and information fields must flow transparently across the TA. The responsibility of the TA is to place these fields in a modified LAPD frame for transmission to its peer entity. The synchronous mode also allows the segmentation of a user message into smaller pieces. The TA may perform this multiplexing operation to avoid the delay involved by waiting for the complete bit stream of the message. The receiving peer entity is required to perform a demultiplexing process at the other end.

The TA also may support bit-transparent operations. This option requires the TA to encapsulate the bits from the user device at the R-reference point. However, no processing of the bits occurs, nor is any error checking performed. The bits are relayed transparently to the peer entity. The transparent mode of operation is to be used if the asynchronous and synchronous modes are not used. The transparent mode of operation may use the HDLC unnumbered information (UI) frame option.

## V.120 Message Format

V.120 uses the frame structure of the Q.921/I.441 Recommendations. This format is illustrated in Figure 8-11. The fields relating to the HDLC frame structure are not discussed here. We shall concentrate on the fields unique to this recommendation.

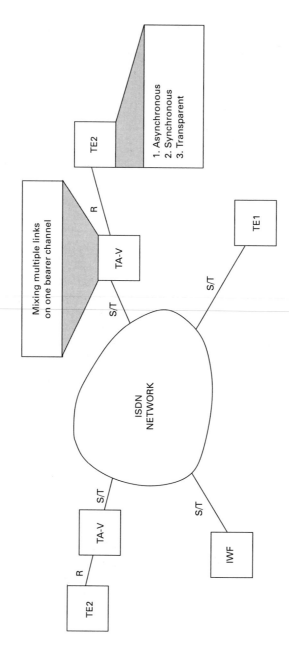

**Figure 8-10.** V.120 Connections

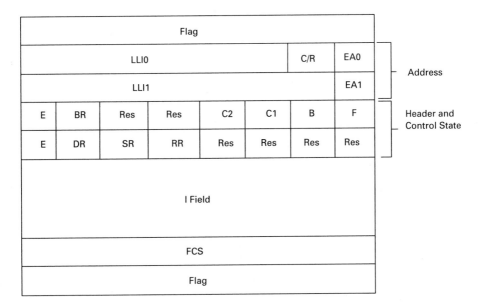

**Figure 8-11** The V.120 Frame Format

The logical link indicator (LLI) is a concatenation of the LLI0 and LLI1 fields. This thirteen-bit field can take the values of 0 to 9,181. The LLI values are similar to the service access point identifier (SAPI) and the terminal end point identifier (TEI) fields that reside in the LAPD frame.

Presently, the following values are reserved:

-        0    End channel signaling
-    1–255    Reserved
-     256    Default LLI
-  257–2,047    For LLI assignment
- 2,048–8,190    Reserved
-   8,191    In-channel layer management

The extended address fields (EA) are used to extend the number of octets in the address. If the value of this bit is zero, it means additional address octets follow. The presence of a 1 value in bit 1 of the address field means that it is the last octet of the address field. As with LAPD, the C/R bit indicates a command (C=0) or response (R=1).

The V.120 header resides in front of the information (I) field as part of HDLC I field. It consists of two parts: (a) the header octet and (b) the control state information octet.

The header octet has eight fields, each one bit in length. The extension bit (E bit) is used to signify that the header has additional state information. If this bit is set to zero, it indicates that the control state information follows. Obviously, the control state information octet is optional.

The break bit (BR) is used in asynchronous applications to accommodate a terminal creating a break signal on the line. If the TA receives a break signal, it changes the BR bit to indicate the break. It must do this in the same frame, or after the queued characters have been set. The asynchronous break signal is mapped by the TA to an HDLC idle condition. If the user device is an HDLC station, the TA sets this bit to 1 if it receives an idle signal from the HDLC station.

The next two bits are reserved and are set to zero. The following two bits are designated as C1 and C2, respectively. These bits are used for diagnostic purposes to notify the TA entities of various types of error conditions that have been detected. The combination of the two bits and their meaning is dependent upon the use of the synchronous, asynchronous, or bit-transparent modes.

The B and F bits (beginning and final) are used to convey information about the segmentation of the message. These bits primarily are used for synchronous mode operations. The values for synchronous modes are as follows:

- 10   Begin frame
- 00   Middle frame
- 01   Final frame
- 11   Single frame

The value mode 11 also pertains to asynchronous and bit-transparent modes of operation.

The second octet of the V.120 header is the control state information octet. It is optional and, as we learned earlier, is designated with coding of the E-extension bit with a value of zero.

Presently, only four bits of this octet are designated for use. They are used as follows:

- Extension bit (E): Used to indicate a further extension of the header octet.
- Data ready bit (DR): Used to indicate that the TE1 interface is activated. At the transmitting end the DR bit is mapped from the V.24 circuit 108/2 data terminal ready (EIA CD). At the receiving end no mapping is required for the DR bit.
- Send ready (SR): Used to indicate that the TE is ready to send data. The SR bit is mapped from the V.24 105 interchange circuit request to send (EIA CA) and the V.24 109 interchange circuit receive line signal detect (EIA CF). At the sending end, this variable is mapped from Circuit 105. At the receiving end, this bit is mapped to Circuit 109.
- Receive ready (RR): Used to indicate that the TE is ready to receive data. The RR bit is not mapped at the sending end. At the receiving end the RR bit maps to the V.24 interchange Circuit 106 ready for sending (EIA CB).
- RES: These bits are reserved for future use.

## SUMMARY

LAPD is the data link layer to support ISDN-based networks. It provides for the safe delivery of ISDN network layer messages between user devices and the ISDN network node. Although closely modeled on HDLC, LAPD has a more elaborate addressing structure in order to handle multipoint devices on a basic rate interface (BRI) channel. Other than the address field—and with a few other differences, such as the use of the HDLC UI frame, different timers, and so on—LAPD is similar to other HDLC protocols.

# 9

# IEEE LAN Link Controls

## INTRODUCTION

Local area networks operate using a variety of link layer protocols. This chapter provides an overview of the more widely used techniques. The emphasis is on the IEEE 802/ISO 8802 Media Access Control (MAC) standards, which form one part of the LAN's data link layer. The MAC standards comprise several hundred pages. It is the intent of this chapter to provide the reader with a summary of the major characteristics of the MAC operations.

## IEEE 802.3 CSMA/CD

A widely used scheme for managing a local area network is *carrier sense multiple access with collision detection* (CSMA/CD). It is based on several concepts of the ALOHA protocol (discussed in the satellite link control chapter), which was designed originally for packet radio systems and later applied to satellite communications. The Xerox Corporation was instrumental in providing the research for CSMA/CD and in developing the first baseband commercial product. The broadband network was developed by MITRE. In 1980, Xerox, the Intel Corporation, and Digital Equipment Corporation jointly published a specification for an Ethernet local network. This specification later was introduced to the IEEE 802 committees, and with several modifications, has found its way into the IEEE 802.3 standard.

## IEEE 802.3 Layers

CSMA/CD Ethernet is organized around the concept of layered protocols (see Figure 9-1). The user layer is provided service by the two CSMA/CD layers, the data link layer and the physical layer. The bottom two layers each consist of two separate entities. The data link layer provides the logic to control the CSMA/CD network. It is medium independent and hence may be broadband or baseband. This layer is divided into the logical link control (LLC) sublayer and the media access control (MAC) sublayer.

The MAC sublayer consists of other sublayers. These sublayers are organized as transmit or receive entities and are illustrated in Figure 9-2. A brief description of the functions of each sublayer follows:

### TRANSMIT DATA ENCAPSULATION

- Accepts data from LLC
- Calculates the CRC value and places it in the FCS field

### TRANSMIT MEDIA ACCESS MANAGEMENT

- Presents a serial bit stream to the physical layer
- Defers transmission when a medium is busy
- Halts transmission when a collision is detected
- Reschedules a retransmission after a collision
- Inserts the PAD field for frames with a LLC length less than a minimum value
- Enforces a collision by sending a jam message

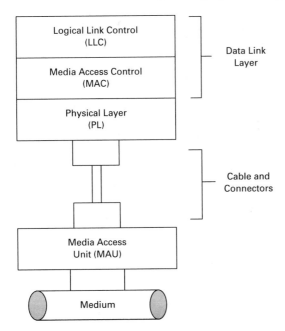

**Figure 9-1.** The CSMA/CD Layers

### RECEIVE DATA DECAPSULATION

- Performs a CRC check
- Recognizes and accepts any frame whose DA field is an address of a station
- Presents data to LLC

### RECEIVE MEDIA ACCESS MANAGEMENT

- Receives a serial bit stream from the physical layer
- Discards frames that are less than the minimum length

The physical layer is medium dependent. It is responsible for such services as introducing the electrical signals onto the channel, providing the timing on the channel, and data encoding and decoding. Like the data link layer, the physical layer is composed of two major entities: the data encoding/decoding entity and the transmit/receive channel access (although the IEEE 802.3 standard combines these entities in its documents). The major functions of these entities are listed on the following page:

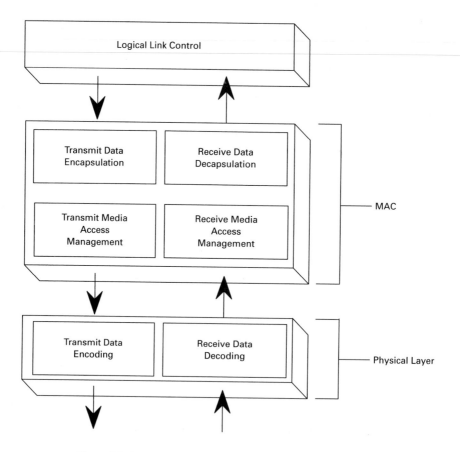

**Figure 9-2.** The CSMA/CD Layers and Sublayers

### DATA ENCODING/DECODING

- Provides the signals to synchronize the stations on the channel (this sync signal is called the *preamble*)
- Encodes the binary data stream to a self-clocking Manchester code at the transmitting site and decodes the Manchester code back to binary code at the receiver.

### CHANNEL ACCESS

- Introduces the physical signal onto the channel on the transmit side and receives the signal on the receive side of the interface
- Senses a carrier on the channel on both the transmit and the receive side (which indicates the channel is occupied)
- Detects a collision on the channel on the transmit side (indicating two signals have interfered with each other)

## IEEE 802.3 Operations

In a CSMA/CD network, each station has both a transmit and receive side to provide the incoming/outgoing flow of data. The transmit side is invoked when a user wishes to transmit data to another DTE on the network; conversely, the receive side is invoked when data are transmitted to the stations on the network.

The transmit data encapsulation entity receives the user data and constructs the MAC frame. It also appends the frame check sequence field to the data and passes the frame to transmit media access management, which buffers the frame until the channel is free. The channel is sensed as free when it sees a carrier sense signal turned off from the transmit channel access entity in the physical layer. After a brief delay, media access management passes the frame to the physical layer.

At the physical layer on the transmit side, data encoding transmits the synchronization signal (preamble). In addition, it encodes the binary data stream to a self-clocking Manchester code. The signal is then passed to transmit channel access, which introduces the signal onto the channel.

The CSMA/CD (MAC) frame is transmitted to all stations connected to the channel. A receiving station senses the preamble, synchronizes itself onto the signal, and turns on the carrier sense signal. Then, receive channel access passes the signal up to data decoding. The data decoding entity translates the Manchester code back to a conventional binary data stream and passes the frame up to the media access management.

Like its counterpart on the transmit side, media access management buffers the frame until the carrier sense signal has been turned off from receive channel access. Media access management now can pass the data up to data decapsulation. Data decapsulation performs an error check on the data to determine if the transmission process created errors. If not, it checks the address field to determine if the frame is destined for its node. If it is, it passes it to the user layer with the destination address (DA), source address (SA), and, of course, the LLC data unit.

Since the CSMA/CD structure is a peer-to-peer network, all stations are vying for the use of the channel when they have data to transmit. The contention can result in the signals from various stations being introduced on the cable at approximately the same time. When this occurs, the signals collide and distort each other. They cannot be received correctly by the stations.

A central aspect of collisions deals with the *collision window*. This term describes the length of time required for the signal to propagate through the channel and to be detected by each station on the network. For example, let us assume that a network has a cable .6 mile (1 Km) long. If stations are situated at the far end of the cable, the furthest station distance is about .6 mile. It takes approximately 4.2 microseconds for a signal to travel this distance. When Station A is ready to transmit, it senses the cable to determine whether a signal is on the circuit. If Station B previously had transmitted its frame onto the channel, but it had not had time to reach Station A, then Station A would assume falsely that the channel was idle and would transmit its packet. In this situation, the two signals would collide.

Under worst-case conditions for a baseband network, the amount of time to detect the collision (and acquire the channel) is twice the propagation delay, since the collided signal must propagate back to the transmitting stations. Propagation delay and collision detection are even longer for a broadband network that uses two cables for send and receive signals. Under worst-case conditions, the time to detect the collision is four times the propagation delay.

Obviously, collision is undesirable, since it creates errors in the network. Moreover, if long frames are transmitted, the collision takes more time on the channel than with the use of short frames. CSMA/CD addresses this problem at the transmit media access management level by stopping the frame transmission immediately upon detecting a collision.

If the signal is sent to all parts of the channel without a collision, the station that transmitted the signal is said to have acquired or seized the channel. Once this occurs, collisions are avoided, since all stations have detected the signal and defer to it. However, in the event of the collision, the transmit channel access component notices the interference on the channel (in the form of voltage abnormalities for a baseband system) and turns on a special collision detect signal to transmit media access management. (A broadband CSMA/CD requires other collision detect methods, such as bit comparisons on the send and receive cables.)

Transmit media access management performs two functions to manage the collision. First, it enforces the collision by transmitting a special bit sequence called the *jam*. The purpose of the jam is to ensure that the duration of the collision is long enough to be noticed by all the other transmitting stations that are involved in the collision. The CSMA/CD LAN requires that the jam be at least 32 but not more than 48 bits. This guarantees that the duration of the collision is sufficient to ensure its detection by all the transmitting stations on the network. Its limited length also ensures that the stations will not interpret it falsely as a valid frame. Any frame containing fewer than 64 bytes (octets) is presumed to be a fragment resulting from a collision and is discarded by any other receiving stations on the link.

Transmit media access management then performs the second function. After the jam is sent, it terminates the transmission and schedules the transmission for a later time, based on a random wait selection. The termination of frame transmission decreases the effect of a long frame collision manifesting itself on the channel for an extended time.

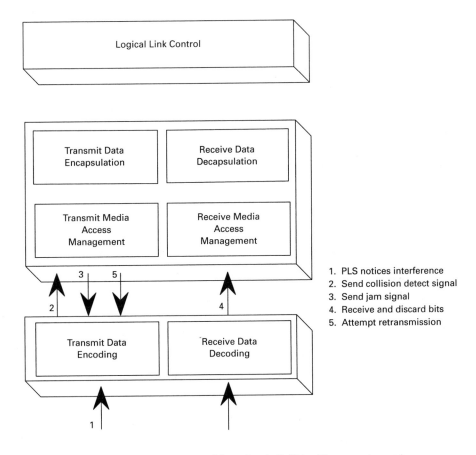

**Figure 9-3.** Sequence of Operations in Collision Management

At the receiving station or stations, the bits resulting from the collision are decoded by the physical layer. The fragmented frames received from the collision are distinguished from valid frames by the receive media access management layer. It notices that the collision fragment is smaller than the shortest valid frame and discards the fragments. Consequently, the jam is used to ensure all transmitting stations notice the collision, and the fragmented frame is transmitted to ensure that any receiving stations ignore the transmission.

Both Ethernet and 802.3 use a 1-persistent technique to manage collisions and channel contention. However, this 1-persistent algorithm is applied to an integral multiple of a slot time (512 bits), and the scheduling of retransmission is performed by a controlled randomizing process called *truncated binary exponential back-off.* After 16 unsuccessful attempts, the station gives up. A summary of the collision management operations is provided in Figure 9-3.

## The 802.3 Frame

The MAC level CSMA/CD frame for 802.3 is shown in Figure 9-4. The *preamble is* transmitted first to achieve medium stabilization and synchronization. The *start frame*

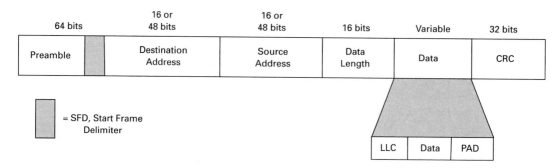

**Figure 9-4.** The 802.3 Frame

*delimiter* (SFD) follows the preamble and indicates the start of the frame. The 16-or 48-bit physical address fields contain the MAC addresses of the *destination* and *source*. The destination address can identify an individual workstation on the network or a group of stations. The *data length* field indicates the length of the LLC and data fields. If the data field is less than a maximum length, the PAD field is added to make up the difference. The *cyclic redundancy check* (CRC) value is contained in the FCS field.

## IEEE 802.4 TOKEN BUS

The token bus LANs are used primarily in manufacturing applications. They use a bus topology, yet provide access to the channel as if it were a ring. The protocol eliminates the collisions found in the carrier sense collision detection systems, but still allows the use of a bus-type channel. The token bus requires no physical ordering of the stations on the channel. The stations can be configured logically to pass the token in any order.

The protocol uses a control frame called an *access token* or *access right.* This token gives a station the exclusive use of the bus. The token-holding station uses the bus for a period of time to send and/or receive data. It then passes the token to a designated station called the *successor station.* In the bus topology, all stations listen and receive the access token, but the only station allowed to use the channel is the successor station. All other stations must await their turn to receive the token. The stations receive the token through a cyclic sequence, which forms a logical ring on the physical bus.

A large user group exists for 802.4. Those interested in obtaining more information can write to the following address:

Manufacturing Automation Protocol (MAP) Chairman
GM Technical Center
Manufacturing Building A/MD 39
30300 Mound Road
Warren, MI 48090-9040

### IEEE 802.4 Layers

The layers of the token bus network are quite similar to the other IEEE 802 networks (see Figure 9-5). Of course, the protocols and interfaces that reside in the layers are different, with the exception of the LLC layer (which is not part of the token bus protocol).

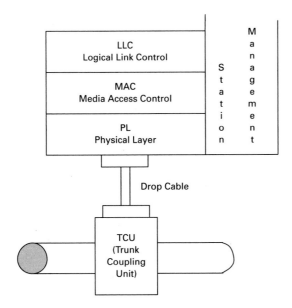

**Figure 9-5.** Layers for Token Bus LANs

This protocol has a station management layer that is used to manage aspects of MAC, LLC, and the physical layers.

The MAC sublayer consists of four major functions: the interface machine (IFM), the access control machine (ACM), the receive machine (RxM), and the transmit machine (TxM).

The ACM is the heart of the token bus system. It determines when to place a frame on the bus and cooperates with the other stations' ACM to control access to the shared bus. It also is responsible for initialization and maintenance of the logical ring, including error detection and fault recovery. In addition, it controls the admission of new stations.

The LLC frames are passed to the ACM by the interface machine (IFM). This component buffers the LLC sublayer requests. The IFM maps "quality of service" parameters from the LLC view to the MAC view and performs address checking on received LLC frames.

The TxM and RxM components have limited functions. The responsibility of the TxM is to transmit the frame to the physical layer. The RxM accepts data from the physical layer and identifies a full frame by detecting the SD and ED. It also checks the FCS field to validate an error-free transmission. If a received frame is an LLC type, it is passed from the RxM component to the IFM.

## IEEE 802.4 Operations

The token bus protocol is a collision-free protocol and uses a special frame called a *token* to govern which station is allowed to send data. The station with the token has control over the network. The IEEE 802.4 determines the logical ring of the physical bus by the numeric value of the addresses. A MAC or LLC data unit provides the facility for the lowest address to hand the token to the highest address. Then, the token is passed from a predecessor station to its successor station.

The token bus is more complex than the CSMA/CD network. It has initialization procedures that determine which station is to receive access to the network in the order of first, second, third, etc. It has ring addition and ring deletion procedures, wherein stations periodically are allowed to insert/remove themselves from the logical ring. Capacity can be allocated through the use of priorities, and several procedures exist for the detection and recovery of faults.

As shown in Figure 9-6, the token (right to transmit) is passed from station to station in descending numerical order of station address. When a station hears a token frame addressed to itself, it may transmit data frames. When a station has completed transmitting data frames, it passes the token to the next station in the logical ring. When a station has the token, it may delegate temporarily its right to transmit to another station by sending a request-with-response data frame.

After each station has completed transmitting any data frames it may have, the station passes the token to its successor by sending a token control frame. After sending the token frame, the station listens for evidence that its successor has heard the token frame and is active. If the sender hears a valid frame following the token, it assumes that its successor has the token and is transmitting. If the token sender does not hear a valid frame following its token pass, it attempts to access the station of the network and may implement measures to pass around the problem station by establishing a new successor. For more serious faults, attempts are made to re-establish the ring.

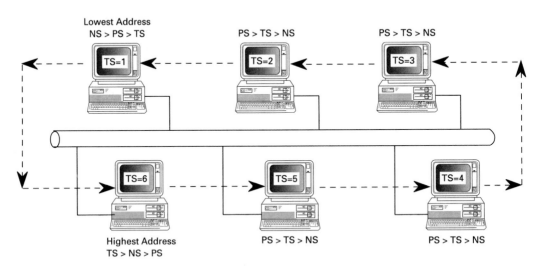

TS = This Station Address
NS = Next Station Address
PS = Previous Station Address

**Figure 9-6.** Token Bus

### The IEEE 802.4 Frame

The PDU for the token bus is quite similar to the PDUs of some of the other IEEE networks (see Figure 9-7). The protocol uses a number of different formats containing various fields to manage the removal and insertion of stations on the logical ring, the check for lost frames, and other diagnostic operations, however. The protocol contains a conventional preamble to provide synchronization and clocking functions. The frame control is used for managing the token and data on the network. Its contents vary depending on whether the frame is a LLC-type frame or a MAC-type frame. Source addresses contain the conventional 2- or 6-octet address spaces. The data unit (information field) contains user data, and its length is variable. The frame check sequence is a 4-octet field used for error detection. And, finally, the ending delimiter provides for other control functions.

The frame begins with a start delimiter. It contains signaling patterns that are always distinguishable from data patterns. The start delimiter field consists of 8 bits where the n value signify nondata bits which are coded. The purpose of the end and start delimiters (ED and SD) is to "frame" the traffic, that is, to distinguish when the frame begins and ends.

The 7th bit of the ED field is the intermediate bit. If this bit is set to 1, it signifies that the station has more transmissions. If it is set to 0, it means that the station has sent its last frame and it will send nothing following the ED. The 8th bit in the ED is called the *error bit.* This is set to 1 by a repeater to indicate that the immediately preceding frame had an FCS error. This is used for the receiving station to treat the frame as invalid.

## IEEE 802.5 TOKEN RING

The token ring LAN has been used for several years. The IEEE 802.5 standard now is implemented in a number of vendors' products. IBM uses a variation of 802.5 in its token ring network.

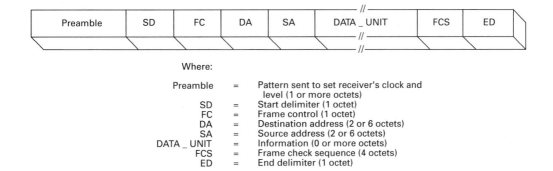

Where:

| | | |
|---|---|---|
| Preamble | = | Pattern sent to set receiver's clock and level (1 or more octets) |
| SD | = | Start delimiter (1 octet) |
| FC | = | Frame control (1 octet) |
| DA | = | Destination address (2 or 6 octets) |
| SA | = | Source address (2 or 6 octets) |
| DATA _ UNIT | = | Information (0 or more octets) |
| FCS | = | Frame check sequence (4 octets) |
| ED | = | End delimiter (1 octet) |

**Figure 9-7.** General Format of Token Bus Frame
(Several other formats used for bus management)

## IEEE 802.5 Layers

The layers for the IEEE 802.5 token ring are in conformance with the overall model of the IEEE network standards (see Figure 9-8). The basic layers consist of logical link control (LLC), media access control (MAC), and the physical layer (PL). In addition, a station management function is available that interfaces with LLC, MAC, and PL.

This figure shows a physical interface for shielded twisted pair. The medium interface cable (MIC) is a series of interchange circuits that are used for sending and receiving traffic between the station and the TCU.

Most token ring vendors provide a 16 Mbit/s or 4 Mbit/s product. Typically, the 16 Mbit/s network is employed with shielded twisted pair and the 4 Mbit/s product is provided with unshielded twisted pair.

## IEEE 802.5 Operations

In a token ring topology, the stations are connected to a concentric ring through a *ring interface unit* (RIU) (see figure 9-8). Each RIU is responsible for monitoring the data passing through it, as well as regenerating the signal and passing it to the next station. If the address in the header of the transmission indicates the data are destined for a station, the interface unit copies the data and passes the information to the user device.

If the ring is idle (that is, no user data are occupying the ring), a "free" token is passed around the ring from node to node. This token indicates that the ring is available.

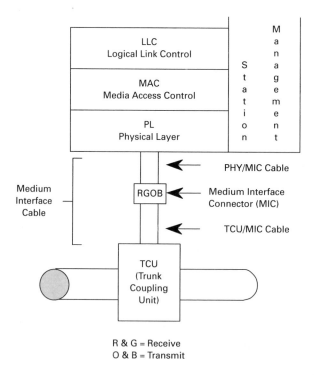

**Figure 9-8.** The Token Ring Layers

Any station with data to transmit can use the token to transmit traffic. The control of the ring is passed sequentially from node to node around the ring.

During the period when the station has the token, it controls the ring. Upon acquiring the token (i.e., marking the token busy), the transmitting station inserts data behind the token and passes the data through the ring (see Figure 9-9). As each RIU monitors the data, it regenerates the transmission, checks the address in the header of the data, and passes the data to the next station.

Some systems remove the token from the ring, place the data on the channel, and then insert the token behind the data. Other user frames can be placed behind the first data element to allow a "piggybacking" effect on the LAN, with multiple user frames circling the ring. The approach requires that the token be placed behind the last data transmission. Piggybacking is useful for large circumferential rings that experience a long delay in the transmission around the ring, but the short propagation delay on a LAN is not worth the added complexity of a multiple token LAN. The 802.5 does not permit piggybacking.

Upon the data's arrival at the transmitting station, this station makes the token free and passes it to the next station on the ring. This requirement prevents one station from

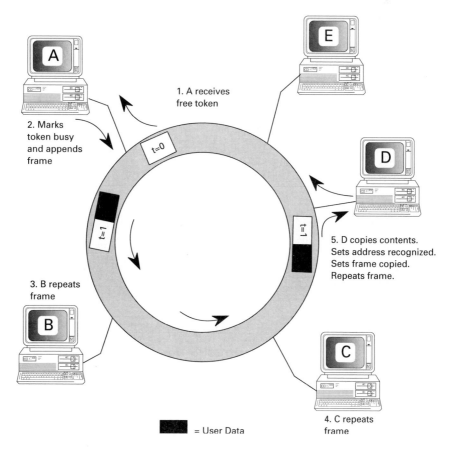

**Figure 9-9.** Seizing the Token

monopolizing the ring. If the token passes around the ring without being used, the station once again can use the token and transmit data.

Thus, each station is guaranteed access to the network in a noncollision manner. If n stations exist on the network, a station is assured of using the network every nth pass of the token.

Many token ring networks (including the 802.5 standard) use priority schemes. The object of the priority is to give each station an opportunity to reserve the use of the ring for the next transmission around the ring. As the token and data circle the ring, each node examines the token, which contains a reservation field. If a node's priority is higher than the priority number in the reservation field, it raises the reservation field number to its level, thus reserving the token on the next round. If another node does not make the reservation field higher, the station is allowed to use the token and channel on the next pass around the ring.

The station with the token is required to store the previous reservation value in a temporary storage area. Upon releasing the token, the station restores the network to its previous lowest priority request. In this manner, once the token is made free for the next round, the station with the highest reservation is allowed to seize the token.

### IEEE 802.5 Frame

The token format, illustrated in Figure 9-10, consists of several fields. We first examine the starting delimiter (SD), the access control (AC), and the ending delimiter (ED). The purpose of the two delimiters is to indicate the beginning and ending of the transmission. The access control contains eight bits. Three bits are used for a priority indicator, three bits are used for a reservation indicator, and one bit is the token bit. When the token bit is set to 0, it indicates that the transmission is a token. When it is set to 1, it indicates that a data unit is being transmitted. The last bit in the access control byte is the monitor bit. This provides for a designated station to monitor the ring for error control and backup purposes. An abort token consists only of the SD and ED. This transmission can be sent at any time to abort a previous transmission.

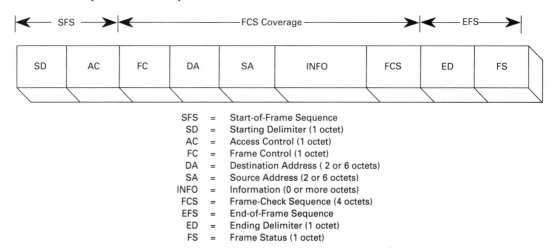

SFS  =  Start-of-Frame Sequence
SD   =  Starting Delimiter (1 octet)
AC   =  Access Control (1 octet)
FC   =  Frame Control (1 octet)
DA   =  Destination Address ( 2 or 6 octets)
SA   =  Source Address (2 or 6 octets)
INFO =  Information (0 or more octets)
FCS  =  Frame-Check Sequence (4 octets)
EFS  =  End-of-Frame Sequence
ED   =  Ending Delimiter (1 octet)
FS   =  Frame Status (1 octet)

**Figure 9-10.**  General Frame Format for the Token Ring

In addition to the SD, AC, and ED, the standard provides for additional fields. The frame control field defines the type of frame (MAC or LLC data unit) and can be used to establish priorities between two LLC peer entities. The address fields identify the sending and receiving stations. The information field contains user data. The FCS field is used for error checking and the frame status field is used to indicate that the receiving station recognized its address and copied the data in the information field.

## IEEE 802.6 METROPOLITAN AREA NETWORK

The Metropolitan Area Network (MAN) standards are sponsored by the IEEE, ANSI, and the regional Bell Operating Companies (BOCs). Although 802.6 was designed initially for a LAN-to-MAN support service, the telephone companies see it as a technology to provide for interconnecting LANs to its central office, and even for the interconnection of telephone switching facilities.

802.6 also forms the basis for the Switched Multi-megabit Data Service (SMDS), which is now being touted as the solution to the "WAN bottleneck." Therefore, the LAN/WAN internetworking problem can be alleviated with the use of 802.6 technology for connecting the WAN to LANs.

The MAN standard is organized around a topology and technique called *dual queue dual bus* (DQDB). This term means that the topology uses two buses. Each of these buses transmits traffic in one direction only. The implementation for MAN provides for transfer rates from 34 to 150 Mbit/s.

The DQDB provides for two types of access. One access is called *prearbitrated services,* which guarantees a certain amount of "bandwidth." This access is useful for isochronous services such as voice and video. The second service is called *queued arbitrated service,* which provides services based on demand. It is designed to accommodate bursty services such as data transmission. Figure 9-11 summarizes the major features of the DQDB architecture.

A MAN is designed with two unidirectional buses. Each bus is independent of the other in the transfer of traffic. The topology can be designed as an open bus or closed bus configuration. Figure 9-12 shows the two alternatives.

Two unidirectional dual buses; capacity twice that of each bus

Buses independent in the transfer of traffic

Looped bus or open bus configurations

DQDB independent of physical layer:
    ANSI D3:  77.736 Mbit/s over coax or fiber
    ANSI SONET STS-3c:  155.520 Mbit/s over single-mode fiber
    CCITT G-703:  34.368 Mbit/s or 139.264 Mbit/s over metallic medium

Access control:
    Prearbitrated (PA) for isochronous services

**Figure 9-11.** Dual Queue Dual Bus (DQDB) Attributes

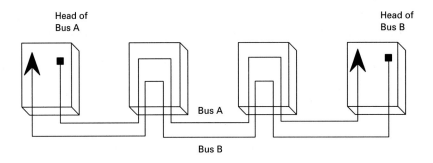

(a) Open Bus Architecture

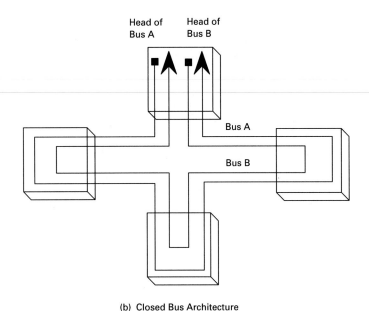

(b) Closed Bus Architecture

**Figure 9-12.** The DQDB Bus Architectures

## The IEEE 802.6 Layers

The MAN layers are modeled on the IEEE 802 architecture. The DQDB layer roughly parallels that of the MAC, although the DQDB layer is considerably more extensive.

The headings at the top of Figure 9-13 show the types of services that are supported by MAN functions. The LLC services are any services coming from the LLC layer. The connection-oriented services are designed to support asynchronous virtual circuit services. The other services are "under study." The isochronous services are designed to support applications that need constant "bandwidth," such as voice and video.

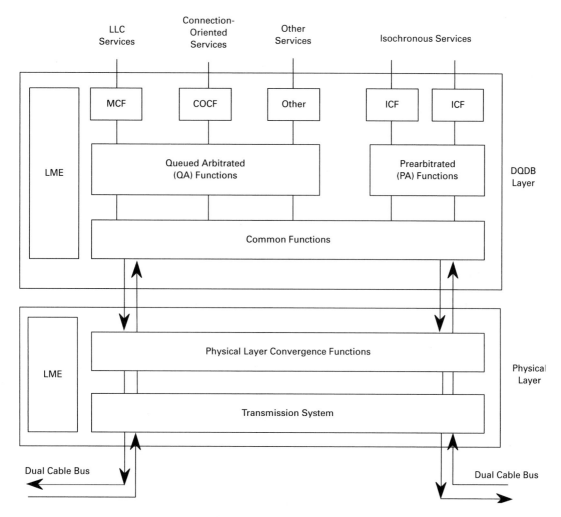

**Figure 9-13.** The MAN Layers

The convergence functions are responsible for taking user formats and changing them to DQDB formats. At the physical layer, the physical layer convergence functions assumes that each transmission system has a different convergence function. Therefore, this operation provides a consistent service to the DQDB layer. The transmission system layer supports the physical media such as DS3, G.703, STS-3C, and so on. The left side of this figure shows the layer management entities (LMEs). As in the spirit of the IEEE model, these LMEs provide the management functions for the various operations.

## The IEEE 802.6 Operations

A node gains access to the network by putting itself in a queue (one queue exists for each bus). When a node is idling, a count is made of the requests that pass on the bus, for example, Bus B. The request counter is incremented by 1 for each queued request. The request counter also is decremented by 1 with each empty slot on Bus A. In order to use Bus A, a node sets a request bit on a slot on Bus B. The downstream nodes notice that this slot is set and they increment their request counters by 1.

Each node keeps a count of the number of downstream requests and balances that with the number of the empty slot. Based on the values in the counters, the nodes are queued to use the bus. To send, a node puts a request on a slot on Bus B and remembers the slot count. By sending the request counter to a countdown counter, the node can locate an empty slot. When the counter = 0, the node uses the slot.

To iterate, as a slot passes across Bus A, the nodes must decrement their counter values. If a node's value was 0, it is allowed to gain access to the bus and use the slot.

If both nodes have a countdown value of 0, the simplest approach is to give the upstream node the service first.

### The IEEE 802.6 Frame

The MAN/DQDB PDU is called a slot. It consists of the segment and a one-octet control field known either as *slot control* or *access control*. This header is added at the transmit convergence common function and serviced by the receive common function of the DQDB layer.

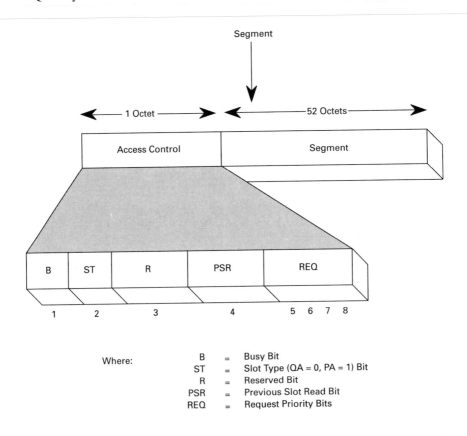

| B | ST | R | PSR | REQ |

| 1 | 2 | 3 | 4 | 5 6 7 8 |

Where:

| | | |
|---|---|---|
| B | = | Busy Bit |
| ST | = | Slot Type (QA = 0, PA = 1) Bit |
| R | = | Reserved Bit |
| PSR | = | Previous Slot Read Bit |
| REQ | = | Request Priority Bits |

**Figure 9-14.** The 802.6 Slot

The header consists of five fields (see Figure 9-14). The first field is a busy bit field, which is set to one to indicate the slot is busy or to zero to indicate there is no information. The ST is the *slot type,* which identifies the slot as queued arbitrated when set to 0, or as prearbitrated when set to 1. The reserved bit is reserved and is not used by 802.6. The PSR is the *previous slot read* bit, which is used to control access to the DQDB. For queued arbitrated applications, the *request field* (REQ) is used to establish a priority for the data.

## SUMMARY

The media access control (MAC) sublayer of a local area network provides the capabilities to manage the traffic on the LAN media. MAC forms the bottom sublayer of the IEE/ISO data link layer. MAC is protocol specific, but media independent. MAC operations vary widely for each local area network implementation.

# 10

# *Logical Link Control (LLC)*

## INTRODUCTION

This chapter introduces the logical link control (LLC) protocol published as IEEE 802.2 and ISO 8802/2. We will learn how LLC rests on top of all the 802/8802 MAC protocols and provides a flexible and convenient interface of the end-user application into and out of a LAN. The LLC Types 1, 2, and 3 are examined, as well as the link service access points (LSAPs). The IEEE and ISO standards are aligned with each other technically. For simplicity, this chapter refers to the IEEE 802.2 standard.

### The Sublayers of the IEEE 802 Data Link Layer

The IEEE efforts have emphasized the need to keep the OSI model and the 802 specifications as compatible as possible. As shown in Figure 10-1, the 802 committees split the data link layer into two sublayers: media access control (MAC) and logical link control (LLC). MAC encompasses 802.3, 802.4, 802.5, and others. The LLC includes 802.2. This sublayer was implemented to make the LLC sublayer independent of a specific LAN access method. The LLC sublayer also is used to provide an interface into or out of the specific MAC protocol.

The MAC/LLC split provides several attractive features. First, it controls access to the shared channel among the autonomous user devices. Second, it provides for a decentralized (peer-to-peer) scheme that reduces the LAN's susceptibility to errors. Third, it provides a more compatible interface with wide area networks, since LLC is a subset of HDLC. Fourth, LLC is independent of a specific access method; MAC (not LLC) is protocol-specific. This approach gives an 802 network a flexible interface with workstations and other networks.

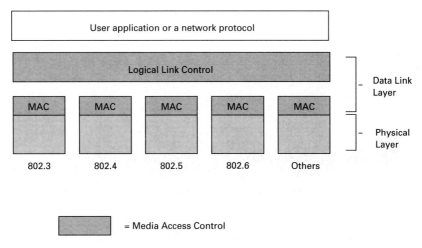

**Figure 10-1.** The LLC and MAC Sublayers

LLC can be implemented in a number of ways on a LAN. At its most basic function, it is used to interface the LAN functions with the user applications. All IEEE 802 LANs require the use of LLC for this interface.

LLC also can be used for some rather elaborate connection management procedures and flow control operations. For example, one type of LLC allows the creation of connections between user stations, as well as the use of positive and negative acknowledgments, sequencing numbers, and flow control operations with sliding windows.

If these functions seem excessive for certain user applications, LLC can be configured to perform minimal levels of service. In this configuration, LLC simply provides a connectionless interface between the user application and MAC.

## MAJOR FUNCTIONS OF LLC

As shown in Figure 10-1, LLC provides the interface to the next upper-layer protocol, which can be a user application, but more often is a network layer protocol such as the widely used Internet Protocol (IP). This interface is supported with several service definitions that are examined later in this chapter. As explained in the previous section, the LLC also provides the interface into the MAC sublayer.

As part of these interfaces, LLC is responsible for the transfer of data between the user or network layer protocol and MAC. By invoking HDLC-type operations (receive ready [RR] and receive not ready [RNR]), LLC can flow-control the adjacent upper layer.

LLC can be configured to support connection-oriented operations between applications running on a LAN. These operations are initiated with the HDLC set asynchronous balanced mode extended frame (SABME). It also can be configured as a connectionless protocol with the HDLC unnumbered information (UI) frame.

In addition, LLC can acknowledge traffic on the LAN (either positive or negative) and can be configured to support the sequencing of protocol data units between two user applications or between the communicating network layer protocols.

## THE LLC SERVICE DEFINITIONS

The IEEE 802.2 specification defines a number of interface options through service definitions that the user application can employ with LLC. These interfaces are modeled with abstract primitives which (in the real world) are implemented with software calls, such as C programming function calls, UNIX system library calls, and so on.

Figure 10-2 shows the LLC primitive sets with state transition diagrams. With this model, the user is any process that is invoking the services of LLC (designated as the "LLC provider"). In Figure 10-2, (a) through (f) show how the user sends request primitives to LLC, which provides various options in returning traffic or delivering data with indication or confirm primitives. A common method for the transfer of data is modeled in (f), in which the request primitive submits data to LLC and LLC delivers the data to the remote user with the indication primitive. Notice that LLC provides a local confirm of the traffic to the local user. In turn, (c) models a connectionless operation in which data are delivered to the end user with an indication primitive, but no confirmation is provided to either party.

Other options available to the user and LLC also are illustrated. Figure 10-2, (a) usually is implemented for sending control information from the user to LLC when the user is not interested in a reply. Also, (d) represents the exchange of control information, with LLC providing a confirm to the user's request. Finally, (b) and (e) are used by LLC to inform one or both users about something that LLC considers important.

The result of a request primitive which invokes a confirm from the remote LLC provider is shown in (g). Be aware that this is not a complete end-to-end acknowledgment, since the confirm did not emanate from the end user, but only from the remote LLC module.

The concept that either user can simultaneously send requests to LLC and LLC will respond to each request with the confirm primitive is modeled in (h).

After 802.2 was initially published, (i) and (j) were added to support a *connectionless-acknowledged service*. This term means that LLC does not set up a connection between two stations, but does provide a "low-level" acknowledgment capability.

The actual implementation of this model depends on a vendor's specific product; thus, one should check the vendor to see how the LLC model is implemented.

We shall have more to say about these operations as we proceed through this chapter.

## CONNECTION OPTIONS WITH LLC TYPES 1, 2, AND 3

At the onset of the IEEE 802 work, it was recognized that a connection-oriented system would limit the scope and power of a local area network. Consequently, two connectionless models now are specified:

- unacknowledged connectionless model

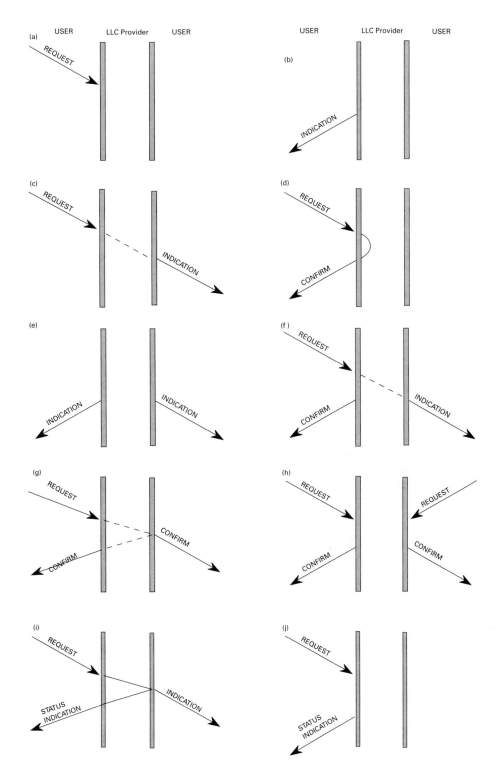

**Figure 10-2.** The 802.2 Service Definitions

Let us consider the reason for this approach. First, many local applications do not need the data integrity provided by a connection-oriented network. For example, sensor equipment can afford to lose occasional data, since the sensor readings typically occur quite frequently and the data loss does not adversely affect the information content. As an illustration, the forest service in Canada uses a "connectionless" system to collect data on lightning strikes. Since several thousand strikes can occur in a very short time span, the loss of a few observations does not bias the data. A second example is inquiry-response systems, such as point-of-sale, which usually perform acknowledgment at the application level. These systems do not need connection-oriented services at the lower levels. Finally, packetized voice can tolerate some packet loss without affecting the quality of the voice reproduction.

A second reason to use a connectionless system is that high-speed application processes cannot tolerate the overhead in establishing and disestablishing the connections. The problem is particularly severe in the local area network, with its high-speed channels and low error rates. Many LAN applications require fast setups with each other. Others require very fast communications between the DTEs.

An acknowledged connectionless service is useful for a number of reasons. Consider the operations of a LAN in a commercial bank. A data link protocol usually maintains state tables, sequence numbers, and windows for each station on the link. It would be impractical to provide this service for every station on the bank's local network. Yet, workstations such as the bank's automated teller machines (ATMs) require they be polled for their transactions. The host computer also must be assured that all transactions are sent and received without errors. The data are too important to use a protocol that does not provide acknowledgments. Additionally, the bank's alarm system needs some type of acknowledgment to assure the computer receives notice of security breaches in the bank. It is too time-consuming to establish a "connection" before sending the alarm data.

## CLASSES OF SERVICE

The 802 LAN standards include four types of service for LLC users:

Type 1:  Unacknowledged Connectionless Service
Type 2:  Connection-mode Service
Type 3:  Acknowledged Connectionless Service
Type 4:  All of the above services

All 802 networks must provide unacknowledged connectionless service (Type 1). Optionally, connection-oriented service can be provided (Type 2). Type 1 networks provide no ACKs, flow control, or error recovery; Type 2 networks provide connection management, ACKs, flow control, and error recovery. The use of LLC Type 2 avails the user of the features of HDLC's set asynchronous balanced model extended (SABME). SABME provides for the following HDLC features: (a) reject (REJ), negative acknowledgments of traffic; (b) receive not ready (RNR), closing data flow; and (c) receive ready (RR), opening data flow. Type 3 networks provide no connection setup and disconnect, but they do provide for immediate acknowledgment of data units. Most Type 1 networks use a higher-level protocol (i.e., the transport layer) to provide connection management functions.

## LOGICAL LINK CONTROL PROTOCOL DATA UNIT (PDU)

The LLC protocol data unit is shown in Figure 10-3. The LLC unit contains a destination service access point address (DSAP), source service access point address (SSAP), control field, and information field. The DSAP is an 8-bit field in which 7 bits are used for the actual SAP address. The first bit of this field is designated as the individual/group bit (I/G). When this bit is set to 0, it identifies an individual DSAP. If the bit is set to 1, it identifies a group of SAPs at a station that can receive data.

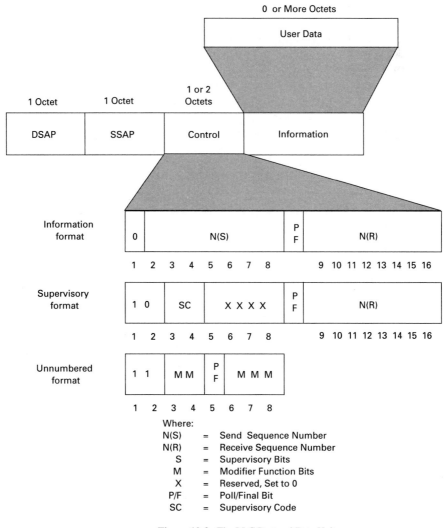

**Figure 10-3.** The LLC Protocol Data Unit

The SSAP also consists of 8 bits. Seven bits identify the source SAP. The first bit of this field is designated as the command/response bit (C/R) and is used to indicate whether the data unit is an HDLC command or an HDLC response.

The HDLC-type commands and responses, established in the control field, depend on whether the LAN is Type 1, 2, or 3. For Type 2, the information format is used to sequence sending traffic with N(S) and to acknowledge traffic with the N(R). For sending Type 1 data, the unnumbered format is used to send an HDLC unnumbered information (UI) data unit. The supervisory format is used for certain of the types to issue flow control data units as well as negative acknowledgments in the event of problems. The UI also is used for Type 3 to provide a simple ACK/NAK capability. The poll/final bit (P/F) generally is implemented in accordance with conventional HDLC rules.

The exchange ID field (XID) (see Figure 10-4) is used with LLC for negotiating certain services and to inform the receiving station about the sending station's intent to employ Type 1 or Type 2 operations. The IEEE security option also is identified in the XID frame, as is the establishment of a receive buffer through the receive window size bits.

The HDLC-type commands and responses, established in the control field, depend on whether the LAN is Type 1, 2, or 3. The instruction sets allowed are shown in Table 10-1 (notice the UI frame for connectionless service and SABME for connection-oriented service). Since this material is covered in considerable detail in the chapter on HDLC (Chapter 6), we need not repeat the explanation here.

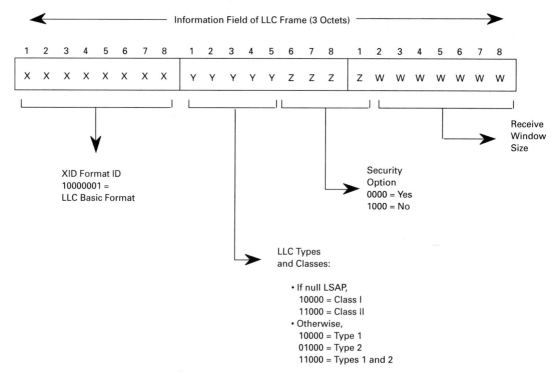

**Figure 10-4.** Information Field of the XID Frame

**TABLE 10-1.** LLC COMMANDS AND RESPONSES

| | | Commands | Responses |
|---|---|---|---|
| Type 1 | | UI | |
| | | XID | XID |
| | | TEST | TEST |
| Type 2 | (I Format) | I | I |
| | (S Format) | RR | RR |
| | | RNR | RNR |
| | | REJ | REJ |
| | (U Format) | SABME | UA, FRMR |
| | | DISC | DM |
| Type 3 | | AC0 | AC0 |
| | | AC1 | AC1 |

## OPERATIONS FOR LLC TYPES 1 AND 3

The operations of LLC Type 2 (SABME) have been explained in previous chapters. Figure 10-5 summarizes the operations for LLC Type 1 and Type 3. With Type 1 operations, traffic is exchanged between the stations with HDLC UI data units. Obviously, UI is connectionless because sequence numbers are not used in the UI format. Moreover, Type 1 does not set up a mapping of the LLC SAPs. For Type 3 operations, there is no connection established between the SAPs, but the AC0 and AC1 fields are used for the sending and acknowledging of traffic. Type 3 is a half-duplex protocol. In this example, Station A sends data to Station B and sequences this one data unit with a value of AC0. Station B acknowledges this data unit by returning a data unit coded as AC1. Station A then is allowed to send its next unit in which it places the value of AC1 in the data unit. In turn, Station B acknowledges this unit by sending back to Station A a data unit coded as AC0.

In effect, the stations "flip-flop" the values of AC0 and AC1 in their ongoing dialogue. LLC Type 3 does not permit more than one data unit to be outstanding at any one time. Consequently, the values of 0 and 1 are sufficient for traffic sequencing and acknowledgment. Those who have studied data link protocols may recognize this operation as part of the once widely used Binary Synchronous Control (BSC) (bisync) protocol.

## LLC SERVICE ACCESS POINTS (SAPs)

Previous chapters have described the functions and operations of service access points. Figure 10-6 shows an example of the relationship of LLC LSAPs in three different LAN stations. The SAPs perform the services of software ports. Their function is to identify the application entity residing above LLC. In this example, Applications X and Y are identified with SAP A1 and A2, respectively. In two other stations, Application Q identified with SAP C1 is logically associated with Application X identified with SAP

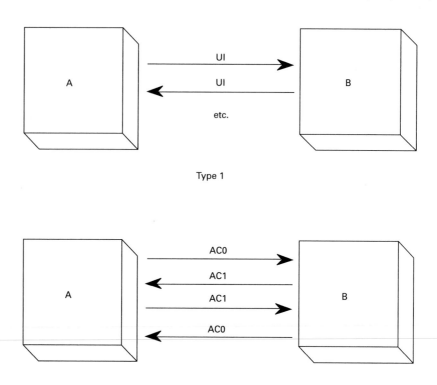

Type 1

Type 3

**Figure 10-5.** Type 1 and Type 3 Operations

A1. Additionally, Application Z identified with SAP B1 is associated with Application Y, which uses SAP A2.

It is possible for SAP numbers to be reused at the same time in a LAN. This possibility could create ambiguity in the identification of SAP sessions. An easy solution to this problem is to concatenate the MAC addresses with the SAP addresses. With this approach, the SAP identifiers are unique.

The IEEE provides a registration service for entities that are common in the LAN communications industry. These "well-known LSAPs" identify widely used protocols that typically run on top of an IEEE 802 network. Table 10-2 shows some examples of well-known LSAPs. There are other well-known LSAPs that are not included here.

The IEEE LSAP architecture is managed through a component hierarchy which consists of the (a) station, (b) SAP, and (c) connect components (see Figure 10-7).

The station component is responsible for processing events which affect an entire LLC module (entity). As examples, (1) the station component manages all SAPs and their connections, and (2) the station component sends and responds to all XID and TEST protocol data units.

The SAP component operates within the station component procedure and is responsible for the management of each MAC destination address, destination SAP/MAC source address, and source SAP pair.

The connect component rests under the SAP component procedure and assumes the responsibility for the specific operations of each SAP component pair.

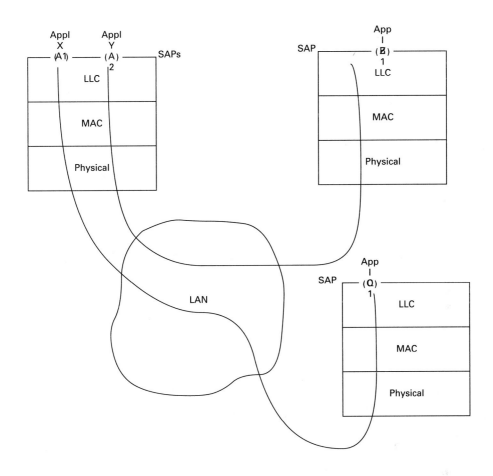

**Figure 10-6.** Mapping LSAPs

**TABLE 10-2.**   WELL-KNOWN LSAPs

| Link SAP | Description |
|---|---|
| IEEE Binary | |
| 00000000 | Null LSAP |
| 01010101 | SNAP (uses 802.2) |
| 01000010 | Bridge spanning tree protocol (802.1) |
| 01000000 | Individual LLC sublayer management |
| 11000000 | Group LLC sublayer management |
| 00100000 | SNA path control |
| 01100000 | DoD Internet Protocol |
| 01110000 | Proway-LAN (NW Maintenance and initialization) |
| 01110010 | EIA-RS511 (factory automation) |
| 01110001 | Proway-LAN (active station list maintenance) |
| 01111111 | OSI network protocol |
| 11111111 | Global DSAP |

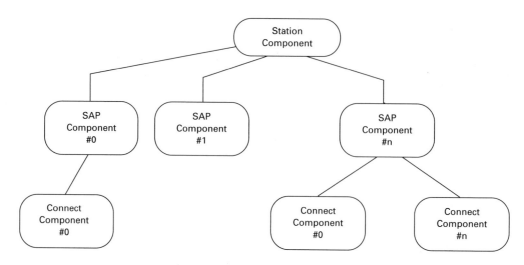

**Figure 10-7.** Structure of SAP Management

## 802 LAYER INTERACTIONS THROUGH PRIMITIVES

The 802 LANs use primitives to specify services. The primitives are defined for both the LLC and MAC sublayers. These primitives for LLC are important to the data link protocol designer, because they provide the tools for "driving" the LLC protocols. As discussed previously, the IEEE and OSI primitives (service definitions) are somewhat abstract and are implemented with programming languages' function calls or an operating system library calls. On a general level, four generic primitives are defined:

Request:      Passed from user to invoke a service.

Indication:   Passed from the service layer to user to indicate an event that is significant to the user.

Response:     Passed by user to acknowledge some procedure invoked by an indication primitive to the user

Confirm:      Passed from the service layer to user to convey the results of previous service request(s).

Table 10-3 lists each of the 802 primitives used with LLC. The following material describes them in more detail.

### Network Layer/LLC Primitives

**Connectionless Unacknowledged Data Transfer.** Two primitives are used for connectionless data transfer:

- DL_UNITDATA.request (source-address, destination-address, data, priority)
- DL_UNITDATA.indication (source-address, destination-address, data, priority)

**TABLE 10-3.** LLC PRIMITIVES

LLC PRIMITIVES

    Connectionless Data Transfer

        DL_UNITDATA.request
        DL_UNITDATA.indication

    Connection-Oriented Services

        DL_CONNECT.request
        DL_CONNECT.indication
        DL_CONNECT.response
        DL_CONNECT.confirm

        DL_DATA.request
        DL_DATA.indication

        DL_CONNECTION_FLOWCONTROL.request
        DL_CONNECTION_FLOWCONTROL.indication

        DL_RESET.request
        DL_RESET.indication
        DL_RESET.response
        DL_RESET.confirm

        DL_DISCONNECT.request
        DL_DISCONNECT.indication

MAC PRIMITIVES

        MA_UNITDATA.request
        MA_UNITDATA.indication
        MA_UNITDATA_STATUS.indication

The request primitive is passed from the network layer to LLC to request a link service data unit (LSDU) be sent to a remote link service access point . The address parameters are equivalent to a combination of the LLC SAP and MAC addresses. The priority field is passed to MAC and implemented (except for 802.3, which has no priority mechanism). The indication primitive is passed from LLC to the network layer to indicate the arrival of a link service data unit from a remote entity. This relationship is depicted in Figure 10-8.

Upon receiving the request primitive, LLC must create an unnumbered information data unit (UI) and pass this data unit to MAC through a MAC/LLC primitive. MAC is responsible for encapsulating the LLC information into a MAC frame and sending it to the physical layer, which places it on the channel. At the receiving end, the process is reversed, and at the LLC/network interface the DL_UNITDATA.indication primitive is formulated from the information in the received UI data unit. It is then passed to the network layer for further processing.

**Connection-Oriented Service.** Four primitives are used to establish a connection-oriented session (see Figure 10-9):

- DL_CONNECT.request (source-address, destination-address, priority)
- DL_CONNECT.indication (source-address, destination-address, priority)
- DL_CONNECT.response (source-address, destination-address, priority)
- DL_CONNECT.confirm (source-address, destination-address, priority)

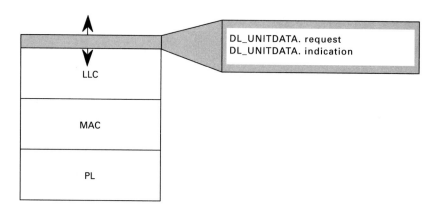

**Figure 10-8.** LCC Primitives for Connectionless Service

Once these primitives have been exchanged, it is the responsibility of the LLC entities to manage the flow control of the data units. The DL_CONNECT.request primitive is used by LLC to create the SABME data unit, which it passes to MAC. At the receiving end, the SABME is passed from MAC to LLC with the DL_CONNECT.indication primitive.

Two primitives are used for connection-oriented data transfer. These primitives are used to pass the LLC information (I) frame between two stations.

- DL_DATA.request (source-address, destination-address, data)
- DL_DATA.indication (source-address, destination-address, data)

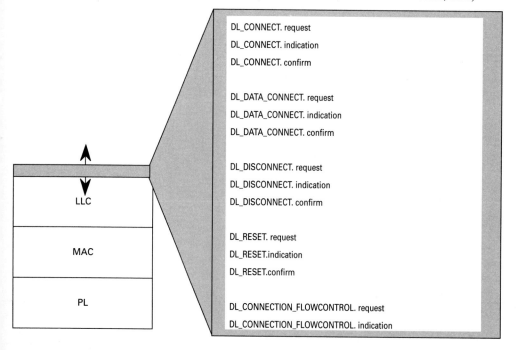

**Figure 10-9.** LLC Primitives for Connection-Oriented Services

Interestingly, no confirmation primitives are returned to the sender. Generally, the MAC sublayer will deliver the data error-free and the LLC ensures it is sent in the proper order. In the event of a problem, the protocol can issue disconnects or resets.

The network layer can control the amount of data it receives from LLC and, likewise, LLC can flow-control the network layer. Two primitives are used for flow control:

- DL_CONNECTION_FLOWCONTROL.request (source-address, destination-address, amount)
- DL_CONNECTION_FLOWCONTROL.indication (source-address, destination-address, amount)

The amount parameter specifies the amount of data the affected entity is allowed to pass. It can be set with each issuance of the request or indication primitive. If set to zero, data transfer is stopped. Although not defined in the LLC standard, the amount field in a DL_CONNECTION-FLOWCONTROL.request primitive should provoke LLC to issue a receive not ready data unit (RNR) if the value indicates that the network layer wishes to reduce the traffic flow.

Four primitives are used to reset a connection:

- DL_RESET.request (source-address, destination-address)
- DL_RESET.indication (source-address, destination-address, reason)
- DL_RESET.response (source-address, destination-address)
- DL_RESET.confirm (source-address, destination-address)

A reset causes all unacknowledged data units to be discarded. LLC does not recover the lost data units, so a higher-level protocol must assume this responsibility. Although not defined in the LLC standard, the reset primitives are used to transport LLC disconnect (DISC) and disconnect mode (DM) data units between the stations, although they may also invoke SABME and UA. One should check with the specific vendor to determine how these primitives are implemented in a product.

Three primitives are used to disconnect the network/LLC session:

- DL_DISCONNECT.request (source-address, destination-address)
- DL_DISCONNECT.indication (source-address, destination-address, reason)
- DL_DISCONNECT.confirm (source-address, destination-address, reason)

The *reason* parameter in the indication primitive states the reason for the disconnection. The disconnect can be initiated either by the LLC user or the LLC service provider. This action terminates the logical connection, and any outstanding data units are discarded.

### Acknowledged Connectionless Data Transfer

The acknowledged connectionless service was added with the 1987 revision to the IEEE 802 standards. It consists of two services:

DL_DATA_ACK     An acknowledged delivery service with no prior connection establishment

DL_REPLY        A poll and response service with no prior connection establishment

The DL_DATA_ACK service allows an LLC user to request an immediate acknowledgment to a transmission. A service-class parameter in the primitive stipulates whether the MAC sublayer is to participate in the acknowledgment (802.4 supports this feature). A status parameter is used by the remote peer LLC entity to indicate whether the protocol data unit was/was not received successfully. The scenario in Figure 10-10 is used for this service.

The DL_REPLY service is quite useful when a user wishes to solicit data from another user. The LLC entity can hold a data unit and pass it to any user that polls for the data, or a user can poll the remote user directly for the data. As examples, the DL_DATA_ACK service would be useful for an electronic mailbox facility; the DL_REPLY service could be used to poll sensor devices on a factory floor.

### LLC/MAC Primitives

The LLC and MAC sublayers use only three primitives to communicate with each other:

* MA_UNITDATA.request (source-address, destination-address, data, priority, service-class)
* MA_UNITDATA.indication (destination-address, source-address, data, reception-status, priority, service-class)
* MA_UNITDATA_STATUS.indication (destination-address, source-address, transmission status, provided-priority, provided-service-class)

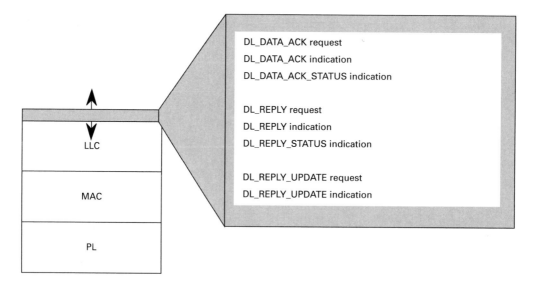

**Figure 10-10.** LCC Primitives for Acknowledged Connectionless Services

The address parameters specify the MAC addresses. The reception-status parameter indicates the success of the transfer. An error would be reported to LLC, which might take remedial action. The transmission-status parameter also is passed to LLC. Its value depends on a vendor's implementation.

Perhaps the most attractive feature of the LLC/MAC arrangement is that the MA_UNITDATA.request primitive is used to send any type of LLC data unit to any type of MAC network. In other words, the interface is portable across MAC protocols.

## SECURITY FEATURES

The LLC protocol has been amended to include a security feature. As shown in Figure 10-11, the LLC sublayer has been divided into yet another sublayer—LLC Control Security (LLCS). Notice from this figure that the service definitions have not been changed, and the LLCS sublayer receives MAC primitives and sends MAC primitives. Therefore, from the architectural standpoint, the addition of LLCS is transparent to the upper-layer LLC and the lower-layer MAC.

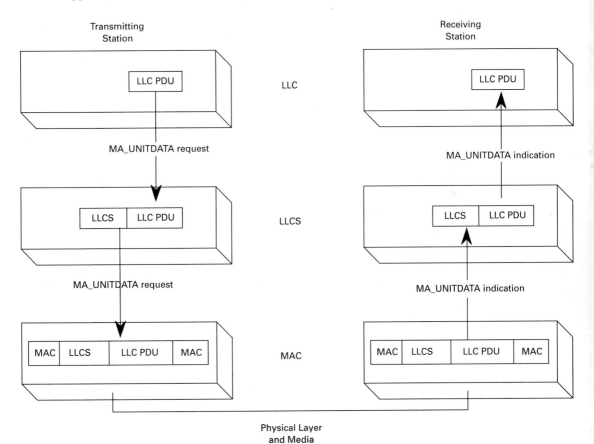

**Figure 10-11.** LCC Security Layers

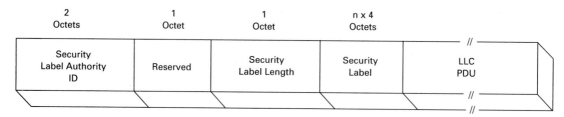

**Figure 10-12.** The LLCS Protocol Data Unit

Figure 10-12 depicts the LLCS protocol data unit (as does Figure 10-11, in a more general manner). The fields labeled *Security Label Authority ID, Security Label Length,* and *Security Label* are not defined explicitly in the standard. They are to be used by the appropriate enterprise in a manner deemed suitable. The security label authority ID is intended to provide a unique identifier of the enterprise that is responsible for assigning security labels to the LLCS protocol data unit. As just mentioned, the security label actual value depends on the actions of the label authority.

## SUMMARY

The logical link control protocol is designed to rest above the media access control protocol. Through the invocation of either Types 1, 2, or 3, the network manager can obtain either connection-oriented services modeled on HDLC's set asynchronous balanced mode or connectionless services through the use of HDLC's unnumbered information frame (UI). Alternately, Type 3 can be used as a connectionless, yet acknowledged, service. This flexibility provides the network user with options for tailoring services to meet the specific needs of the upper-layer protocols.

# *11*

# *LAPM*

## INTRODUCTION

This chapter examines a relatively new link protocol called V.42. It also is known as *link access procedure for modems*, or LAPM. The architecture of LAPM is examined, as well as the V.42 primitives. The relationship of LAPM to HDLC is discussed and a companion protocol, used for data compression (V.42*bis*), is reviewed.

## PURPOSE OF V.42

V.42 has aroused considerable interest in the user community because it addresses two problems that have developed with the increased use of asynchronous devices (and especially asynchronous personal computers): (a) the absence of a standardized asynchronous-to-synchronous conversion protocol, and (b) the need for a more sophisticated error-detection process for asynchronous systems than exists with simple echo checks and parity checks. V.42 is designed to perform asynchronous-synchronous code conversion, as well as error detection and retransmission of damaged data. V.42 is the culmination of several years of efforts by CCITT, working in conjunction with users and vendors.

The link setup of V.42 is shown in Figure 11-1, which illustrates that error detection and correction have been moved to the physical level, at the DCE. This means asynchronous link protocols using parity and echo checks that usually reside in the DTE can be replaced by V.42. In effect, the data link control layer is removed from the user device.

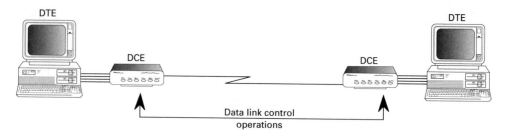

**Figure 11-1.** Data Link Control at the DCE

V.42 includes the conventional services found in a data link control protocol:

- use of a link control protocol for sequencing and flow control
- inclusion of a cyclic redundancy check for error detection
- use of V.14 for asynchronous-to-synchronous conversion
- transmission of synchronous data on the communications link
- use of flags to delineate the frame on the link from other signals
- provision for retransmission of data by the sender in the event of error detection by the receiver

The error-detecting DCE contains four major components, which are illustrated in Figure 11-2.

- A signal converter
- An error control function
- A control function
- A V.24 interface

The V.42 Recommendation establishes the error control function as the service provider and the control function as the service user. These terms are used in the context of the OSI model.

The V.24 interface provides the connection to the DTE. Data are exchanged on the interface in a start-stop format. The signal converter is the interface to the telephone line.

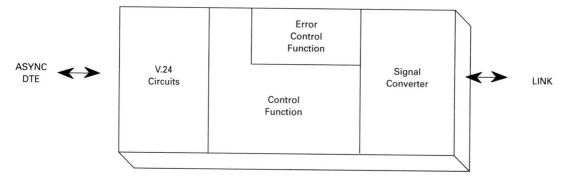

**Figure 11-2.** The Error Control Modem (V.42 & LAPM)

It is designed to operate on a 2-wire, point-to-point leased circuit (although this author sees no reason that the specification could not be used on dial-up, with V.25, V.25*bis*, or EIA 366 dial-up procedures established for an initial handshake). The control function coordinates and controls the other DCE functions. The error control function is responsible for the error correction protocol.

## RESPONSIBILITIES OF THE CONTROL FUNCTION AND ERROR CONTROL FUNCTION

The *control function* is the "operating system" of V.42. It is responsible for conducting a handshake with the remote DCE to determine whether it is capable of supporting a V.42 error-correcting scheme. It also is responsible for falling back to a non-error-correcting mode in the event the DCE cannot support error-correcting schemes or asynchronous-to-synchronous conversion schemes. It is responsible for negotiating the procedures to be used between the DCEs. It manages the delivery of the data between the error-control function and the V.24 interface. It ensures that data are not lost during this transfer. Also, it provides the synchronous-to-asynchronous conversion between the V.24 interface and the error control function. It provides and coordinates loopback testing and, if necessary, it renegotiates parameters that govern the operations of the DCEs during the connection. Finally, it is responsible for releasing the connection.

The *error control function* is like most conventional line protocols published by CCITT and is unaware of the actions just described. Its responsibility is to deliver the traffic safely across the interface, to negotiate the link level operational parameters, and to perform error correction and retransmission of corrupted data. It is responsible for responding to loopback testing and releasing of the connection as dictated by the control function.

## LAPM

V.42 implements a link control protocol called LAPM (*link access procedure for modems*). It is based on the HDLC family of protocols and also was derived from the LAPD specification (which is part of the CCITT ISDN Recommendations). Figure 11-3 shows the format for the LAPM XID frame. This frame is used during the handshaking operation between the two modems. We examine XID shortly.

LAPM uses the HDLC balanced asynchronous class (BA). It makes use of HDLC functional extensions BA 1, 2, 4, 7, and 10. This mode is identical to LAPD. Also, it permits an optional procedure using HDLC functional extensions 3, 12, and 14.

The principal difference between LAPM and a conventional HDLC implementation is the use of the address field. The address field consists of the data link identifier, the C/R bit, and the address extension bit. The C/R bit is a command/response bit that identifies the frame as either a command or response. The DLCI value is used to transfer information between the V.42 interfaces. Currently, DLCI is set to 0 to identify a DTE-to-DTE interface. Other values are permitted within the limits defined in the recommendation. The address extension bit can be set to 1 to designate another octet for DLCI.

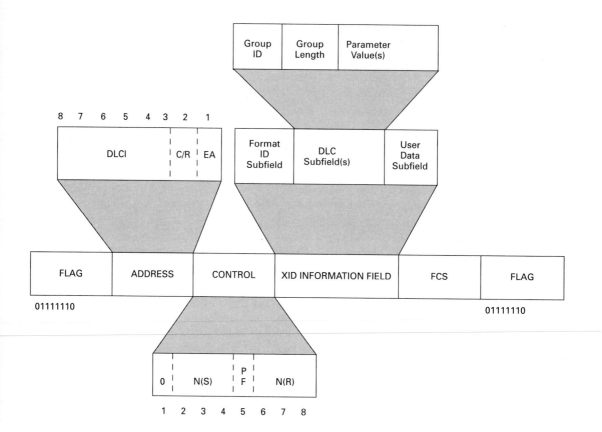

FLAG: DELINEATES BEGINNING AND ENDING OF FRAME
ADDRESS: IDENTIFIES V.24 INTERFACES
CONTROL: USED FOR SEQUENCING, FLOW CONTROL
INFORMATION: USER DATA OR CONTROL HEADERS
FCS: FRAME CHECK SEQUENCE (FOR ERROR CHECKING)
N(S): SENDING SEQUENCE NUMBER
N(R): RECEIVING SEQUENCE NUMBER
P/F: THE POLL OR FINAL BIT
C/R: COMMAND/RESPONSE BIT
EA: ADDRESS FIELD EXTENSION
DLCI:  DATA LINK CONNECTION IDENTIFIER

**Figure 11-3.** The LAPM XID Frame

The format of the XID frame in Figure 11-3 appears to be quite complex, but basically it involves only a few fields (some of which are yet to be defined in the recommendation). We focus on the XID information field because it contains the parameters used to negotiate a number of features between the two peer entities. The I field of the XID frame consists of:

- Format identifier subfield (FI): An 8-bit field to designate the format of the I field. It has been set up to allow 128 different formats to be defined by the ISO and 128 other formats to be defined by users. Currently, only a "general purpose" format has been established (with a value of 10000010).

- Group identifier: Specifies a user data subfield in conjunction with the general format FI.
- Group length (GL): Gives the length of the parameter field.
- Parameter field: Composed of parameter identifier(s) (PI), parameter length(s) (PL), parameter value(s) (PV). These fields are used to establish the maximum length of the I field, the transmit and receive window sizes, etc.
- User data subfield: At present, the only value defined in this field is: (a) 1 = manufacturer's ID not assigned by CCITT, (b) 0 = manufacturer's ID assigned by CCITT.

V.42 includes an appendix that defines an alternate procedure to LAPM. This procedure is based on the Microcom MNP protocol. This appendix was included by the CCITT due to the prevalence of MNP in many personal computer systems. The CCITT states that the alternate protocol is fully compatible with MNP. CCITT also states that it does not intend to provide updates and enhancements to this appendix.

## V.42 Primitives

The communications between the control function and the error control function occur through OSI-type primitives. These primitives are used by the control function to direct the actions of the error control function and for the error control function to inform the control function of its activities. The V.42 primitives are summarized in Table 11-1.

### Establishing Communications Between the DCEs

The establishment of the V.42 session proceeds through two phases: (a) the detection phase, and (b) the protocol establishment phase.

**Detection Phase.** The detection phase is performed transparently by the control function: the user DTE and the error control function are not aware of the operation. It uses conventional dial-and-answer techniques found in many modems today. It does not define the specific dial-and-answer standard, but defers to the particular modulation recommendations.

Naturally enough, the originating DCE becomes the originator and the answering DCE becomes the answerer. The roles assumed during this carrier handshake depend on the specific modem standards.

**TABLE 11-1.** V.42 PRIMITIVES

| Primitive | Function |
| --- | --- |
| L-ESTABLISH | Establishes a connection between error-correcting entities |
| L-DATA | Transfers data |
| L-RELEASE | Releases the connection between the entities |
| L-SIGNAL | Sends a break signal |
| L-SETPARM | Establishes or negotiates parameters for a session |
| L-TEST | Sets up a look-back test between entities |

Several detection operations are shown in Figure 11-4. The originator begins the handshaking operations when the dial-and-answer procedures are finished. This means circuits *ready for sending* (RFS) and *received signal detector* (RSD) are in the ON condition. The originator control function then sends out a special bit pattern called the

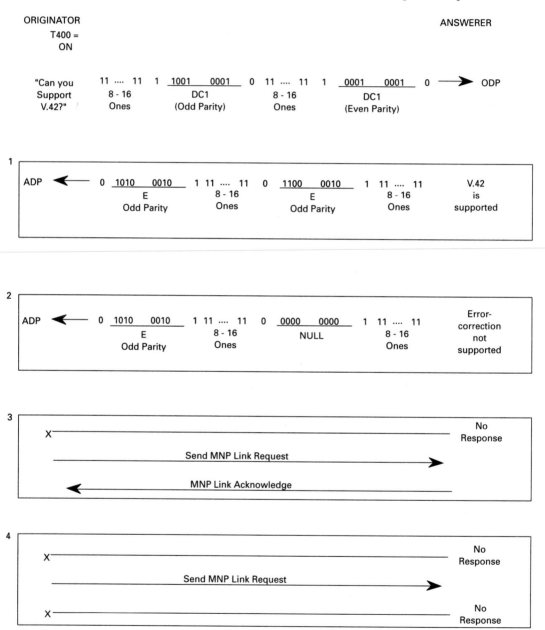

**Figure 11-4.** The Detection Phase

*originator detection pattern* (ODP). The pattern is a ASCII DC1 with even parity followed by 8–16 binary ones, followed by another DC1 with odd parity, and followed by 8–16 ones. This is used by the receiving DCE as a "hello." If the originating DCE does not receive a response to this bit pattern, it may or may not fall back to a non-error-correcting mode. Whatever the case may be, it assumes that V.42 capability does not exist in the remote DCE.

The remote DCE, upon receiving the ODP, becomes the answerer. If it is "smart" enough to understand that the originating DCE is capable of error-correcting operations, it sends back an *answer detection pattern* (ADP) to indicate: (1) if V.42 is supported, (2) if no error-correcting protocol is desired, or if there are other codes that are reserved for future use. Let us assume that it transmits back the pattern indicating V.42 is supported. The two DCEs now have completed the detection phase and the second phase is entered.

**Protocol Establishment Phase.** After the completion of the detection phase, the protocol establishment phase is used to establish the logical link and negotiate the parameters for the operation. At this point the V.42 primitives are invoked.

The protocol establishment phase is shown in Figure 11-5. This figure shows that 18 discrete steps are involved. Keep in mind that this is only one scenario, showing a typical connection establishment and transfer of data along with some negotiation of parameters. Several other scenarios are available. The following discussion summarizes the operations depicted in Figure 11-5.

The first six steps are used to establish the logical connection between the two DCEs, as well as the link layer connection. The transmitting control function gets things started by sending the L-ESTABLISH request primitive to its error control function. This primitive is mapped to a LAPM set asynchronous balanced mode extended command frame (SABME). This frame is transferred to the remote ECF, which maps the frame to a link establishment indication primitive (L-ESTAB Ind). In Step 4, the remote control function responds with a link establishment response primitive (L-ESTAB Res). Its supporting ECF maps this primitive to a LAPM unnumbered acknowledgment frame (UA). This frame is transmitted across the link, where it is received by the local ECF. The UA frame is then mapped to the link establishment confirm primitive (L-ESTAB Conf). These operations complete the initial handshaking between the two DCEs.

Next, the control function may choose to negotiate parameters for the session.

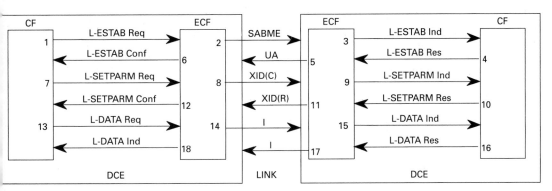

**Figure 11-5.** The V.42 Protocol Establishment Phase

Figure 11-5 shows that it sends a L-SET parameter request primitive. Its ECF uses this primitive to create an XID LAPM frame. The parameters in this frame are used by the receiving DCE to determine several operating constraints to be used during the session. As can be seen from the figure, the receiving ECF receives the XID frame and maps it to an L-SET parameter indication primitive.

In Step 10, the remote control function responds with L-SET parameter response, which is mapped to the XID response frame in Step 11. To complete this part of the process, the frame is sent to the local ECF, which maps the XID frame to the L-SET parameter confirm primitive.

The parameters that are negotiated in Steps 9 through 10 are as follows:

- Detection phase timer (T400): Determines the amount of time the ECF waits for the originator detection pattern (ODP) or the answer detection pattern (ADP). The default value is 750 ms.

- Detection timer (T401): Determines the amount of time the DCE waits for an acknowledgment from remote station before resorting to remedial actions.

- Maximum retransmissions (N400): Determines the number of times the DCE will retransmit a frame requiring a response.

- Maximum number of octets in an I field (N401): Determines the number of octets that can be carried in the I field of an I frame, an XID frame, a UI frame, or a test frame. Default is 128 octets.

- Window size (k): Determines the number of I frames that can be outstanding before an acknowledgment is required. The default value is 15.

- Reply delay timer (T402): Determines the amount of time the receiving DCE will wait before transmitting a reply to a previously transmitted frame. This timer ensures that the transmitting DCE's T401 timer does not expire needlessly and transmit redundant frames.

- N activity timer (T403): Determines the amount of time a DCE will allow the channel to be idle, that is, not transmitting any valid frames. The purpose of this timer is to detect faults as early as possible.

We assume that all has gone well in the negotiation of the session parameters. The remaining operations in the figure depict the transfer of data using the data primitives and the LAPM information frames.

Note that the operating parameters deal with activities that should remain transparent to the end user. Of course, systems personnel are quite interested in these parameters, but again they are beyond (and should be kept beyond) the end user. Indeed, this standard does not stipulate (with the exception of the manufacturer's ID) any values that must reside in the I field.

For data transfer, V.42 simply accepts the user information across the transmit lead of V.24 and encapsulates it into the I field of LAPM for safe transport across the link to the receiving DCE. Of course, we learned earlier in this chapter that this is the principal function of V.42 that is, it is an error-correcting protocol.

## V.42*BIS*

During the work on V.42, which was completed in 1988, the CCITT study group XVII decided that a data compression enhancement was needed to further the performance of error-correcting modems. Consequently, a number of existing schemes were analyzed, notably British Telecom's BTLZ, Hayes' system, Microcom's MNP5 and MNP7, and the ACT Formula. The decision was made to use the BTLZ algorithm, which we examine shortly. V.42*bis* was not published in the *Blue Book,* but has undergone rapid development and now is an approved standard.

The V.42*bis* data compression recommendation has a compression ratio of 3:1 to 4:1 (based on the use of ASCII text). The recommendation requires approximately 3K of memory. The dictionary size for the characters and strings can be as little as 512 bytes and as great as 2,048 bytes. The designer must analyze the trade-offs between smaller and larger dictionaries and must consider the fact that the larger dictionaries provide better performance with higher compression ratios, even though they consume more memory. Keep in mind that V.42*bis* permits the same software to be used on different size dictionaries.

As depicted in Figure 11-6, the V.42*bis* model is quite similar to the V.42 model. The only additional functional module is, logically enough, the data compression function.

The V.42*bis* compression algorithm works on strings of characters. It does not work on character substitution, but encodes a string of characters with a fixed-length code word. The system also uses a dictionary to store frequently occurring character strings along with a code to represent the character strings.

Figure 11-7 depicts a general view of the operations of the transmit modem and the receive modem. A character string is matched against the directory on the transmit side and an attempt is made to match this character string to a string existing in the dictionary. If a code word is found that matches a character string, it is sent to another buffer for assembly with other previously matched code words. The code words are placed in the LAPM frame and transmitted to the receiving modem.

The lower portion of this figure shows the operations at the receiving modem. The code words are used to perform a "look up" in the receiving modem's dictionary. The code word *value* reveals a particular string. This permits the code word to be mapped back to the original character string.

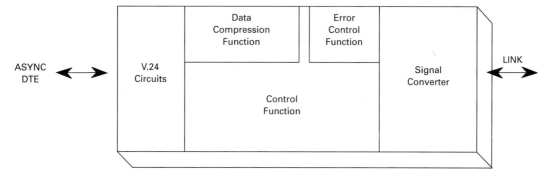

**Figure 11-6.** The V.42*bis* Model

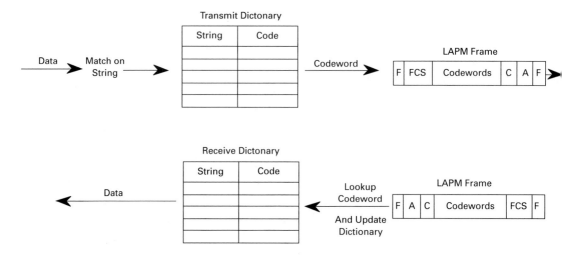

**Figure 11-7.** Transmit and Receive Operations

The dictionaries must be updated in both modems. When the dictionary in the sending modem detects the first character in the data stream that does not match an entry in the dictionary, it forwards the character string that did match with the appropriate code word and then uses the unmatched character to produce one more concatenated string in the dictionary.

The receive directory finds the string that matches the code word. However, the transmit side is one step ahead of the receive side. Therefore, at the receiving modem, the first character of the next received code word must be used to update the receive side dictionary. The V.42*bis* receiver always assumes that the first character of each string is to be used to update the previous character string.

For our purposes, the main point is that LAPM carries the compressed data as the contents of the I field in the LAPM frame.

## SUMMARY

The link access procedure for modems (LAPM) provides several features for asynchronous interfaces. Not only will it work with V.14 to translate asynchronous to synchronous transmission formats, it also provides a HDLC SABM capability for managing the traffic between two modems. LAPM is published as part of the V.42 Recommendation by the CCITT.

In addition, V.42*bis* can be implemented for data compression capabilities in the modem, as well. The combination of these features provides a powerful tool for interfacing asynchronous and synchronous systems across the communications link.

# 12

# Wireless Link Controls and SS7

## INTRODUCTION

This chapter reviews a number of link layer protocols used on wireless systems. For satellite systems, the emphasis is the ALOHA protocol, as well as slotted ALOHA and several derivations. In addition, *time division multiple access* (TDMA) techniques are examined in relation to how they are used in some satellite circuits. The chapter examines *satellite delay units* (SDU) and how they can be used to more effectively utilize the satellite link. Cellular systems also are discussed, as well as the GSM standards. In addition, the SS7 specification is included in this chapter. Even though it typically is used on hard-wire systems, it is also employed on GSM.

## AN INTRODUCTION TO SATELLITE COMMUNICATIONS

It should prove helpful to provide a brief tutorial on satellite communications. Those already familiar with the topic may choose to skip to the next section. In essence, satellite communications is microwave relay communications from an earth station to a satellite station and back to another earth station (or, for that matter, back to the same earth station).

The technology provides for a large communications capacity. Through the use of the microwave frequency bands, several thousand voice-grade channels can be placed on a satellite station.

The satellite also has the capacity for a broadcast transmission. The transmitting antenna can send signals to a wide geographical area. Applications such as electronic mail and distributed systems find the broadcast capability quite useful.

Transmission cost is independent of distance between the earth sites. For example, it is immaterial if two sites are 100 or 1000 miles apart, as long as they are serviced by the same communications satellite. The signals transmitted from the satellite can be received by all stations, regardless of their distance from each other.

The stations experience a significant signal propagation delay. Since many satellites are positioned 22,300 miles above the earth, the transmission has to travel into space and return. A round-trip transmission requires a minimum of about 240 milliseconds (ms), and could be greater as the signal travels through other components. This may affect certain link layer protocols, as we shall see shortly.

The broadcast aspect of satellite communications may present security problems, since all stations under the satellite antenna can receive the broadcasts. Consequently, transmissions often are changed (encrypted) for satellite channels.

## Geosynchronous Systems

Many satellites are in a geosynchronous orbit. They rotate around the earth at 6,900 miles (11,040 Km) per hour and remain positioned over the same point above the equator. Thus, the earth stations' antenna can remain in one position, since the satellite's motion relative to the earth's position is fixed. Furthermore, a single geosynchronous satellite with nondirectional antenna can cover about 30% of the earth's surface. The geosynchronous orbit requires a rocket launch of 22,300 miles (35,680 Km) into space. Geosynchronous satellites can achieve worldwide coverage (some limited areas in the polar regions are not covered) with three satellites spaced at 120° intervals from each other.

## POLLING/SELECTION ON SATELLITE SYSTEMS

Satellite communications can be controlled by polling/selection techniques. The traffic is managed by an earth station (designated as a primary site) sending polls and selects to the satellite for relaying back to secondary earth stations. An alternate approach (not used much) is to have the satellite station provide the polls and selects to control the network. Let us examine both approaches to determine the advantages and disadvantages of polling/selection in satellite systems.

First, we assume a satellite computer performs the polling and selection. Since the satellite is located 22,300 miles (35,680 Km) above the earth and the signal propagates at a rate of 186,000 miles (297,600 Km) per second, it takes a minimum of 120 milliseconds (ms) for the poll or select to reach an earth station (22,300 miles ÷ 186,000 mps = .120 seconds, or 35,680 ÷ 297,600 = 120 seconds). It requires another 120 ms for the response to the poll and select to reach the communications satellite. Consequently, each polling and selection cycle takes 240 ms. Assuming n users are to be polled and selected within the network, a full polling and selection cycle would take .240 × n seconds. If 100 users were using the satellite system, it would require .240 × 100, or 24 seconds, for a full polling/selection cycle to take place. Obviously, the delay presents some rather serious response time problems. If a ground station controls the polls and selects, the performance is even worse, since the poll or select is sent up to the satellite and down to the earth station. Consequently, with 100 users in the network, a ground station controller would require 48 seconds for the full polling/selection cycle.

The delay is quite evident for a half-duplex session in which only two stations are using the channel. If User A from one station sends a frame on the satellite channel to User B at another site, User A must pause and wait for an acknowledgment. If the two users are sending multiple frames to each other (as in a file-transfer batch transmission), the accumulated delays create an extended time to complete the process, which reduces the effective utilization of the channel. The widely used half-duplex binary synchronous control protocol (BSC or bisync) experiences considerable utilization degradation on a satellite channel. Assuming a 9.6 Kbit/s channel, the BSC link efficiency is as shown in Table 12-1.

The larger the block or frame size, the better the channel utilization, because the larger blocks mask the delay effect of the long-distance circuit. Half-duplex delay does not create a problem on short-distance channels with short delays (of 10 ms., for example). It is more evident on circuits of several hundred miles (40 ms. delay) to several thousand miles (500 ms. delay, or more).

The use of a full-duplex protocol decreases the response time and increases the throughput. The full-duplex system allows the overlapping of transmissions and acknowledgments across a channel and substantially can reduce the amount of delay incurred in the polling cycle. For example, one station can be polled, and while the poll is being transmitted to that station, yet another station can transmit data on the return channel. If timers and windows are established properly, full-duplex line protocols "mask" the propagation delay.

Window management is an important consideration. For example, if a system is transmitting 1,000 bit frames and the channel is operating at 50,000 bits per second, the channel provides the speed for multiple frames to be sent on the up and down links in succession before any responses or data are transmitted back. High-speed channels actually increase the effect of propagation delay. Consequently, the window closes faster with high-speed channels and short blocks of data.

In order to prevent the channel from becoming idle, the conventional link protocol window of seven often is expanded. The window expansion prevents the transmitting side from closing its window sequencing option by expanding the window from n to 127; that is, 127 frames can be transmitted in succession without any acknowledgment from the receiver. The expanded window allows the system to compensate for the propagation delay and provides for more efficient channel utilization.

Expanded windows present some additional problems, however. In the event of an error, the Go-Back-N (REJ) technique discussed in Chapter 3 necessitates the

**TABLE 12-1.** CHANNEL UTILIZATION WITH HALF-DUPLEX

| Block (Frame) Size | 10 ms. Delay | 38 ms. Delay | 500 ms. Delay |
|---|---|---|---|
| 40 bytes | 76.9% | 46.7% | 6.2% |
| 132 bytes | 91.7% | 74.3% | 18.0% |
| 516 bytes | 97.7% | 91.9% | 46.2% |

retransmission of one or more frames. For example, if the transmitting site sends Frames 1 through 40, and Frame 6 is in error, then Frames 6 through 40 must be retransmitted. With the alternate method Selective Reject (SREJ), the receiving station is tasked with queuing several frames to await the retransmission of the single frame. In our example, Frames 7 through 40 must be held at the receiver site until Frame 6 is retransmitted, because the frames must be passed to the user in sequential order.

To place this discussion in its proper perspective, it must be emphasized that the newer satellite services exhibit low *bit error rates* (BER). For example, a high-performance satellite service has a BER ranging from $1:10^7$ to $1:10^9$. Consequently, the REJ/SREJ problem is not as serious on a satellite link as it would be on a lower-quality long-distance medium.

## ALOHA

In the early 1970s, Norman Abramson, at the University of Hawaii, devised a technique for uncoordinated users to effectively compete for a channel. The approach is called the ALOHA system; it is so named because the word ALOHA is an Hawaiian greeting without regard to whether a person is arriving or departing. The original ALOHA technique used a ground-based radio packet system, rather than satellites, but the ideas are applicable to any channel media when users are contending for its use.

The premise of ALOHA is that users are acting on a peer-to-peer basis—they have equal access to the channel. A user station transmits whenever it has data to send. Since the channel is not allocated by any primary/secondary structure, it is possible (and probable) that users occasionally will transmit at approximately the same time. Simultaneous transmission results in the signals interfering and distorting each other as the separate signals propagate up to the satellite transponder. These "collisions" necessitate the retransmission of the damaged frames. (The term "packet" is used in place of "frame" under the ALOHA scheme.) Since the users of the satellite link know exactly what was transmitted onto the up-link channel and when it was transmitted, they only need listen to the down-link channel at a prescribed time to determine whether the broadcast packet arrived without damage.

If the packet is damaged due to a collision, the stations are required to retransmit the damaged packet. In essence, the idea is to listen to the down-link channel one up-and-down delay time after the packet was sent. If the packet is destroyed, the transmitting site is required to wait a short random period and then to retransmit. The randomized wait period diminishes the chances of the competing stations colliding again, since the waiting times likely will differ and result in retransmissions at different times. When traffic increases, the randomized waits can be increased to diminish the collisions.

Figure 12-1 depicts a typical ALOHA system using satellite communications. Stations A and B are transmitting packets on a shared channel. The down-link channel shows that Packet 1 from station A is transmitted up and down safely; Packet 2 from station B also is transmitted without error. However, the second packet from A and the first packet from B are transmitted at approximately the same time. As the transmissions of the two stations are narrowcasted up to the satellite station, the signals interfere with each other, resulting in a collision.

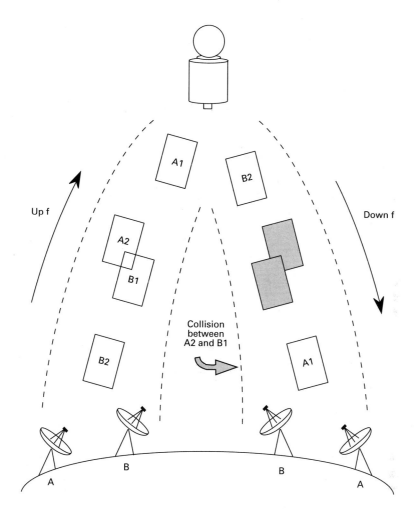

**Figure 12-1.** Random ALOHA on Satellite Links

The satellite station is not responsible for error detection or error correction; it transmits what it receives from the up-link. On the down-link, stations A and B note the packets have collided and, upon waiting a random period of time (usually a few milliseconds), attempt to retransmit. This approach is quite effective when the users are uncoordinated and are sending traffic in bursts, such as data from keyboard terminals.

## Calculating Delay on an ALOHA Channel

We assume a packet initially is transmitted (which takes t seconds) and is received after Nt seconds of transmission delay. If interference occurs, the sender waits a random period (between 0 and K packet times) before retransmitting. On the average, a wait of (1 + K) t/2 seconds takes place before another retransmission can occur.

Let us assume further that s represents channel throughput; that is, the amount of traffic successfully delivered. The value g represents total traffic, including successful and unsuccessful deliveries. Therefore, the ratio g/s represents the number of times each packet has to be retransmitted before a successful delivery occurs.

Given these assumptions, the *total average delay* (TAD) through an ALOHA channel is computed as:

$$TAD = t/2[1 + e^{2g}(1 + 2N) + K(e^{2g} - 1)]$$

Where: t = packet length in seconds; g = total traffic (bits per second); N = propagation delay in packet lengths; K = retransmission protocol delay in packet lengths; e = 2.718 (base of natural logarithms).

Figure 12-2 plots several ALOHA channel delay scenarios, with a channel rate of 50 Kbit/s and a packet length of 1000 bits. The value t is 20 ms (1000/50000 = .02). The figure reveals that little delay is encountered with a light load on the channel. As traffic increases, more collisions occur and the delay lengthens. The curves show the packet retransmission delay (K) increases as throughput (s) increases.

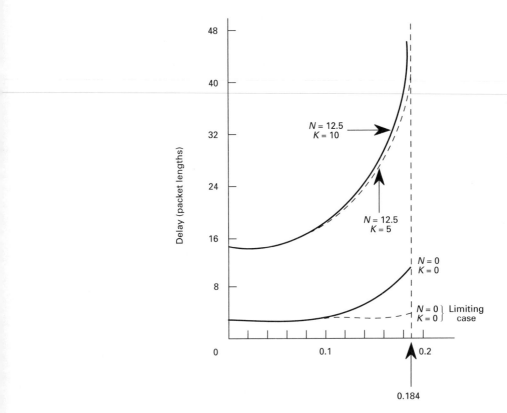

ALOHA channel throughput, *S*

N = Round-trip satellite delay, in packet lengths
K = Protocol retransmission, delay (maximum waiting before retransmitting a collided packet), in packet lengths

**Figure 12-2.** An ALOHA Channel Delay versus Throughput [ROSN82]

Random ALOHA experiences considerable degradation of throughput when the channel is heavily utilized. However, keep in mind that what is transmitted across the channel is all end-user data. Unlike the primary/secondary polling systems, ALOHA uses no polls, selects, or negative responses to polls. Only end-user information is transmitted. Nonetheless, the pure random scheme can be improved by adapting a more efficient strategy for using the uncoordinated channel, called Slotted ALOHA.

Slotted ALOHA requires that common clocks be established at the earth stations and at the satellite. The clocks are synchronized to send traffic at specific periods. For example, the clocks may require that packets are transmitted only on 20 ms. (.020 second) increments. In this example, the 20 ms. increment is derived from a 50,000-bit/s channel and 1,000-bit packets (1,000 ÷ 50,000 = .020 second).

The 20 ms. increment is referred to as the *packet duration,* which is the time in which the packet is transmitted on the channel. All stations are required to transmit at the beginning of a slot period. A packet cannot be transmitted if it overlaps more than one slot.

The Slotted ALOHA approach increases throughput substantially on the channel, because if packets overlap or collide, they do so completely; at most, only one slot is damaged. However, like pure Random ALOHA, the Slotted ALOHA does offer opportunities for collisions. For example, if two stations transmit in the same clock period, their packets collide. As in the pure Random ALOHA approach, the stations are required to wait a random period of time before attempting to seize a slot for retransmission.

Another refinement to Slotted ALOHA is Slotted ALOHA with Nonowner. The channel slots are combined into an ALOHA frame. The ALOHA frame must equal or exceed the up-and-down propagation delay. This relationship is defined as:

$$AFL \geq PD$$

or

$$NSL * SLT \geq PD$$

Where: AFL = ALOHA frame length; PD = the up-and-down propagation delay; NSL = number of slots in an ALOHA frame; and SLT = time interval of a slot.

Consequently, a 1,000-bit packet lasting 20 ms. would require a minimum of 12 slots to make up the ALOHA frame: 12 slots $\times$ 20 ms. = 240 ms. The 240 ms. period represents the minimum up-and-down propagation delay (120 ms. (up) + 120 ms. (down) = 240 ms.).

Slotted ALOHA with Nonowner requires that a station select an empty slot in the frame. Once the user has seized the slot, it is reserved for the user for successive frames until the user relinquishes the slot. The relinquishment occurs by the station sending a protocol control code, such as EOT (*end of transmission*). Upon receiving an EOT, the next frame transmitted is empty for that particular slot. A user station then is allowed to contend for the slot with the next subsequent frame. The only collisions occurring on Slotted ALOHA with Nonowner are when stations pick the same slot in the 240 ms. frame.

Another variation of Slotted ALOHA is Slotted ALOHA with Owner. The slots of each frame now are owned by users. The user has exclusive use of that slot within the frame as long as the user has data to transmit. In the event that the user relinquishes the slot, it is so indicated with an established code. The slot becomes empty and is available for any other user to seize it. Once another user has seized the slot, that user has exclusive rights to the use of the slot, until the original owner seizes the slot. The rightful owner can claim the slot at any time by beginning transmissions within the designated slot in the frame. The relinquishment is required when the rightful owner transmits. Obviously, the first time the owner transmits in the slot a collision may occur. On the subsequent frame, the rightful owner retransmits. The relinquishing station then must look for another free slot, or must go to other slots if they are owned. This refined approach of ALOHA is classified as a peer-to-peer priority structure, since some stations can be given priority ownership over other stations.

## TIME DIVISION MULTIPLE ACCESS (TDMA)

COMSAT initiated work on TDMA in the mid-1960s. Since then, scores of TDMA systems have been implemented worldwide. Even though FDMA still is the prevalent technique for signaling, TDMA is used more on new systems. TDMA shares a satellite transponder by dividing access into time slots. Each earth terminal is designated a time, and its transmission burst is timed precisely into the slot. Our example of TDMA is the Satellite Business System (SBS).

TDMA assigns slots as needed. However, unlike the ALOHA system, the slots are assigned by a primary station called the *reference* (REF). As depicted in Figure 12-3, the reference station accepts requests from the other stations, and based on the nature of the traffic and available channel capacity, the REF assigns these requests to specific frames for subsequent transmission. Every 20 frames, the reference station is assigned to each transponder of the system. SBS provides for as many as ten active transponders per satellite.

Figure 12-3 also shows the earth station components. The major components consist of the port adapter, the satellite communications controller (SCC), a burst modem, the transmit/receive device, and an antenna.

The port adapter is responsible for interfacing the user lines into the earth station. The adapter accepts voice images at a rate of 32 Kbit/s and data at rates varying from 2.4 Kbit/s to 1.544 Mbit/s.

All digital images are passed to the satellite communications controller, which is a software-oriented unit that consolidates the functions of timing, station assignment, switching, and processing of voice and data calls. It calculates channel requirements based on the number of voice connections, the number of data ports available, and the number of queued data connection requests. It then assigns these requests to TDMA frames.

The burst modem sends out a 48 Mbit/s signal with 15 ms. frames (.015 second) under the direction of the satellite controller. Thus, each transponder has the capability of operating at 48 megabits per second (see Figure 12-4).

The transmit/receive antennas are responsible for transmitting and receiving the up-and-down channel links. SBS operates at 14 gigahertz on the up link and 12 gigahertz on the down link. This transmission band was chosen because it is relatively free from other

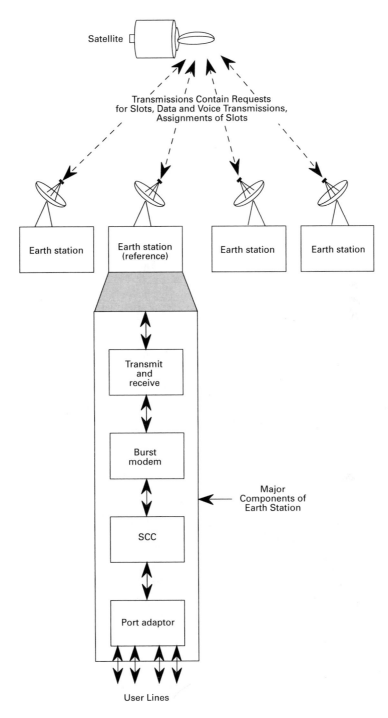

**Figure 12-3.** Satellite Business Systems (SBS) TDMA

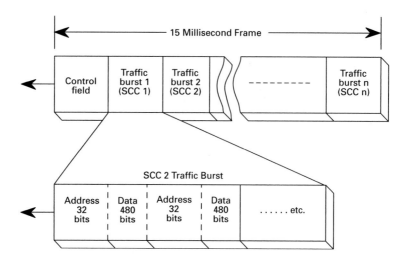

**Figure 12-4.** The TDMA Frame

satellite transmissions and because it allows the earth stations to operate relatively free from the terrestrial microwave operations of 4/6 gigahertz.

On a 15 ms. frame, the reference station (REF) transmits an assignment set for all SCCs using the transponder. As mentioned earlier, this transmission is sent every 20 frames. The assignment set specifies the capacity and position of each SCC's traffic burst to the transponder. Recall that assignments are made in response to the requests received in earlier frames. The control field of the frame contains the assignments and the requests from the competing stations. The remainder of the frame consists of the traffic, which contains the traffic bursts from each SCC that was assigned a position by the reference station.

The traffic is packed in 512-bit channels consisting of a 32-bit destination address and 480 bits of data. The 480-bit data frame was chosen to accommodate the requirement for a voice transmission rate of 32 kilobits per second [480 $\times$ (1 second/.015 slot) = 32,000].

The 32 kilobits per second rate uses only a small fraction of the total 48 megabit channel capacity. Consequently, many voice and data transmissions can be *time division multiplexed* (TDM) efficiently onto the high-speed 48 Mbit/s channel.

## Satellite-Switched Time Division Multiple Access (SS/TDMA)

SS/TDMA uses TDMA and multibeam antennae. The antennae cover several geographical zones. A switch at the satellite connects the up link and down link channels by switching the configuration as necessary. SS/TDMA also may use communications channels directly between the satellites. Often, communicating ground stations are not visible by the same satellite. An *intersatellite link* (ISL) can be used to directly link up two satellites. The combination of SS/TDMA and ISL appears very promising, and the 1990s likely will see operational systems.

## SATELLITE DELAY UNITS (SDUs)

Since half-duplex protocols such as bisync are used widely today, satellite vendors have developed methods to compensate for the inherent inefficiency of a half-duplex system on the satellite circuit. The satellite delay compensation unit (SDU) is one such tool. Assume Stations A and B are to communicate through a satellite channel. However, instead of communicating directly with each other, the two stations transmit and receive through a SDU. The SDU is connected to each of the stations through a land-based terrestrial link, such as microwave or optical fibers. Consequently, the delay of signal transmission between the DTE and the SDU is very short.

The SDU actually is a protocol converter. It accepts bisync traffic from Station A and Station B and buffers the traffic locally. When Station A sends a select command to Station B, the SDU servicing Station A immediately acknowledges the select with an ACK0. The data are transmitted, checked for errors at the SDU, and then acknowledged. The SDU for A then transmits the data using its own protocol through the satellite circuit for transmission down to the down link SDU (B). The SDU for B provides an error check and responds with an acknowledgment. The SDU servicing Station B then goes through the same sequence of events that DTE A and SDU A performed—it sends a Select to Station B, which acknowledges the Select, receives the data, checks for errors, and responds with an ACK0.

The satellite delay compensation units provide some immunity from the cumulative effects of delay on half-duplex protocols. However, certain protocols, even though they may be half-duplex, may not benefit from the SDU compensation. For example, if half-duplex messages, such as bisync, are sent one at a time for an interactive session, there is no cumulative effect on the delay of these transmissions, even though the long delay could be a problem for extremely high-speed applications. However, half-duplex systems that utilize batch transmission, such as many of the IBM 3270 family devices, can benefit substantially from the use of the SDU, because the session between the DTEs usually encompasses many blocks of transmission. In batch systems, the transmitting SDU can receive and buffer an entire file before it activates the remote SDU session. Likewise, the receiving SDU can buffer the batch file completely and then establish the session with the receiving DTE.

## CELLULAR COMMUNICATIONS

Even the familiar cellular telephone system uses a data link control to manage the calls made to and from mobile telephones. Cellular radio was conceived as a terrestrial voice telephone network. Its purpose is to upgrade the existing mobile radio-telephone system. The idea goes back to 1972 when the FCC recognized the demand for mobile telephones was exceeding the frequencies available.

The FCC then opened up frequencies initially in the 800-900 MHz band, and schemes were developed to reuse the same frequencies in the same geographical vicinity. In 1979, a prototype network was built in Chicago by AT&T. In a few short years, cellular radio has grown to reach all metropolitan areas, and systems are being developed for nationwide service.

A cellular radio network is structured around the concept of "cells" (see Figure 12-5). Each cell is a geographical area with a low-power transmitter. The mobile telephone in the automobile or truck communicates with the transmitter, which, in turn, communicates with the *Mobile Telephone Switching Office* (MTSO). The MTSO is an extension of the telephone central office, and the mobile channel appears to be the same as a wire line to the stored program control logic (SPC) at the telephone office.

As the mobile unit passes through the network, the user is assigned a frequency for use during transit through each cell. Since each cell has its own low-power transmitter, the signals for nonadjacent cells do not interfere with each other. As a consequence, the noncontiguous cells can use the same frequencies.

## Cellular Radio's Link Control Operation

The purpose of the data link control channel for a cellular radio system is to manage the calls between the MTSO, the cell site, and the mobile unit. The channel is used (a) to establish a handshake between mobile unit and the MTSO to determine which channel is to be used during the session, (b) to release the channel as the vehicle crosses cells, and (c) to terminate the call.

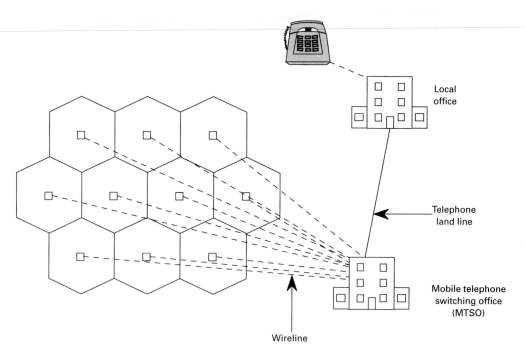

**Figure 12-5.** Cellular Radio

### Cellular Radio and Data Transmission

Cellular radio technology was designed for voice communications. Two major problems must be addressed for data communications:

- Radio fading causes the loss of several characters of data.
- The handing-off to another cell entails a "blanked-out" period of 300 to 900 ms. This period is insignificant for voice, but causes the loss of data.

Several systems now are available to deal with the loss of data in mobile systems. Some are designed around the Hayes modem specification. All systems entail some type of error correction scheme, and a retransmission occurs if the error correction effort does not repair the corrupted data.

## INFRARED

The use of infrared frequencies for short-haul transmission is another option that has proved quite successful for some applications. The system is built around optical transceivers that transmit and receive at relatively short distances (approximately one mile, maximum).

Infrared has several attractive features. First, the signals are not subject to microwave interference and the FCC does not require the users to obtain permission to use the frequency spectrum. Second, unlike hard-wire systems, infrared requires no cable pulling and, consequently, the user may not have to obtain rights-of-way for infrared installation. Third, the systems are relatively inexpensive and easy to install. Fourth, the systems operate at relatively high data rates, typically in the Mbit/s range.

However, the distance is limited to about one mile due to a myriad of factors. The signal experiences scattering due to fog, smog, and dust. It also can experience shimmer due to air temperature variations which change the reflective index of the air. Rain, too, will cause a distortion of the signal.

Notwithstanding, infrared works quite well for special, short-distance applications. As of this writing, several commercial systems have been introduced for local area networks. For example, a number of offerings are available for connecting Apple's Macintosh computers through an infrared LAN.

## GROUP SPECIALE MOBILE (GSM)

Europe has led the way for the implementation of the Group Speciale Mobile (GSM) digital cellular system. Current technology with radio operates in the frequency bands of 800 MHz to 900 MHz, with 25 MHz allocated for each band and a 25 MHz channel-spacing channel. This is the technique used with the American Advanced Mobile Phone System (AMPS). The spacing used on the TACS in the frequency range of 870-890 MHz restricts AMPS to 666 channels.

The European digital cellular technology uses approximately 10 MHz of a frequency band (although some cellular operators have allocated 25 MHz) and provides multiple access with narrow band TDMA. Each of the GSM channels is supported with a 200 KHz carrier and divided into timeslots of about 577 microseconds. These time slots are grouped into eight units to form a TDMA frame. The ISDN channel concepts are used in GSM. The ISDN terminal types of TE1 and TE2 are supported.

This emerging technology will provide for enhanced functionality beyond that which exists in the analog technology. For example, calls could be transferred from one unit to another; calls may be queued. There may be indications of calls received. Third party calls may be used, as well as conference calls. In addition, GSM supports closed subscriber groups and priority groups. GSM also will allow the use of operator-assisted message service and the transfer of calls to voice mail systems.

GSM also is designed to interface with the integrated services digital network (ISDN). Indeed, much of the technology for some of the GSM components was derived from ISDN terminal adapter (TA) technology.

The GSM standards body is a part of the European Telecommunications Standards Institute (ETSI) and the Consultative Committee on International Telegraphy and Telephony (CCITT). These organizations have established the topology, architecture, and standards for GSM, which is illustrated in Figure 12-6.

The GSM structure is divided into two major systems: the base station subsystem (BSS) and the network subsystem (NSS). The BSS consists of the mobile stations, the base transceiver stations (BTS), and the base station controllers (BSC). Its purpose is to

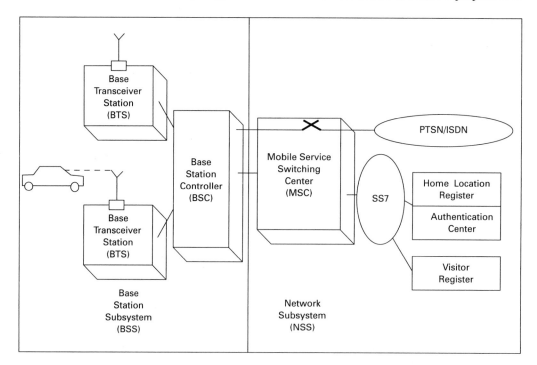

**Figure 12-6.** GSM Architecture

provide digital signaling to and from the mobile units and to hide the radio subsystem from the network subsystem.

In turn, the NSS is made up of Signaling System Number 7 (SS7), the mobile service center (MSC), telephone and ISDN networks, the home location register, the authentication center, and the visitor register.

The MSC is responsible for handling the switching functions for the calls to and from the mobile subscribers. The MSCs also provide interfaces into ISDNs and the public telephone switched networks (PTSNs). It is responsible for handling the functions between the BSCs and the components in the network subsystem.

The home location register consists of data bases that contain information about the subscribers. This register participates in establishing calls with the subscribers. The visitor register is a local data base that is associated with an MSC and supports the setting up of calls, as well. As a mobile unit enters an area, the visitor register exchanges information with the home location register in order for the system to track the mobile units as they roam between cells.

The authentication center is responsible for providing security, data encryption, and subscriber authentication. Generally, they are colocated with the home location register.

### Data Link Controls in GSM

The data link controls used in GSM are variations of TDMA described earlier in this chapter (except considerably more elaborate). In addition, the SS7 data link control protocol is employed in the communications between the MSC and the home location register, the authentication center, and the visitor register. This protocol is described in the next section.

## THE SS7 DATA LINK CONTROL PROTOCOL

The SS7 link control is not just a protocol for wireless operations. However, since it is part of GSM Network Subsystem (NSS), this chapter is as appropriate as any for its inclusion. Be aware, however, that SS7 and its data link layer can be employed in hard-wire or wireless systems.

### Overview of SS7

SS7 defines the procedures for the setup and clearing of a call between telephone users. It performs these functions by exchanging telephone control messages and signals between the SS7 telephone exchange and SS7 *signaling transfer points* (STPs). At the broadest level, the SS7 telephone signaling messages are made up of (a) telephone signaling message types and, within the types, (b) the identification of specific components relevant to the telephone call. Q.722 describes these components, and they are summarized in Table 12-2.

**TABLE 12-2.** GENERAL FUNCTIONS OF SS7 MESSAGES AND SIGNALS

| Message Components |
| --- |
| • Identifiers of: circuits signaling points, called and calling parties, incoming trunks, and transit exchanges |
| • Control codes to set up and clear down a call |
| • Called party's number |
| • Indicator that called party's line is out of service |
| • Indication of national, international, or other subscriber |
| • Indication that called party has cleared |
| • Nature of circuit (satellite/terrestrial) |
| • Indication that called party cleared, then went off-hook again |
| • Use of echo-suppression |
| • Notification to reset a faulty circuit |
| • Language of assistance operators |
| • Status identifiers (calling line identity incomplete; all addresses complete; use of coin station; network congestion; no digital path available; number not in use; blocking signals for certain conditions) |
| • Circuit continuity check |
| • Call forwarding (and previous routes of the call) |
| • Provision for an all-digital path |
| • Security access calls (called *closed user group* [CUG]) |
| • Malicious call identification |
| • Request to hold the connection |
| • Charging information |
| • Indication that a called party's line is free |
| • Call setup failure |
| • Subscriber busy signal |

## SS7 Operations

The SS7 data link is a full-duplex, digital transmission channel operating at 64 Kbit/s. The SS7 link operates on both terrestrial and satellite links. The actual digital signals on the link are derived from pulse code modulation multiplexing equipment or from equipment that employs a frame structure.

The link must be dedicated to SS7. In accordance with the idea of clear channel signaling, no other transmission can be transferred with the signaling messages. Extraneous equipment must be disabled or removed from an SS7 link.

The SS7 network functions are called signaling network functions and fall into two categories:

- Signaling message-handling functions: direct the message transfer to the proper link or user part

- Signaling network management functions: control the message routing and the configuration of the SS7 network

Figure 12-7 depicts an SS7 signaling network. The switching nodes in the network are referred to as *signaling points,* which are connected by the Level 2 signaling links (discussed in the next section). If multiple parallel links connect the signaling points, they are called a *signaling link set.* A group of links with identical characteristics are referred to as a *link group.*

A message is generated at a user part function, known as the *originating point*, and is sent to another user part function, known as the *destination point*. The intermediate nodes are signaling transfer points (STP).

The STPs use information in the message to determine its routing. A routing label contains the identification of the originating and destination points. A code also is used to manage load sharing within the network. The routing label is used by the STP in combination with predetermined routing data to make the routing decisions. The route is fixed, unless failures occur in the network. In this situation, the routing is modified by Level 3 functions. The load-sharing logic (and code in the label) permit the distribution of the traffic to a particular destination to be distributed to two or more output signaling links.

The following are the major functions of the SS7 network layer:

- Message routing: Selects the link to be used for each message.
- Message distribution: Selects the user part at the destination point (by checking the service indicator code).
- Message discrimination: Determines at each signaling point whether the message is to be forwarded to message routing or message distribution.
- Signaling traffic management: Controls the message routing functions of flow control, rerouting, changeover to a less faulty link, and recovery from link failure.
- Signaling link management: Manages the activity of the Level 2 function. Provides logical interface between Level 2 and Level 3.
- Signaling route management: Transfers status information about signaling routes to remote signaling points.

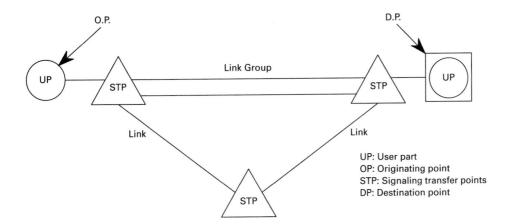

**Figure 12-7.** SS7 Level 3 (Q.704)

## SS7 Level 2 (Q.703)

Q.703 describes the procedures for transferring SS7 signaling messages across one link. Q.703 has many similarities to the HDLC protocol (High-Level Data Link Control). For example, both protocols use flags, error checks, and sending/receiving sequence numbers. The messages are transferred in variable length signal units (SUs), and the primary task of this level is to ensure their error-free delivery. The SUs are one of three types (see Figure 12-8):

- Message signal unit (MSU)
- Link status signal unit (LSSU)
- Fill-in signal unit (FISU)

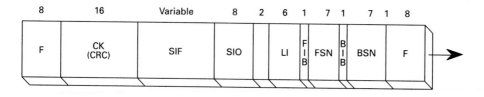

(a) Message Signal Unit (MSU)

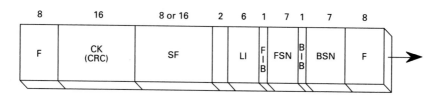

(b) Link Status Signal Unit (LSSU)

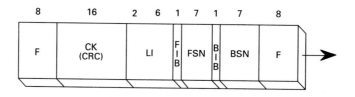

(c) Fill-in Signal Unit (FISU)

CK = Check bits                          FIB = Forward indicator bit
F = Flag                                 SF = Status field
LI = Length Indicator                    SIF = Signalling information field
BSN = Backward sequence number           SIO = Service information octet
FSN = Forward sequence number            CRC = Cycle redundancy check
BIB = Backward indicator bit

Note: Numbers over each field signify the number of bits for that field.

**Figure 12-8.** SS7 Signal Units

The MSU carries the actual signaling message forward to the user parts (UP). Q.703 transfers the MSU across the link and determines whether the message is uncorrupted. If the message is damaged during the transfer, it is retransmitted. The LSSU and FISU do not transport User Part (UP) signals; they are used to provide Level 2 control and status signal units between the Level 2 Q.703 protocols at each end of the link.

All SUs begin and end with the 8-bit flag and all SUs use a $X^{16} + X^{12} + X^5 + 1$ cyclic redundancy check (CRC.) (Chapter 7 explains CRC.) Two sequence numbers are used to provide flow control and user message accountability. The *backward sequence number* (BSN) acknowledges a message and the *forward sequence number* (FSN) identifies the service unit in which it resides. The BSN and FSN perform the same functions as the N(R) and N(S) fields that are used in many other Level 2 protocols (HDLC, SDLC, LAPB, etc.). They are used with the *forward indicator bit* (FIB) and the *backward indicator bit* (BIB) to perform sequencing and acknowledging functions. The FSN/FIB are associated with the BSN/BIB in one direction. They are independent of the FSN/FIB and BSN/BIB in the other direction. This concept permits independent flow across both directions of the full-duplex link.

The *length indicator* (LI) field specifies the number of octets that follow up to the CK (CRC) field.

The *service information octet* (SIO) is divided into two fields. The service indicator is used by Level 3 to perform message distribution and routing functions. The values identify the type of message. For example, the user parts (UP) are identified, such as ISDN user part, telephone user part, and so on. The subservice field also contains four bits and is used by signaling message-handling functions to distinguish between international and national messages.

The *signaling information field* (SIF) contents depend on which user part is contained in the service unit. It is used by Level 3 for routing control.

The *status field* (SF) is an 8-bit field, in which three bits are used to activate and restore the link and to ensure link alignment, that is, proper recognition and delineation of the flags and the service units' contents.

## SUMMARY

The conventional polling protocol is too slow and cumbersome for use over satellite channels for the transmission of data. Techniques such as ALOHA and TDMA often are employed in place of the conventional link control protocols. Cellular systems also use data link controls. Most are based on some form of TDMA and/or LAPD. The SS7 technology is employed on both hard-wire and wireless networks and uses SS7 signal units in its data link control layer.

# 13

# *Frame Relay*

## INTRODUCTION

This chapter examines the frame relay protocol. It discusses the pros and cons of using frame relay and compares frame relay both to X.25 and to other data link control protocols. It explains how frame relay is employed in private and public data networks, as well as the ways the frame relay standards published by the CCITT and ANSI are being used.

## WHY FRAME RELAY?

Frame relay has gained increased attention in the past few years. It is designed to address several problems that exist in some data communications systems. We summarize these problems in the following discussion.

Transmission systems today are experiencing far fewer errors and problems than they did in the 1970s and 1980s. During that period, link layer and network layer protocols were developed and implemented to cope with error-prone transmission circuits and unreliable networks. However, with the increased use of optical fibers and highly conditioned lines, protocols that expend resources to deal with errors become less important. Indeed, the case can be made that these protocols are "overkill" for modern communications networks.

The second factor that has contributed to the increased use of frame relay is the need for higher-capacity network interfaces (in bits/second). The technology of the 1970s and 1980s focused on kilobit transmission rates that are inadequate to serve applications that need large transmissions of data, such as bit-mapped graphics, telemetry systems, and large data base transfers.

The technology developed with wide area networks during the last two decades was designed to cope with noisy lines and relatively slow speed interfaces. Today, the WAN is becoming a bottleneck, as LANs operate in the megabit range. With some exceptions, WANs are restricted to the kilobit range.

In addition, many of the protocols that exist today were designed to support relatively "unintelligent" devices, such as nonprogrammable terminals. Today, terminals and workstations operate with powerful microprocessors and have many capabilities. They are able to handle extensive tasks that were heretofore delegated to network components.

Frame relay is designed to eliminate and/or combine certain operations residing in the data link layer, as well as most of the operations that a conventional connection-oriented network layer performs. It implements the operational aspects of statistical multiplexing found in the X.25 protocol and the efficiency of circuit switching found in TDM protocols.

The result is increased throughput, decreased delay, and the saving of "CPU cycles" within the network, because some services are eliminated.

The frame relay link operations are much simpler than the conventional data link control, essentially, performing two operations: (a) it uses flags to check for the presence of the frame on the link, and (b) it performs an FCS check. If the FCS check reveals an error, the frame is discarded and the link layer takes no remedial action. Figure 13-1 shows the operations on a frame relay link.

One might wonder about the sense of discarding traffic and not taking any remedial action. After all, most users do not like to lose data. The idea of frame relay is to place the responsibility for data integrity in another layer. Under most circumstances, the transport layer assumes this responsibility. But let there be no confusion: if one cares for one's data, error checking must be performed somewhere, because errors do occur. If error checking is not performed by the network, it must be performed by the user.

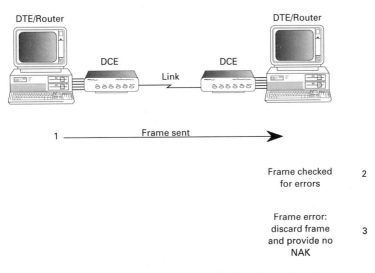

**Figure 13-1.** The Frame Relay Operations

If the main features of frame relay were the simple elimination of ACKing and NAKing, the technology would not have made much of an impact in the industry. However, frame relay is used also as a supporting technology for public and private network offerings that provide customers "bandwidth" on demand—a technology that is quite attractive for bursty data communications systems.

## THE FRAME RELAY LAYERS

Figure 13-2 shows the frame relay layers. On the left is a depiction of a typical data communications protocol stack that encompasses the physical, data link, and network layers. These layers perform conventional operations. For example, the physical layer is responsible for terminating traffic, providing connectors, as well as physical signaling. The data link layer is responsible for error checking and retransmission of errored traffic that may occur on the communications link. The network layer is responsible for managing the traffic within the network, establishing virtual connections, and negotiating quality of services between the network and the users.

In contrast, the frame relay stack virtually eliminates (no pun intended) the network layer and several aspects of the data link layer. Small wonder that frame relay is fast—it does very little.

## PERMANENT VIRTUAL CIRCUIT (PVC) OPERATIONS

Figure 13-3 illustrates one network layer operation that is essential for frame relay operations: the identification of virtual connections. Frame relay uses the *data link*

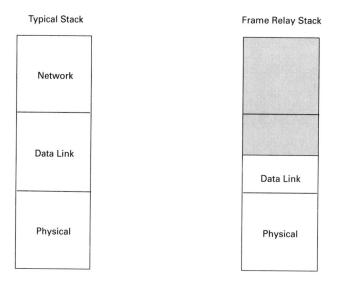

**Figure 13-2.** The Frame Relay Layers

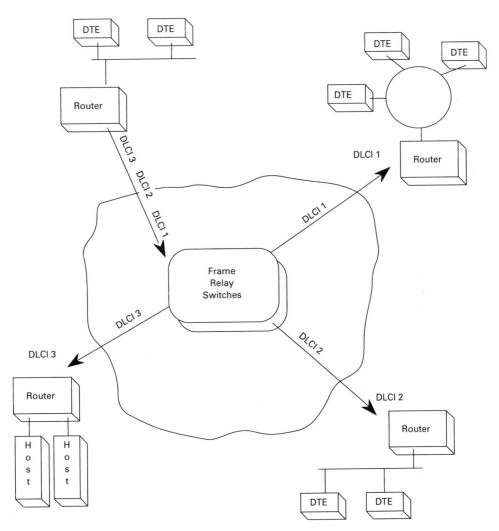

**Figure 13-3.** Permanent Virtual Circuits

*connection identifier* (DLCI) to identify the destination address. This 10-bit number corresponds to the virtual circuit number in the network layer protocol.

The DLCIs are premapped to a destination node, a technique known as a *permanent virtual circuit*. This process simplifies the operations at the routers because they need only to consult their routing table, check the DLCI in the table, and route the traffic to the proper output port based on this address.

Inside the network, the same scheme is used, although the frame relay switches need not maintain a strict virtual relationship in the network. Connectionless operations can be implemented to allow for dynamic and robust routing between the frame relay switches. The only requirement is to make certain the frame arrives at the port designated in the DLCI.

## THE FRAME RELAY FRAME FORMAT

The frame relay frame resembles many other protocols that use the HDLC frame format (see Figure 13-4). It contains the beginning and ending flag fields, which are used to delimit and recognize the frame on the communications link. It does not contain a separate address field; the address field is contained in the control field. Together they are designated as the frame relay header. The information field contains user data. The frame check sequence (FCS), like other link layer protocols, is used to determine whether the frame has been damaged during transmission on the communications link.

The frame relay header consists of seven fields:

- *DLCI:* The data link connection identifier identifies the destination virtual circuit user (which is typically a router attached to a LAN, but can be any machine with a frame relay interface)
- *C/R:* The command response bit (which is not used by the frame relay network)
- *EA:* The address extension bits
- *FECN:* The forward explicit congestion notification bit
- *BECN:* The backward explicit congestion notification bit
- *DE:* The discard eligibility indicator bit

## CONGESTION CONTROL

Earlier discussions in this chapter emphasized that frame relay eliminates most of the functions of the network layer. It so happens that one of the main functions of this layer is the use of flow-control mechanisms to prevent user devices from introducing excessive traffic into the network, thus avoiding congestion and the resultant loss of performance. A network still must deal with congestion control, a problem that typically is handled at the network layer. Most networks provide transmission rules for their users that include agreements concerning the quantity of traffic that can be sent to the network before the

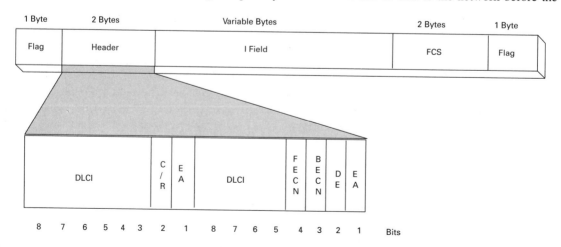

**Figure 13-4.** The Frame Relay Frame

traffic flow is regulated (flow-controlled). Flow control is an essential ingredient to prevent congestion in a network. Congestion is a problem that network administrators avoid almost at any cost because it results in severe degradation of the network, both in throughput and response time.

Queuing theory demonstrates that the offered load to the network may increase linearly, with resulting throughput also increasing . . . but only to a point. As the traffic (offered load) in the network reaches a certain point, mild congestion begins to occur, with the resulting drop in throughput. If this proceeded in a linear fashion, it would not be so complex a problem. However, at a point at which utilization of the network reaches a certain level, throughput drops exponentially due to serious congestion and the buildup of the servers (queues).

Therefore, even simple networks such as frame relay-based networks should provide some mechanism of informing components in the network when congestion is occurring. In addition, they should provide a flow-control mechanism.

The congestion and flow-control feature is optional. Vendors choosing not to implement this operation still will comply with the standard. However, if other flow-control measures are not implemented in the network, the use of this particular option becomes quite important.

## The FECN and BECN Bits

Two mechanisms are employed to (a) notify users, routers, and frame relay switches about congestion, and (b) take corrective action. Both capabilities are achieved by the *backward explicit congestion notification* (BECN) bit and the *forward explicit congestion notification* (FECN) bit.

Assume that a frame relay switch in Figure 13-5 is starting to experience congestion problems due to its buffers (queues) becoming full and/or experiencing a problem with memory management. It may inform both the upstream nodes and the downstream nodes of the problem by the use of the FECN and BECN bits, respectively. The BECN bit is turned on in the frame and is sent downstream to notify (potentially) the source of the traffic that the congestion exists at a switch. This operation would permit the source to flow-control its traffic until the congestion problem is solved.

In addition, the FECN bit may be set and placed in a frame and sent to the upstream node to inform it that congestion is occurring downstream. One might question why the FECN is used to notify upstream devices that congestion is occurring downstream. After all, the downstream device is the one creating the traffic problem. The answer is that remedial action might be taken at the upstream device as well, depending upon the machine. For example, this FECN bit could be passed to an upper-layer protocol (such as the transport layer) which will allow it to (a) slow down its acknowledgments (which, in some protocols, would close the transmit window at the sending device) or (b) establish its own more restrictive flow-control agreement with its communications source machine (which also is allowed, in some protocols).

An obvious solution to the problem is for the source machines to flow-control themselves to ameliorate the network congestion problem.

A potential problem is encountered with the user of the BECN, because it is intended to be piggybacked on a frame coming from the upstream area and destined for the downstream area. Consequently, flow-control to the downstream node cannot be

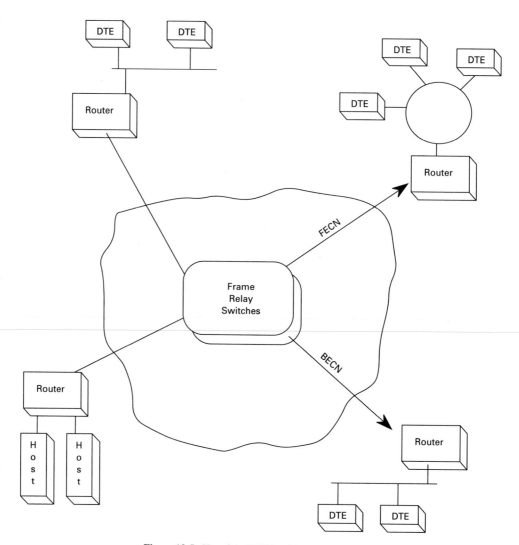

**Figure 13-5.** Use of the FECN and BECN Bits

achieved unless the upstream node is sending data. This rather awkward aspect of the frame relay rules prompted the ANSI committee to add another feature to its consolidated link layer management (CLLM) operation.

The DLCI 1023 number is reserved for the frame relay node to notify the downstream node about various operations, problems, and so on. This allows the network to send traffic to a user device or its router, irrespective of receiving traffic from the upstream. CLLM includes the diagnostic code in the frame to describe the problem encountered by the network. In our example, this would identify excessive congestion, but it could identify other problems as well, such as failure of a processor or a link. In addition, the ANSI approach lists the DLCIs that should flow-control their traffic.

Some vendors rely on the transport layer to flow-control the end-user devices. Since, typically, the transport layer resides in the end-user machine, if the BECN bit is to be acted upon by the transport layer, a means could be devised for the BECN signal to be received and recognized by the transport layer. Presently, most systems do not inform the transport layer.

This approach, while simple in concept, may not be so easy to implement. It requires both modification to user transport layers and additional coding, with the potential result of nonconformance to transport layer standards.

Notwithstanding, a vendor certainly may choose to make the user machine aware of the BECN operation. If so, the receiving transport layer then can adjust its credit window to the downstream originator. This approach would work quite well with ISO/CCITT transport layer Class 4, as well as TCP, since these protocols require that the sending device adjust its credit window to that of the receiving device.

While this approach is feasible technically, it does present additional problems for the end-user device by increasing its responsibilities.

In addition, frame relay does not address the issue of the discarding of traffic and its effect on the downstream (originator) module. In many transport layer protocols, the nonreceipt of acknowledgments from the destination device will result in time-outs at the sender, with the resulting retransmission of (in this example) discarded PDUs. Thus, the network congestion problem is compounded: the valid traffic is thrown away due to congestion, yet this same traffic is reintroduced.

Clearly, a potentially vexing problem results from this approach. In short, the originating site needs to adjust the rate at which it sends traffic. Consequently, the BECN bit is a very important component for efficient frame relay operations.

The designer must give serious consideration to how FECN and BECN operate in conjunction with the originating and destination transport layer modules.

### The Discard Eligibility (DE) Bit

Since congestion can be a major problem in any demand-driven network, frame relay adapts the approach of discarding traffic to avoid congestion problems. In some instances, it is desirable to discern which data units in the user's traffic should be discarded.

The approach currently used by frame relay is to implement the *discard eligibility* (DE) bit (see Figure 13-6). How the DE bit is acted upon is an implementation-specific decision. However, in most instances the DE bit is turned to 1 to indicate to the network that, in the event of problems, the packet with this bit is "more eligible" for being discarded than others in which the bit is set to 0. In some implementations, the network turns on the D bit for use inside the network.

Of course, the DE bit need not be implemented. When congestion occurs, a node simply may throw away traffic at random. Not only is this unfair, it may entail discarding critical data. Even more important, it has no ability to discern which sending ports must initiate error recovery.

### The Committed Information Rate

While an end user might be allowed to manipulate the DE bit, a better approach is for the network to use this bit to aid in determining what to do with the traffic. One method is the

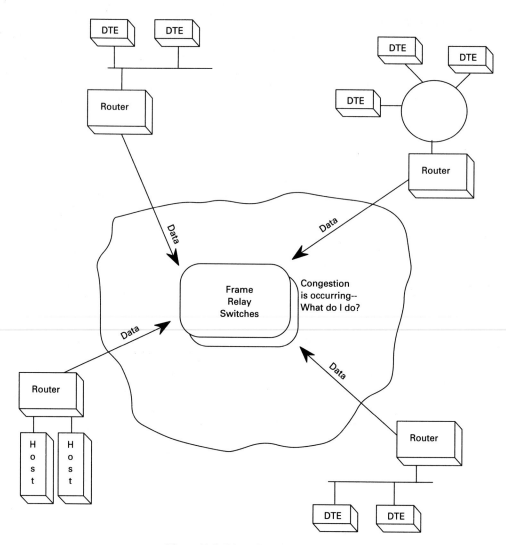

**Figure 13-6.** Discarding Traffic

technique called the *committed information rate* (CIR). An end user estimates the amount of traffic that it will be sending during a period of time. The network measures this traffic during a time interval. If it is less than the CIR value, the network will not alter the DE bit. If the rate exceeds the CIR value during the specified period of time, the network will allow the traffic to go through, unless it is congested. If the network is congested, this traffic will be discarded.

The CIR is a tool used by frame relay networks to (a) regulate the flow of traffic, (b) allow the user some choice in user throughput rate, and (c) determine certain pricing structures for the frame relay service.

The vast majority of frame relay networks provide the user with a guaranteed service (relating to throughput) if the user's input rate is below some predefined CIR. If the user exceeds the CIR for some period of time, the network may discard traffic beyond that of the CIR. The clause "may discard" means that the network most likely will not discard traffic if it has sufficient resources to transport the user traffic during the time the CIR is exceeded.

In most implementations, the current rate of a user's input might exceed not only the CIR, but also some permitted maximum rate. If this situation occurs, the network may discard all excess traffic beyond the permitted rate.

## THE CCITT AND ANSI LAYERS

Frame relay service is provided through the ISDN C-plane (control plane) procedures and U-plane (user plane) procedures (see Figure 13-7). Virtual calls may be established as needed, in which case they are negotiated during call setup through the C-plane procedures. Additionally, C-plane procedures can be established on a permanent virtual call basis. In this circumstance, the DLCI and associated quality of service parameters must be defined by administrative specific operations.

For frame relay, the network does not support the full features of Q.922 Layer 2 protocol. It supports only core aspects of Q.922 (be aware that Q.922 is an enhancement of Q.921).

Core service offerings can be made either on basic access or primary access interfaces and on ISDN channels B, D, and H.

The idea of providing core functions is that a frame relay and bearer service is provided if no user functions are implemented above the core function in the network. That is, functions above those that are stipulated in the core functions must be implemented on an end-to-end basis, not on a user-to-network basis.

In its simplest form, this architecture is designed to simplify procedures established in other standards, yet allow these other standards to provide additional services that are

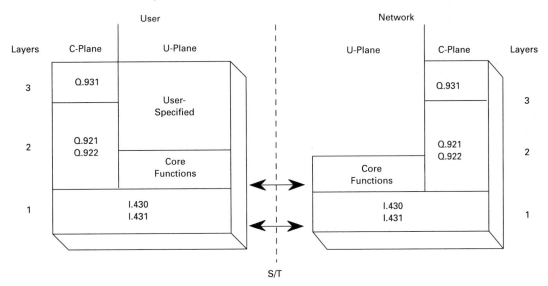

**Figure 13-7.** The CCITT Frame Relay Model

negotiated (if needed) in the C-plane before any data transfer occurs. Thereafter, data transfer occurring in the U-plane is performed on a very simple connectionless basis.

ANSI bases its frame relay platform on the CCITT Q.921/Q.922 standards. ANSI document T1.602 is the counterpart to CCITT's Q.921/Q.922. ANSI's implementation of the ISDN physical layer is published in ANSI T1.601-1988, *Integrated Services Digital Network-Basic Access Interface for Use on Metallic Loops for Application on the Network Side of the NT (Layer 1 specification).*

As shown in Figure 13-8, the C-plane uses the D channel in accordance with ANSI T1.601-1988. The U-plane can use any channel (that is, the B, D, or H channel). Typically, additional requirements will be placed on terminals (such as sequencing and flow control) because the core functions do not provide these services.

## THE CONSOLIDATED LINK LAYER MANAGEMENT MESSAGE (CLLM)

The *consolidated link layer management message* (CLLM) has been developed by the CCITT and ANSI to provide some additional functions for the frame relay service. CLLM is based on the use of HDLC XID frames and is derived from the ISO 8885 standard. This standard is one aspect of HDLC that describes the use of the XID frame information field contents and its format. Figure 13-9 shows the format of the CLLM control field.

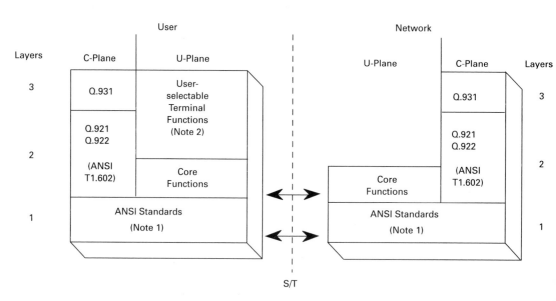

Note 1:  C-Plane uses D Channel (see Q.921 and ANSI T1.601-1988).
        U-Plane uses D, B, or H channel.
Note 2:  Additional requirements (such as congestion control) may be
        placed on terminals.

**Figure 13-8.** The ANSI Frame Relay Model

| Octet | Bits | Field Description |
|---|---|---|
| | 87654321 | |
| 1 | 111110R0 | Address |
| 2 | 11110001 | Address |
| 3 | 10101111 | HDLC XID control |
| 4 | 10000010 | Format identifier (130) |
| 5 | 00001111 | Group identifier (15) |
| 6 | | Group length |
| 7 | | Group length |
| 8 | 00000000 | Parameter identifier (0) |
| 9 | 00000100 | Parameter length (4) |
| 10 | 01101001 | Parameter value (105) |
| 11 | 00110001 | Parameter value (49) |
| 12 | 00110010 | Parameter value (50) |
| 13 | 00110010 | Parameter value (50) |
| 14 | 00000010 | Parameter identifier (2, cause id) |
| 15 | 00000001 | Parameter length (1) |
| 16 | | Cause value (congestion, failure, etc.) |
| 17 | 00000011 | Parameter value (3, DLCI identifer) |
| 18 | | Parameter length |
| 19 | | DLCI value |
| 20 | | DLCI value |
| etc | | etc |
| 2n+17 | | DLCI value (nth DLCI) |
| 2n+18 | | DLCI value (nth DLCI) |
| 2n+19 | | FCS |
| 2n+20 | | FCS |

**Figure 13-9.** The CLLM Format

The cause code field (octet 16 of the frame) is used for these operations (Figure 13-10). The cause code allows a node that is experiencing congestion or other problems to report the type of problem, although it can be seen from this figure that the nature of the problem that can be reported is limited to a few codes.

One code is particularly interesting—the unknown cause. Of course, the use of such a code is not unusual in network operations, but to state that an unknown problem is for the "short term" or the "long term" seems to indicate that the reporter of the problem suffers from a lack of clairvoyance and, at the same time, possesses an ample supply of it. It seems to say, "I do not know what the problem is, but it will last a long (short) time."

Whatever the rationale for this code, the frame relay protocol states that the cause code is to be coded "short term" if the sender anticipates a transient problem and "long term" if the sender anticipates a problem that is not simply transient. In any event, the decision of how to use this field is network dependent.

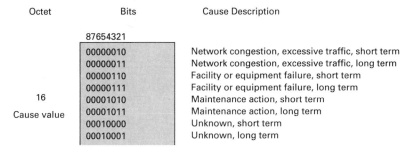

| Octet | Bits | Cause Description |
|---|---|---|
| | 87654321 | |
| | 00000010 | Network congestion, excessive traffic, short term |
| | 00000011 | Network congestion, excessive traffic, long term |
| | 00000110 | Facility or equipment failure, short term |
| | 00000111 | Facility or equipment failure, long term |
| 16 | 00001010 | Maintenance action, short term |
| | 00001011 | Maintenance action, long term |
| Cause value | 00010000 | Unknown, short term |
| | 00010001 | Unknown, long term |

**Figure 13-10.** The Cause Code

## RELATIONSHIP OF USER AND NETWORK LAYERS

Figure 13-11 shows the relationship of the layers located at the end-user host machines, the frame relay nodes (the routers), and the frame relay switches (the network nodes). Notice that the transport layer resides in the host machines. The network layer resides in the host machines and the routers.

Vendors vary regarding which network protocol is placed in the switch, although typically it is a connectionless routing protocol like the Internet Protocol (IP) or a vendor's implementation of an IP-like protocol.

## ENCAPSULATING DATAGRAMS INTO THE FRAME RELAY FRAME

The Internet has published a standard for the encapsulation of interconnected traffic over a frame relay network. The method is quite simple. The network protocol simply encapsulates the datagrams into the Q.922 frame. This frame contains information that identifies the protocol data unit that is within the frame. The Network Protocol ID (NPID) field contains the values for the protocols that may reside within the frame. This standard is published as *Request for Comments* (RFC) *1294*.

The frame relay stations are permitted to exchange HDLC XID frames in accordance with Q.922. Probably you already are aware that the XID frame allows certain parameters to be negotiated between stations, such as the retransmission timer (T200), the maximum frame size (N201), and the number of outstanding I frames (K). If these values are not negotiated, they must operate with default values specified in Q.922:

- N201 = 260 Octets
- K: 3: 16 Kilobit per second link, 7: 64 Kilobit per second link, 32: 384 Kilobit per second link, 40: 1.536 center megabit per second link or above.
- T200 = 1.5 seconds

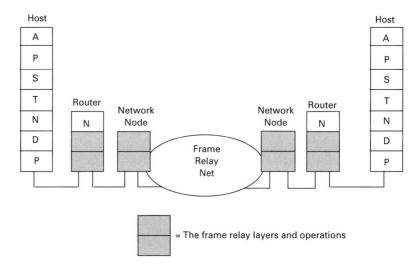

**Figure 13-11.** The User and Network Layers

## SUMMARY

Frame relay is a "lean" solution to the wide area network bottleneck problem. If the user recognizes that frame relay offers a minimal level of service and accepts this scenario, frame relay can provide a cost-effective high bandwidth capacity for hosts or LANs across wide area networks. Frame relay's philosophy is to do very little in the network and to make the user device do quite a lot. Again, if this is accepted, frame relay should be an appropriate method for interfacing local and wide area networks. Perhaps its main attraction is that the frame relay technology is being used with different pricing strategies for bandwidth on demand from the frame relay vendors.

# 14

# Internet Link Controls

## INTRODUCTION

This chapter provides an overview of link layer protocol operations defined in the Internet. As a general statement, most of the Internet protocols (sometimes known as the TCP/IP suite of protocols) do not define what is required at the link layer, but some documents have been published by the Internet authorities to clarify procedures for certain link layer and network operations. This chapter reviews the major aspects of these protocols.

## OVERVIEW OF TCP/IP

In order to comprehend the protocols discussed in this chapter, one must have at least a basic understanding of the TCP/IP protocols. This section provides an overview of these protocols. Those already knowledgeable in this area might choose to skip to the next section.

### The Internet Protocol (IP)

The Internet Protocol (IP) is a routing protocol. It is designed to route traffic within a network or between networks. Figure 14-1 shows a router positioned among Networks A, B, and C. Networks A, B, and C often are called *subnetworks*. The term does not mean that they provide fewer functions than a conventional network. Rather, it means that the subnetworks contribute to the overall operations for internetworking. Stated another way, the subnetworks comprise an internetwork or an internet.

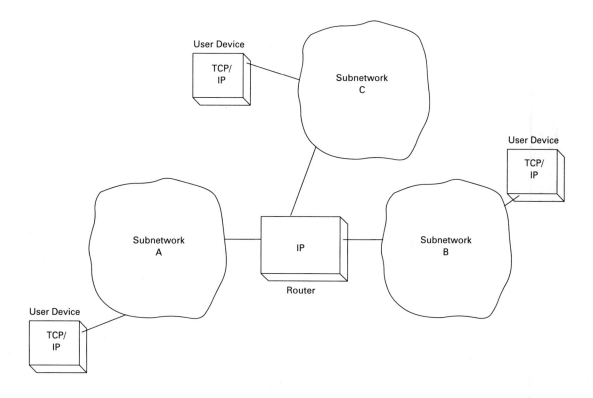

**Figure 14-1.** A Typical Internet Configuration

IP is designed to remain transparent to the end-user application. Indeed, the end-user application resides in the host machines connected to the networks.

IP is designed to rest on top of the underlying subnetwork–insofar as possible in a transparent manner. This means that IP assumes little about the characteristics of the underlying network or networks. From the design standpoint this is quite attractive to engineers, because it keeps the subnetworks relatively independent of IP.

The transparency is achieved by encapsulation. The data sent by the host computer are encapsulated into an IP datagram. The IP header identifies the address of the receiving host computer. The IP datagram and header are further encapsulated into the specific protocol of the transit network. For example, a transit network could be an X.25 network or an Ethernet LAN.

After the transit network has delivered the traffic to an IP router, its link control information is stripped away. The gateway then uses the destination address in the datagram header to determine where to route the traffic. Typically, it then passes the datagram to a subnetwork by invoking a subnetwork access protocol (for example, Ethernet on a LAN, or X.25 on a WAN). This protocol is used to encapsulate the datagram header and user data into the headers and trailers that are used by the subnetwork. This process is repeated at each gateway and, eventually, the datagram arrives at the final destination where it is delivered to the receiving station.

## The Transmission Control Protocol (TCP)

The Transmission Control Protocol (TCP) resides in the transport layer of the conventional seven-layer model. It is situated above IP and below the upper layers. Figure 14-1 also illustrates that TCP is not loaded into the router. It is designed to reside in the host computer or in a machine that is tasked with end-to-end integrity of the transfer of user data. In practice, TCP usually is placed in the user host machine.

The figure also shows that TCP is designed to run over the IP. Since IP is a connectionless protocol, the tasks of reliability, flow control, sequencing, session opens, and closes are given to TCP. Although TCP and IP are tied together so closely that they are used in the same context "TCP/IP," TCP also can support other protocols. For example, another connectionless protocol, such as the ISO 8473 (*Connectionless Network Protocol* or CLNP), could operate with TCP (with adjustments to the interface between the modules).

TCP is a *connection-oriented protocol*. This term refers to the fact that TCP maintains status and state information about each user data stream flowing into and out of the TCP module. The term used in this context also means TCP is responsible for the end-to-end transfer of data across one network or multiple networks to a receiving user application (or the next upper-layer protocol).

TCP is also a data management protocol. It is responsible for the *reliable transfer* of each of the characters passed to it from an upper layer (characters also are called bytes or octets). Consequently, it uses sequence numbers and positive acknowledgments.

A sequence number is assigned to each octet transmitted. The receiving TCP module uses a checksum routine to check the data for damage that may have occurred during the transmission process. If the data are acceptable, TCP returns a positive acknowledgment (ACK) to the sending TCP module. If the data are damaged, the receiving TCP discards the data and uses a sequence number to inform the sending TCP about the problem. Like many other connection-oriented protocols, TCP uses timers to ensure that the lapse of time is not excessive before remedial measures are taken for either the transmission of acknowledgments from the receiving site and/or the retransmission of data at the transmitting site.

## THE POINT-TO-POINT PROTOCOL (PPP)

The *point-to-point protocol* (PPP) was implemented to solve a problem that evolved in the industry during the last decade. With the rapid growth of internetworking, several vendors and standards organizations developed a number of network layer protocols. The Internet protocol is the most widely used of these. However, machines (such as routers) typically run more than one network layer protocol. While IP is a given on most machines, routers also run network layer protocols developed by companies such as Xerox, 3Com, Novell, and others. Machines communicating with each other did not readily know which network layer protocols were available during a session.

In addition, until the advent of PPP, the industry did not have a standard means to define a *point-to-point encapsulation protocol*. This term means that a protocol carries or encapsulates a network layer PDU in its I field and uses another field in the frame to identify which network layer PDU resides in the I field. The PPP standard solves these two problems.

PPP is used to encapsulate network layer datagrams over a serial communications link. The protocol allows two machines on a point-to-point communications channel to negotiate the particular types of network layer protocols (such as IP) that are to be used during a session. After this negotiation occurs, PPP is used to carry the network layer protocol data units (PDUs) in the I field of an HDLC-type frame. This protocol supports either bit-oriented synchronous transmission or asynchronous (start/stop) transmission. It can be used on switched or dial-up links. It requires a full-duplex capability.

PPP is divided into three major components. The first component deals with the HDLC frame and how it is used for encapsulating datagrams in the I field of the frame. The second major component of PPP is the *Link Control Protocol* (LCP), which is used to establish the link, to test the link for various quality of service features, to configure the link, and to disestablish the link. The third major component is a generic family of *Network Control Protocols* (NCPs) for establishing which network layer protocols are to be used for the connection.

PPP supports the simultaneous use of network protocols. For example, the protocol allows two users to negotiate the simultaneous use of the Internet Protocol (IP), DEC's Decnet IV network layer, IPX, XNS, and so on.

## PPP PHYSICAL LAYER

The point-to-point protocol places no restriction on what is to be used at the physical layer. For example, EIA 232D, V.35, or RS422 can be applied across the DTE/DCE interface. The physical layer must be either a dedicated or circuit-switched link, and it must operate in duplex mode. Either asynchronous start/stop or synchronous bit transmission is permitted. PPP can operate across higher-speed or lower-speed networks at the physical layer. Indeed, the physical layer is transparent to PPP operations.

## PPP AND THE DATA LINK LAYER

As introduced earlier, the PPP PDU uses the HDLC frame as stipulated in ISO 3309-1979 (and amended by ISO 3309-1984/PDAD1).

Since several chapters in this book have explained HDLC in detail, this chapter is restricted to showing the frame format and its relationship to PPP. Figure 14-2 shows this format. The flag sequence is the standard HDLC flag of 01111110 (Hex 7e); the addresses field is set to all 1s (Hex ff), which signifies all the stations' addresses. PPP does not use individual station addresses because it is a point-to-point protocol. The control field is set to identify a HDLC unnumbered information (UI) command. Its value is 00000011 (Hex 03).

The protocol field is used to identify the PDU that is encapsulated into the I field of the frame. The values in this field are assigned through the *Internet Request* for *Comments* (RFC) *1060*. On a more general note, the field values are assigned initially in

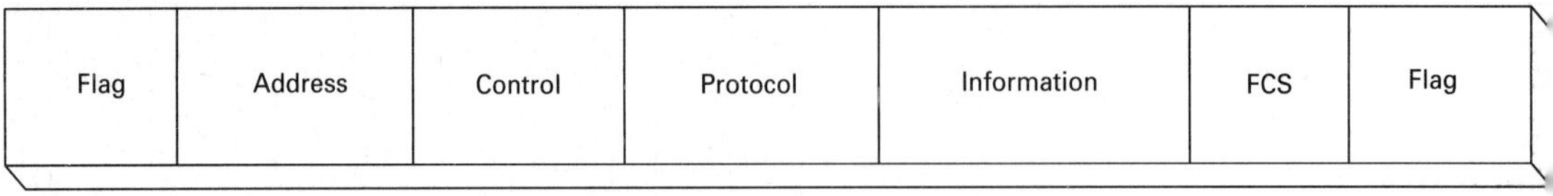

| Flag | Address | Control | Protocol | Information | FCS | Flag |
|------|---------|---------|----------|-------------|-----|------|

```
        Flag  = 01111110
     Address  = 11111111
     Control  = 00000011
    Protocol  = See RFC 1060
 Information  = Network layer PDU
         FCS  = 16 bits
```

**Figure 14-2.** The PPP Frame Format

accordance with Table 14-1. As suggested in this table, the values beginning with a 0 identify the network protocol that resided in the I field. Values beginning with 8 identify a control protocol that is used to negotiate the protocols that actually will be used. More will be said about this control protocol shortly. The leading value of c identifies the protocol as the Link Control Protocol (LCP).

As one might expect, the protocol field is not defined in the HDLC standard. It simply uses the ISO 3309 rules for the address extension field.

The I field contains the user data (the datagram) for the protocol that is identified in the protocol field. Once negotiations have occurred between two stations and these stations agree as to which network layer protocols will be used, then the information field

**TABLE 14-1.** INITIAL ASSIGNMENT OF PROTOCOL FIELD

| Hex Value | Protocol |
|-----------|----------|
| 0001-001f | Reserved |
| 0021 | Internet Protocol |
| 0023 | OSI Network Layer |
| 0025 | Xerox NS IDP |
| 0027 | DECnet Phase IV |
| 0029 | AppleTalk |
| 002b | Novell IPX |
| 002d | Van Jacobson Compressed TCP/IP 1 |
| 002f | Van Jacobson Compressed TCP/IP 2 |
| 8021 | Internet Protocol Control Protocol |
| 8023 | OSI Network Layer Control Protocol |
| 8025 | Xerox NS IDP Control Protocol |
| 8027 | DECnet Phase IV Control Protocol |
| 8029 | AppleTalk Control Protocol |
| 802b | Novell IPX Control Protocol |
| 802d | Reserved |
| 802f | Reserved |
| c021 | Link Control Protocol |
| c023 | User/Password Authentication Protocol |

actually contains the datagram. For negotiations, the protocol value is set to either a leading 8, 0, or c (as discussed in the previous paragraph) and the I field contains the control values used to perform the various types of negotiations. The maximum default length for the I field is 1,500 octets. Other values may be used if the PPP implementers agree. The *frame check sequence* (FCS) field is used for error detection. As with most HDLC FCS checks, the calculations are performed on the following fields: address, control, protocol, and I fields.

## PPP LINK CONTROL PROTOCOL (LCP)

LCP was introduced briefly earlier in this chapter. To iterate, its purpose is to support the establishment of the connection and to allow for certain configuration options to be negotiated. The protocol also maintains the connection and provides procedures for terminating the connection. In order to perform these functions, LCP is organized into four phases:

- Phase 1: Link establishment and configuration negotiation
- Phase 2: Link quality determination
- Phase 3: Network layer protocol configuration negotiation
- Phase 4: Link termination

### Link Establishment and Configuration Negotiation

PPP requires that LCP be executed to open the connection between two stations before any network layer traffic is exchanged. This requires a series of message exchanges called *configure packets*. After these packets have been exchanged and a configure acknowledge packet has been sent and received between the stations, the connection is considered to be in an open state and the exchange of datagrams can begin. LCP confines itself only to link operations. It does not understand how to negotiate the implementation of network layer protocols. Indeed, it does not care about the upper-layer negotiations relating to the network protocols.

### Link Quality Determination

This phase is optional and allows LCP to check if the link is of sufficient quality to bring up the network layer. Although the link quality determination phase is defined in the standard, the actual implementation procedures are not specified. This tool exists to provide an LCP echo request and an LCP echo-type packet. These packets are defined within the protocol and exist within the state transition tables of the protocol. The user should understand that their actual implementation is not defined in the standard, however.

### Network Layer Protocol Configuration Negotiation

After the link establishment (and if the link quality determination phase is implemented), this phase allows the two stations to negotiate/configure the protocols that will be used at the network layer. This is performed by the appropriate network control protocol (NCP). The particular protocol that is used here depends on which family of NCPs is implemented. The identification of the particular protocol used is established in the protocol field in accordance with the 8NNN values described earlier in Table 14-1.

## Link Termination

LCP also is responsible for terminating the link connection. It is allowed to perform the termination at its discretion. Unless problems have occurred that create this event, the link termination usually is provided by an upper-layer protocol or a user-operated network control center (which notices problems and terminates the connection).

## LCP Protocol Rules and State Transition Table

LCP's behavior is governed by a state transition table. Table 14-2 is a replica of this state transition table (published in RFC 1171). The protocol works with the interactions of events and states. In this table, the states are listed horizontally and the events are read vertically as columns. The contents within the table are read in the following manner: the entry for each column row may first show the action resulting from an event occurring against a state, followed by a slash and a value that indicates the resulting state. In some entries, two actions are shown tied together with the & sign, and then are followed with a slash showing the resultant state.

**TABLE 14-2.** THE PPP LINK STATE TRANSITION TABLE

| Events | Closed | Listen | Req-Sent | Ack-Rcvd | Ack-Sent | Open | Closing |
|--------|--------|--------|----------|----------|----------|------|---------|
| AO | scr/3 | scr/3 | 3 | 4 | 5 | 6 | scr/3 |
| PO | 2 | 2 | 2* | 4 | 5 | 6 | sta/3* |
| C | 1 | 1 | 1* | 1 | str/7 | str/7 | 7 |
| TO | 1 | 2 | scr/3 | scr/3 | scr/3 | 6 | str/7* |
| PLD | 1 | 1 | 1 | 1 | 1 | 1 | 1 |
| RCR+ | sta/1 | scr&sca/5 | sca/5 | sca/6 | sca/5 | scr&sca/5 | 7 |
| RCR- | sta/1 | scr&scn/3 | scn/3 | scn/4 | scn/3 | scr&scn/3 | 7 |
| RCA | sta/1 | sta/2 | 4 | scr/3 | 6 | scr/3 | 7 |
| RCN | sta/1 | sta/2 | scr/3 | scr/3 | scr/5 | scr/3 | 7 |
| RTR | sta/1 | sta/2 | sta/3 | sta/3 | sta/3 | sta/1 | sta/7 |
| RTA | 1 | 2 | 3 | 3 | 3 | 1 | 1 |
| RCJ | 1 | 2 | 1 | 1 | 1 | 1 | 1 |
| RUC | scj/1 | scj/2 | scj/1 | scj/1 | scj/1 | scj/1 | 1 scj/7 |
| RER | sta/1 | sta/2 | 3 | 4 | 5 | ser/6 | 7 |

Notes:
RCR+    Receive-Configure-Request (Good)
RCR-    Receive-Configure-Request (Bad)
RCJ     Receive-Code-Reject
RUC     Receive-Unknown-Code
RER     Receive-Echo-Request
scj     Send-Code-Reject
ser     Send-Echo-Reply
*       Special attention necessary, see detailed text

The following explanation summarizes the events listed in Table 14-2. The Active-Open (AO), Passive-Open (PO), and Close (C) are events that govern the LCP connections between the two peers. The difference between the AO and the PO is that with the AO, the LCP immediately attempts to open connections, while with the PO the LCP waits for its peer to initiate the sending of traffic.

LCP uses a Time-out (TO) event to manage operations in which certain packets are not received by one of the peer entities. As one example, the Receive-Configure-Request (RCR) packet is used between the entities to open an LCP connection and perhaps specify network configuration options. If an acknowledgment to this request is not received, the time-out event will occur and allow the resending of the request.

The configuration requests operations (RCR, RCA, RCN) are used to set up a connection, specify network configuration, and acknowledge either positively or negatively the request.

LCP connections are closed and acknowledged by the receive terminate request (RTR) and the Receive-Terminate-Ack (RTA).

In the event that a code identifying a network protocol cannot be accepted, a LCP peer may send the Receive-Code-Reject (RCJ). In addition, if a packet is received that cannot be decoded, the Receive-Unknown-Code (RUC) packet may be sent.

Finally, two other events are used to provide the following services. The Receive-Echo-Request (RER) is used to indicate that echo request packets have been received from an LCP peer. The Physical-Layer-Down (PLD) event occurs if the lower physical layer is not operational.

In addition, the table shows the actions permitted in the protocol. We summarize these actions briefly in the following section. The configure actions (*scr, sca,* and *scn*) are packets that are sent between the LCP peers to request the opening of a connection and to establish networking configuration options. The operation provides for positive and negative acknowledgments with scas and scns, respectively.

Connection termination operations are supported by the two packets termed *Send-Terminate-Req* and *Send-Terminate-Ack,* also known as str and sta, respectively.

For the rejection of a packet because of an unknown code, the Send-Code-Reject packet is transmitted to the peer LCP. This table shows it coded as scj. Finally, echo operations are provided through the Send-Echo-Reply packet (ser). This operation acknowledges the receipt of the echo request.

## The LCP Packet

The PPP frame I field is used to carry the link control protocol packet. The protocol field in the frame must contain hex C021 to indicate the I field carries link control protocol information. The format for the field is shown in Figure 14-3. The code field must be coded to identify the type of LCP packet that is encapsulated into the frame. As an example, the code would indicate whether the frame contains a configure request, which likely would be followed by a configure ACK or NAK. Additionally, the code could indicate (for example) an echo request data unit. Naturally, the next frame probably would identify the echo reply. Each of the packets discussed in the previous section are described with codes.

The *identifier field* is a value that is used to match requests and replies. The *length field* defines the length of the LCP packet, which includes code, identifier, and data

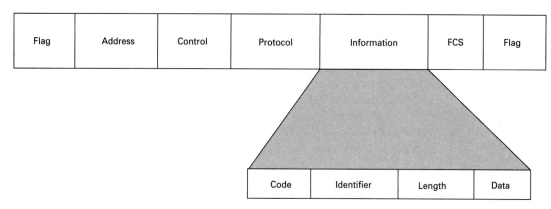

**Figure 14-3.** The Link Control Protocol Packet

fields. The *data field* values are determined on the contents of the *code field*. Refer to RFC 1171 for the values of the data field.

## THE IP CONTROL PROTOCOL (IPCP)

The Internet authorities use a variation of LCP called the IP control protocol (IPCP). It rests on the assumption that the LCP has completed its actions and has entered a network layer protocol configuration negotiation phase. At this time the machines can negotiate their configuration options. The IPCP uses the same format of the LCP data unit, except that the data link layer protocol field is coded as 8021 to identify the IPCP. The code field contains only codes for configure request, configure ack, configure NAK, configure reject, terminate request, terminate ACK, and code reject. Other LCP codes are discarded. The IPCP configuration option values are published in the RFC 1060 (assigned numbers).

## EXAMPLE OF A PPP OPERATION

Figure 14-4 shows an example of how PPP can be used to support network configuration operations. Routers exchange the PPP frames to determine which network layer protocols are supported. In this example, two routers negotiate the use of the Internet Protocol (IP) and its OSI counterpart, ISO 8473, the Connectionless Network Protocol (CLNP). The LCP operations are invoked first to set up and test the link. Next, NCP operations are invoked to negotiate which network protocols are to be used between the machines. After this negotiation is complete, datagrams are exchanged. At any point, either router can terminate the session.

## THE DYNAMICALLY SWITCHED LINK CONTROL PROTOCOL (DSLCP)

Another protocol published as an RFC by the Internet is the *Dynamically Switched Link Control Protocol* (DSLCP). This is not an approved standard published by the Internet

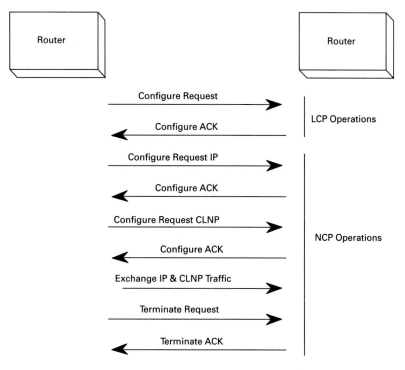

**Figure 14-4.** Example of a PPP Link Operation

Activities Board. As of this writing, it is considered as an experimental protocol. However, due to its obvious usefulness, it is likely that this will become a standard in the future. The pioneering work for this protocol should be credited to Cray Research Inc., which developed these concepts to address the need for an on-demand, high bandwidth data transfer capability. It is one of several solutions in the industry today to combat low-speed wide area technology.

In most countries, leasing high-speed facilities is not cost-effective for many enterprises. Consequently, many companies must use low-cost and low-speed communications facilities between computers. This works well enough for certain applications, but is insufficient for applications that require a high bandwidth for data transfer.

DSLCP provides procedures wherein a user may access low-speed and low-cost links to a computer and then obtain the results from the computer (for example, large file transfers or high-intensity graphics) through a high bandwidth return channel.

This approach allows a high-speed, circuit-switched network to send traffic back to a device, but only when the medium is needed for the transfer. The scenario is for an individual to dial in to a relatively low-speed telephone link or (more likely) an internet through conventional low-speed modems and to invoke programs to prepare the remote device for the return of traffic, then to allocate dynamically a high-speed system to return the traffic on a broadband medium.

DSLCP operates with link controllers. These link controllers use the DSLCP messages to establish a T1 or T3 link, to keep the link up during data transfer, and then to tear down the link as appropriate.

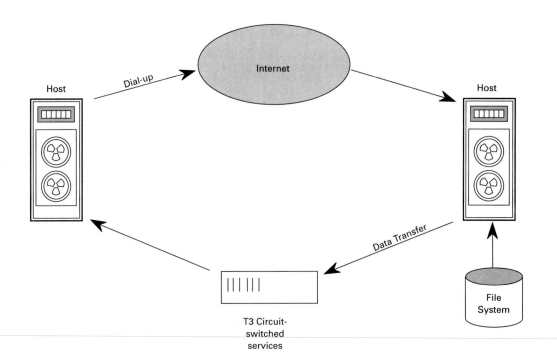

**Figure 14-5.** Bandwidth by Request

The philosophy behind Cray's design is to keep the transport provider isolated from the ongoing link set up and tear down operations. These operations are the responsibility of DSLCP controllers. The transport provider need only inform DSLCP about the actions desired. It then is left to DSLCP to perform these operations.

This idea is illustrated in Figure 14-5. The user logs on to the conventional network into a computer facility. It invokes the necessary requests to develop (for example) a file server's access to a file to return bulk data. After the request is made, the server invokes a circuit-switched service to allocate dynamically a T3 link (or a T1) back to the requester. This link is made available for the duration of the transfer and then released for other activities.

The message format for DSLCP is shown in Figure 14-6. The following provides a description of each of the fields in the DSLCP message. The identifier field is 16 bits in length. It is used to identify uniquely the link setup transactions. It is assigned by the DSLCP and is used with end point addresses for an unambiguous identifier. The total length field also consists of 16 bits. It includes the total length of the message, including both the header and the body.

The function field is 16 bits in length. Its function is to bring up or down a circuit. Therefore, its values are 0 for "bring up" or 1 for "bring down". The event status field is 16 bits in length. It is used to respond to a request for a "bring up" or "bring down" message. It provides for five possible values:

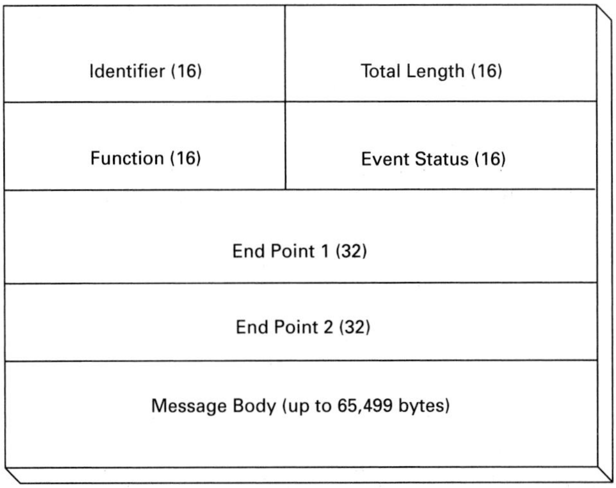

| Identifier (16) | Total Length (16) |
|---|---|
| Function (16) | Event Status (16) |
| End Point 1 (32) | |
| End Point 2 (32) | |
| Message Body (up to 65,499 bytes) | |

**Figure 14-6.** The DSLCP Control Message Format

- 2 = set up request succeeded
- 3 = set up request failed
- 4 = tear down request succeeded
- 5 = tear down request failed
- 7 = network is down.

The DSLCP message contains two end point addresses. They are 32 bits each, and for this protocol are configured with internet addresses that identify the two communicating parties involved in the transaction.

The message body is ASCII string text with a length up to 65,499 bytes. The link controller interprets this field, and its value depends upon the particular implementation within an enterprise.

## SUMMARY

Although the Internet Activities Board and the associated task forces do not become involved to any great extent with data link protocol standards, the Point-to-Point Protocol (PPP) is published as an RFC and is used extensively throughout the industry. The Dynamically Switched Link Control Protocol (DSLCP) is a newcomer that was developed by Cray. Although not a formal Internet standard, its value likely will lead to its success.

# 15

# SDLC, DDCMP, and AppleTalk

## INTRODUCTION

This chapter examines three widely used data link control protocols: SDLC, from IBM, DDCMP from Digital, and AppleTalk from Apple. The decision to include these protocols in this book was not based on any preconceived idea about their importance or merits, but rather on the interest shown by my clients and seminar delegates. The chapter proceeds in a straightforward manner to examine each of these protocols.

## SYNCHRONOUS DATA LINK CONTROL (SDLC)

SDLC (*Synchronous Data Link Control*) is IBM's widely used version of the High Level Data Link Control (HDLC) set of standards. Those who have not done so should read Chapter 6 of this book, since SDLC is based on the HDLC standard. My intent in this description of SDLC is to save readers some time and my publisher some paper by referring to the HDLC material as it pertains to SDLC.

SDLC is implemented in several ways, depending upon IBM's wish to tailor its link control protocol to the specific customer need and the appropriate product to meet the need. It can be used on point-to-point or multipoint links, and on switched or dedicated circuits.

One of the more prevalent SDLC implementations is the use of the HDLC Unbalanced Normal Response Mode, which means the link is managed by one primary station. In addition, SDLC uses several options of HDLC. One of its classifications (for example) is UN-1,2,4,5,6,12, but it does use other HDLC operations.

For the SDLC unbalanced operations, turn to Chapter 6. For SDLC balanced operations, refer to both Chapter 6 and Chapter 7. Again, be aware that IBM has implemented several renditions of SDLC.

## SDLC Transmission States

SDLC manages the link connections between the stations with the use of transmission states. One of four states describe the connection at any given time:

- Active: Traffic is flowing between the stations
- Disconnected: Station is physically disconnected from the link
- Idle: Traffic is not being sent; instead, continuous 1s are transmitted
- Transient: The time between the secondary station receiving a frame and sending a response back to the primary station

## SDLC Addresses

Each secondary station on an SDLC link is configured with one send address and one to several receive addresses. These addresses are link layer addresses and identify only the specific stations that are attached to the link. Other addresses are used in the SNA upper layers for further identification of SNA resources.

The use of several receive addresses permits broadcasting and multicasting operations. These operations are illustrated in Figure 15-1. All stations are associated with address A. In Figure 15-1(a), the frame sent from the host (primary station) to the workstations (secondary stations) is copied by all the stations, because the destination address in the frame is A. This operation is a broadcast: all stations receive the traffic. The multicast operation is shown in Figure 15-1(b). The destination address in the frame is C. Consequently, three stations copy the frame. The station that is associated with addresses A and D does not receive this traffic.

## Loop Operations

The term "HDLC Family" becomes blurred when discussing SDLC, because SDLC uses several operations that are not found in the HDLC standards. These commands and responses provide the ability to establish a loop topology and to perform loop or ring polling operations.

Figure 15-2(a) illustrates a loop configuration. The primary station is connected only to the first and last stations on the loop. A station passes data around the loop to the next station. The primary station can send data to one or more secondary stations, but the secondary stations can send data only to the primary station.

Some IBM equipment uses the hub go-ahead configuration shown in Figure 15-2 (b). The secondary stations are daisy-chained through the inbound channel. The primary station communicates with the secondary stations through the outbound channel.

SDLC uses the addressing rules of HDLC, but adds some additional features to manage multipoint links: (a) individual address; (b) group addresses; and (c) broadcast addresses. The individual address is used in the same manner as in HDLC. The secondary

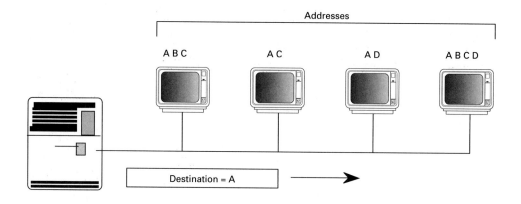

(a) Broadcast: all stations receive

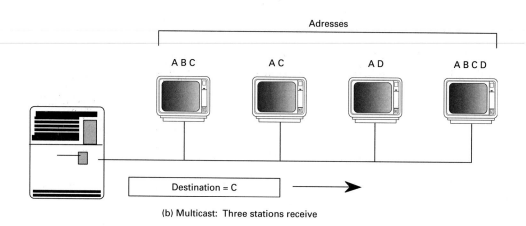

(b) Multicast: Three stations receive

**Figure 15-1.** Broadcast and Multicast Operations

station sends its own address; the primary station sends the address of the secondary station. The group address is used to send traffic to more than one station, that is, to a group of stations. If all stations are to receive the traffic, a broadcast address can be placed in the address field of the frame. All stations would then copy the broadcast frame.

## SDLC Frames

SDLC uses the same frame format as HDLC. The information (I) field contains SDLC control data or the basic transmission unit (BTU) that is passed down from the path control layer.

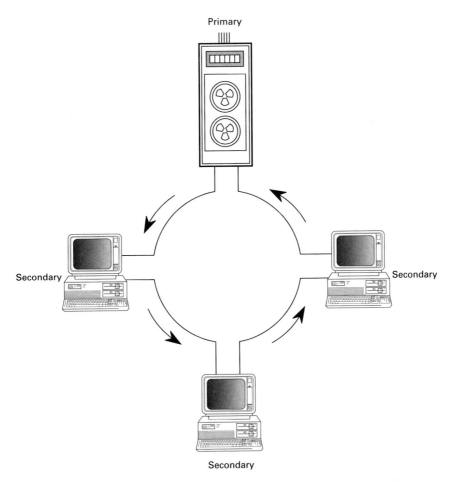

(a) SDLC Loop Operations

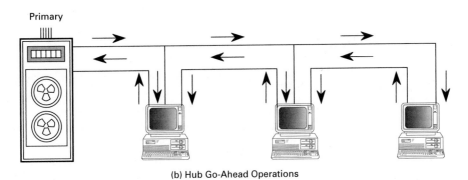

(b) Hub Go-Ahead Operations

**Figure 15-2.** SDLC Operations

SDLC allows an extension of the single byte address field. The address extension is implemented by setting the last bit of the address byte to 1. This setting indicates that another address byte follows. The last address byte sets the last bit in its byte to 0.

This brief discussion is not meant to slight SDLC. It simply reflects the fact that many of the operations of SDLC are based on HDLC. The point has been made many times in this book that HDLC serves as the foundation for many data link control protocols, and SDLC is no exception.

## DIGITAL DATA COMMUNICATIONS MESSAGE PROTOCOL (DDCMP)

The Digital Data Communications Message Protocol (DDCMP), developed by DEC in 1974, is an example of a character-count protocol. It does not have the problem of data/text transparency, since it specifies the length of the user data field with the count field. The receiver need not examine the contents of the text, but merely counts the specified number of bytes in the field. It then knows the next field is the error-check (data checksum field).

### DDCMP Messages

As illustrated in Figure 15-3, DDCMP has a simpler message format convention than its predecessor, the bisync protocol (see Chapter 5). It has one message format and uses the class field in the frame to designate one of three message types:

SOH:  Designates a data message
ENQ:  Identifies the message as a control message, with the control field replacing the count field (more on the control field shortly)
DLE:  Identifies the message as a maintenance message used for special purposes

### Data Message

The formats for the DDCMP data message are illustrated in Figure 15-3. (DEC uses the term *message* to describe its protocol data unit; this text has used the term *frame*). The fields within the message provide the following functions:

- The SOH identifies the message as a data message.
- The count field gives the length of the data field from 1 to 16,383 bytes.
- The flags are called the *sync flag* and the *select flag*. The sync flag indicates the frame will be followed by SYN characters. The select flag is used on half-duplex and multipoint lines to indicate the last data message in a transmission.
- The receive (RESP) and transmit (NUM) numbers are used to sequence the transmitted messages and to acknowledge previously received messages.

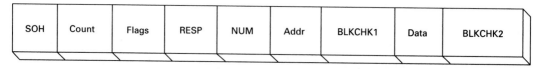

| SOH | Count | Flags | RESP | NUM | Addr | BLKCHK1 | Data | BLKCHK2 |

**Figure 15-3.** The DDCMP Format

- The address field identifies a specific station on a multipoint line. The field is not used on a point-to-point line.
- The BLKCHK1 field is used to perform a CRC-16 frame check sequence on the message header. A separate check is performed on the header to ensure the count field is not damaged.
- The data field contains the user data, and the BLKCHK2 is the CRC-16 frame check sequence on the data field.

## Control Messages

DDCMP uses five control messages to manage the link activity. These messages perform the following tasks on the link:

- Acknowledge message (ACK): This message acknowledges the data messages that have passed the FCS check. The message is utilized when no data messages are forthcoming from the station. The message conveys the same information as the RESP field in the data message.
- Negative acknowledged message (NAK): This message is used to convey a negative acknowledgment (NAK) to the transmitting DDCMP module. A NAK TYPE is available to indicate the cause of the error. Like several other protocols discussed in this chapter, the NAK message also acknowledges previously transmitted messages.
- Reply to message number (REP): This message is used to request a status message from the other station. The message is sent under three conditions: (1) the transmitting node has sent a data message, or (2) has not received an acknowledgment of the data message, or (3) the timer allotted for an acknowledgment has expired.
- Start message (STRT): This message is used for initial contact, and for establishment of the link and synchronization. The DDCMP station sends this message during the initial link setup.
- Start acknowledge message (STACK): This message is sent in response to the start messages. It informs the other DDCMP station that the transmitting node has completed its initialization. This message is quite similar to the HDLC/SDLC UA frame.

## Maintenance Message

The maintenance message is used by DEC's maintenance operation protocol (MOP), which is part of the Network Management layer in the DECnet layered architecture. DDCMP encapsulates the MOP data into the data field.

Table 15-1 contrasts the use of the fields for the control and data messages. In some instances, the fields are used for the same purpose.

## DDCMP Link Operations

DDCMP operates like HDLC in several respects. For example, it uses sliding windows,

**TABLE 15-1.** DDCMP DATA AND CONTROL TYPES

| Data | | Control | |
| --- | --- | --- | --- |
| Field | Use | Field | Use |
| SYN SYN | Synchronization | SYN SYN | Synchronization |
| SOH | Identifier | ENQ | Identifier |
| Count | Length of Data | Control | Note 1 |
| SYNC | Note 1 | SYNC | Note 1 |
| Select | Last Frame | Select | Not Used |
| Response # | Last Received Frame | Response # | ACKs or NAKs |
| Sequence # | Number for this Frame | Sequence # | Used with REP |
| Address | Secondary Station Address | Address | Secondary Station Address |
| Header Checksum | Error Check | Header Checksum | Error Check |
| Data | User Data | Data | Not Used |
| Data Checksum | Error Check | Data Checksum | Not Used |

Note 1: The SYNC bit indicates if the frame will be followed by SYN characters. The control field in a control frame specifies several control functions.

inclusive acknowledgments, and piggybacking. DEC has designed DDCMP around three functional components for link operations: (1) framing, (2) link management, and (3) message exchange. The framing component is similar to the functions of framing and other protocols discussed in this chapter. It locates the beginning and end of the message. In addition, it locates certain bit, byte, or messages within the communications signal itself. DDCMP uses the conventional start/stop transmissions to synchronize individual bytes on asynchronous links. It uses the bisync type character SYN for synchronization on synchronous links. Also it synchronizes messages by searching for one of the three starting bytes after achieving byte synchronization. These bytes are SOH, ENQ, and DLE.

The link management module of DDCMP is responsible for the ongoing transmission and reception of messages between the stations on the link. It manages the conventional link management functions of data flow, window management, addressing, and so on.

The last module of the DDCMP is the message exchange module. This module is used for sequencing operations and for error checking. It is invoked after framing is accomplished.

A typical DDCMP link operation occurs as follows: The transmitting station increments the message number and places it into the NUM field of the data message. The message is framed, transmitted, and a timer is started. The receiving station frames the message, then checks the received CRC value against a computed CRC value. If this value checks satisfactorily, it does the sequence check of the NUM field with an expected receive count variable. If all goes correctly, the receiver then returns a positive acknowledgment message with the ACK'd number. It then increments its respective count variable to N+1.

If the message does not pass these checks, then, as with other protocols in this chapter, the receiver simply ignores the message (or, under certain conditions, it may send an immediate NAK message). Ordinarily, it follows one of three procedures:

**(1)** If the transmitting station receives a positive acknowledgment, it checks the number received to see if the acknowledgment is in receipt of an outstanding message. If this is the case, it assumes that this message and lower-numbered messages have been receipted. If all outstanding messages are not acknowledged, the timer is stopped. However, if any message remains outstanding, the timer is restarted.

**(2)** If the transmitting station receives nothing, the timer expires, and it will then send an REP message to initiate error recovery.

**(3)** The transmitter might receive the negative acknowledgment. If so, it must retransmit the message and all higher-numbered messages. One might recognize this concept as the SDLC/HDLC/LAPB reject (Go-back-N) option.

DDCMP allows window control, as well, in the sense that several data messages may be sent before requiring an acknowledgment of the first data message. As stated before, acknowledgment of the highest-numbered message implies acknowledgment of all lower-numbered messages.

## APPLETALK LINK LAYER PROTOCOLS

AppleTalk was designed by the Apple Computer Corporation to allow the sharing of files and printers and the sending of traffic between computers. The designers of AppleTalk had several goals in mind when they designed the network. First was the desire to offer a very simple network that was easy to implement, yet one that would provide several types of connectivity and would support different types of protocols. Yet another design goal was to develop a "plug and play" operation, in which the AppleTalk user would not have to be concerned with the details of configuration and system generation operations. Rather, through the use of simple menus and icons, AppleTalk could be initiated and configured quite easily.

Another design goal was to establish a peer-to-peer network and to eliminate the cumbersome master-slave and polling-selection technologies that existed prior to the advent of AppleTalk.

In addition, the AppleTalk designers established a layered protocol approach to the architecture of AppleTalk in order to provide for the independence of the layers–especially the independence of the physical layer from the upper layers.

Another design goal for AppleTalk was the ability to add third party packages to the network. This approach is Apple's term for "open architecture."

Actually, the term *AppleTalk* refers to three different types of networks furnished by Apple: LocalTalk, EtherTalk, and TokenTalk. LocalTalk was the first offering from Apple. This network was designed to be inexpensive and to provide modest data rates in the kilobit range. The product usually is built into most of Apple's network offerings. It is fairly limited both in distance and in the number of devices that can be attached.

EtherTalk was brought into the AppleTalk product line to provide a more powerful local area network. It operates with the conventional Ethernet protocol and can run on thick or thin coax or twisted pair. As with all Ethernet networks, the EtherTalk network operates at 10 megabits per second (Mbit/s).

TokenTalk is the last entry into the AppleTalk arena. It is designed as a high-performance network based on the IEEE 802.5 standard and also uses logical link control (LLC).

AppleTalk is a widely used network protocol because of its use in the products of Apple, Inc. It contains many services other than lower-level network services. It provides upper-layer protocol services such as presentation, application, and session layer products. AppleTalk can operate at 230.4 Kbit/s for some users who do not need a large bandwidth capability (with LocalTalk), or it can be configured with a 10 Mbit/s topology (with EtherTalk). It can be configured with TokenTalk, as well. Figure 15-4 summarizes the major features of the AppleTalk implementations.

## The AppleTalk Layers

Figure 15-5 shows a rough approximation of the AppleTalk layers to the layers of the OSI model. One could question whether some of the transport layer protocols fit the transport layer or the application layer. Notwithstanding, the figure provides a useful model for comparison purposes.

The network functions are supported principally by the *AppleTalk link access protocol* (ALAP), which is a combination of an Ethernet protocol and an HDLC link layer protocol. ELAP and TLAP provide other options.

The network layer services also are provided by the *datagram delivery protocol* (DDP). Much of the logic of DDP is oriented toward internetworking to connect bridges and routers into an AppleTalk internet. DDP is responsible for routing datagrams within the internet and for accessing the routing table maintenance protocol (RTMP), which is a route discovery protocol.

At the transport layer, AppleTalk supports a naming service called the *name binding protocol* (NBP). In addition, it supports the *AppleTalk translation protocol* (ATP), which is an end-to-end reliable connection-oriented protocol.

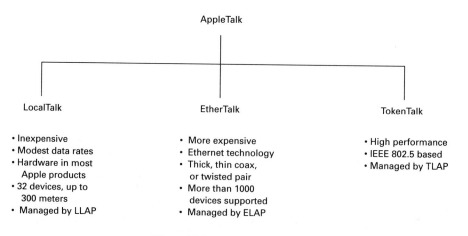

**Figure 15-4.** AppleTalk Networks

OSI Model                                              AppleTalk

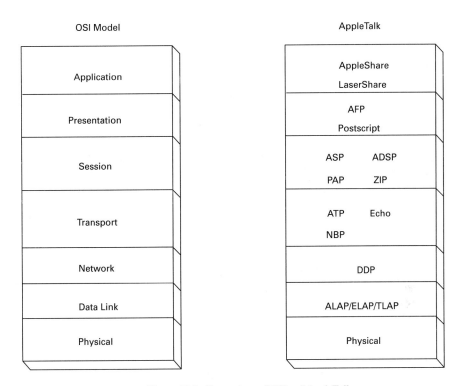

**Figure 15-5.** Comparison of OSI and AppleTalk

AppleTalk supports a variety of protocols dealing with exchanging information between AppleTalk zones. The *zone information protocol* (ZIP) defines how information within zones is generated, managed, and deleted. The *AppleTalk session protocol* (ASP) is a session layer protocol responsible for managing sessions between entities, and for exchanging traffic without duplications and in the proper sequence. The *printer access protocol* (PAP) provides printer servers, while the echo protocol provides diagnostic services. The ADSP provides for stream protocol services similar to the ASP function.

## The AppleTalk Operations and Frames

This section takes a slightly different approach to the examination of the link layer operations of AppleTalk than did the previous sections in this chapter. It will be more convenient to describe AppleTalk by combining the discussions of AppleTalk operations and AppleTalk frames, because several different protocols and supporting frames are utilized in the AppleTalk network.

As shown in Figure 15-6, the AppleTalk link access protocol (ALAP) is a link layer protocol used to manage data transmission and reception on the AppleTalk network. This layer also is called the LLAP (*LocalTalk link access protocol*) in some literature, and in many of Apple's documents, as well. ALAP uses CSMA/CD logic to manage the traffic. Before sending a frame, a station examines the carrier on the medium to determine whether the medium is available. It then waits a random interval before transmitting. It senses the medium again and, if the medium is still free, the station transmits the frame.

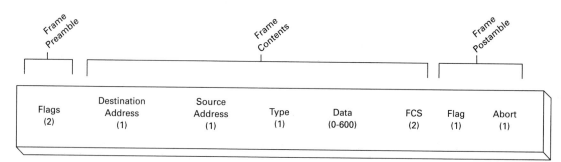

**Figure 15-6.** The ALAP Frame (also called LLAP)

Each station is assigned a 1-byte address value, called a node ID. The node ID is assigned each time the station is turned on. The station generates the *node ID* through a random number algorithm and then sends an inquiry control frame onto the network to determine whether the node ID is being used. If the node ID is used, the station tries again with the same routine.

Like other link layer protocols, ALAP uses flags to identify the beginning of a frame. Also, it uses bit stuffing to ensure that no pseudo-flag exists within the flag.

The ALAP frame contains a 1-byte type field. This field identifies the type of frame (such as an acknowledgment, a node ID inquiry, a request to send, a clear to send, etc.)

ALAP also uses a 2-byte *frame check sequence* (FCS) field for calculating a CRC value. AppleTalk provides an error check through a frame check sequence operation. (FCS). Each node that receives a protocol data unit is required to perform the FCS check. If the FCS check passes, the node then checks to see whether the destination address is destined for that node. If it is destined for that node, it processes the protocol data unit and passes the data unit to upper-layer protocols. If the FCS reveals that an error has occurred on the communications channel, the traffic is discarded and no other action takes place. Therefore, the AppleTalk link layer does not recover from errors.

## Managing Traffic on LocalTalk

The LocalTalk implementation of AppleTalk uses a concept known as *request to send/clear to send* (RTS/CTS) to manage the traffic on the communications channel. These terms have nothing to do with the same terms used in physical layer operations, such as EIA-232-D and V.24.

The process works as follows: a station wishing to transmit traffic on LocalTalk first must send a RTS packet. Contained in this packet is a destination address for the receiving node. This PDU is broadcast to all stations. If the receiving station notes that the destination address is equal to that station's address, it must send back a CTS packet. Other stations check to see whether the address is not equal to their address and ignore the RTS packet.

The originator of the RTS packet then receives the CTS packet from the remote node. It performs a frame check sequence (FCS) check and, if the FCS check reveals no error has occurred, it then is allowed to send data. However, if it never receives a CTS packet, then it assumes something is amiss on the channel (such as a collision of traffic) and it will try again by resending the RTS. Figure 15-7 depicts RTS/CTS operation.

## Upper AppleTalk Layers

While network layers are not the primary subject of this book, it is instructive to note that AppleTalk employs a network layer routing protocol, called the *datagram delivery protocol* (DDP). This protocol is similar to the Internet Protocol (IP) in that it is a datagram protocol providing a best effort delivery, but providing no error recovery.

DDP uses several of the concepts dealing with Internet sockets, as well. A socket is used to identify an entity that is to send and receive datagrams on an AppleTalk internet. The DDP packet must contain both a 1-byte destination socket and source socket number. In addition, DDP utilizes network numbers to determine the destination of the packet.

AppleTalk supports its own internet address scheme by concatenating the network number, the node ID, and the socket number.

DDP uses the *routing table maintenance protocol* (RTMP) to route traffic on the internet. RTMP maintains a routing table that contains the network ID, the number of hops to reach that network, and the next router that will receive the packet for relaying to

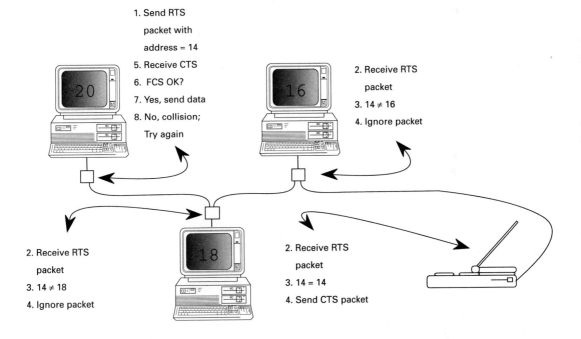

Where:

RTS is a Request-to-send packet

CTS is a Clear-to-send packet

**Figure 15-7.** The Request-to-send/Clear-to-send Operations

the destination network. Routes in the table are refreshed periodically and old entries are discarded.

AppleTalk employs a transport layer protocol that is called the AppleTalk transaction protocol (ATP). ATP rests above the DDP layer and is responsible for recovering from the connectionless DDP operations. Each ATP packet is assigned a 16-bit value which is placed in a transaction ID field. This value is used to correlate a transmitted packet with its associated response.

ATP employs a retransmission timer to ensure a response is received and processed within a period of time.

In addition, an ATP packet contains a command/control field. This field is coded to identify the type of packet being transmitted. It can identify a packet such as requests, responses, and end of message, as well as indications of how to store and to respond to these types of packets.

Another field used to control the traffic is called the *bit map/sequence number.* It is coded in a transaction request to indicate the number of packets expected in the corresponding response. It is coded in the response to indicate the number of packets being transmitted in the response.

Interestingly, ATP carries two user fields. The 4-byte user field is available for higher-level protocols. ATP does not define its context. The data field contains end-user data.

## SUMMARY

SDLC from IBM, DDCMP from Digital, and AppleTalk from Apple are widely used data link protocols. SDLC and DDCMP are designed for use on local or wide area links. AppleTalk, with LLAP, ELAP, or TLAP is a local area network protocol.

# *Index*